# BEHAVE YOURSELF

Here is an open invitation to you to become involved in solving your own problems by using the techniques of modern behavioral science. No longer must you sit back passively, waiting for anxieties and fears to go away or trying to ignore them. No longer must you look upon undesired habits, such as overeating and smoking, as problems you are doomed to go on living with. By directly changing your behavior, you can remove obstacles to your own self-realization and enhance your self-respect.

**You've got to learn how to find happiness—it won't find you. And this is the book that shows you how by putting your life where it belongs—in your hands. . . .**

# BT BEHAVIOR THERAPY

*Strategies for Solving Problems in Living*

SPENCER A. RATHUS and JEFFREY S. NEVID received their doctorates in psychology from the State University of New York and were staff members at Samaritan Hospital in the New York State Capital District. Dr. Rathus has been a faculty member in the Department of Psychiatry at Albany Medical College. He is presently a professor in the Northeastern University College of Criminal Justice, and in private practice in Newton, Massachusetts. Dr. Nevid was a post-doctoral Fellow at Northwestern University and is presently a psychology professor at Hofstra University in Hempstead, N.Y., and in private practice at the Institute for Cognitive Behavior Therapy, in Hempstead and Manhattan.

## SIGNET Books You'll Want to Read

# BT BEHAVIOR THERAPY

## Strategies for Solving Problems in Living

by
SPENCER A. RATHUS, Ph.D.
and
JEFFREY S. NEVID, Ph.D.

A SIGNET BOOK
NEW AMERICAN LIBRARY
TIMES MIRROR

SIGNET TRADEMARK REG. U.S. PAT. OFF. AND FOREIGN COUNTRIES
REGISTERED TRADEMARK—MARCA REGISTRADA
HECHO EN CHICAGO, U.S.A.

SIGNET, SIGNET CLASSICS, MENTOR, PLUME, MERIDIAN AND NAL BOOKS *are published by The New American Library, Inc.,* 1633 *Broadway, New York, New York* 10019

FIRST SIGNET PRINTING, JUNE, 1978

4   5   6   7   8   9   10   11   12

PRINTED IN THE UNITED STATES OF AMERICA

*FOR LOIS, AMY, AND OUR PARENTS*

# Acknowledgments

The techniques of behavior therapy represent the combined efforts of thousands of researchers and practitioners over the past fifty years. Among the many scientists whose work has shaped the concepts and strategies presented in this book, we would like to express our special gratitude to Joseph Cautela, Richard Clark, Barbara Davis, Albert Ellis, Charles Ferster, Cyril Franks, Vito Gioia, Israel Goldiamond, Mary Harris, Daniel Horn, Edmund Jacobson, Virginia Johnson, Mary Cover Jones, Frederick Kanfer, Helen Singer Kaplan, Arnold Lazarus, Michael Mahoney, James Mancuso, John Masters, William Masters, Bernard Mausner, Donald Meichenbaum, Ellen Platt, David Rimm, Andrew Salter, Richard Stuart, Janet Wollersheim, and Joseph Wolpe.

We thank *The Counseling Psychologist* for permitting us to use excerpts from S. A. Rathus, "Principles and Practices of Assertive Training: An Eclectic Overview," Vol. 5, No. 4 (1975), pp. 9–20; Academic Press for permitting us to reprint the Rathus Assertiveness Schedule (RAS) from S. A. Rathus, "A 30-Item Schedule for Assessing Assertive Behavior," *Behavior Therapy*, Vol. 4 (1973), pp. 398–406; and Harper & Row for allowing us to quote from the book *The Inner World of Daydreaming* by Jerome Singer (copyright © 1975). The illustrations in this book were based on drawings which appeared originally in *The New Sex Therapy* by Helen Singer Kaplan, M.D., Ph.D. (Brunner/Mazel, New York, 1974), and in *Human Sexual Inadequacy* by Masters and Johnson (Little, Brown and Company, Boston, 1970), for the use of which we thank all the parties involved.

We also wish to thank our editor at Doubleday & Company, Joseph Gonzalez, for his continued interest in our manuscript. And, finally, our warmest appreciation goes to our wives, Lois and Amy, who were always there with the right word at the right time.

# Contents

# PROGRESSIVE SELF-RELAXATION (PSR): THE BASIC BT STRATEGY FOR HANDLING ANXIETY

## ADDITIONAL BT STRATEGIES FOR DEALING WITH ANXIETY

# 3
# BT STRATEGIES FOR REDUCING FEARS

## 4
## BT STRATEGIES FOR
## GETTING TO SLEEP WITHOUT DRUGS

# 5

# ASSERT YOURSELF

# THE EIGHT-WEEK PROGRAM FOR GREATER ASSERTIVENESS

## ATTACKING SPECIFIC PROBLEM AREAS

THE RATHUS ASSERTIVENESS SCHEDULE (RAS)

# 6

# BT PROGRAMS
# FOR GREATER
# SEXUAL FULFILLMENT

## THE MISERY OF SEX

## MALE SEXUAL PROBLEMS
### Impotence

### Premature Ejaculation

### Painful Intercourse

### Vaginismus

## MYTHS THAT INTERFERE WITH SEXUAL FULFILLMENT

# 7
## BEHAVE YOURSELF:
## BT Strategies for Making
## and Breaking Habits

## BT SELF-CONTROL: A SUMMING UP

# 8
# FAT
## The BT Way to Take It Off and Keep It Off

### BEHAVIORAL WEIGHT REDUCTION: THE THEORY AND EVIDENCE

### BEHAVIORAL WEIGHT CONTROL: EMPIRICAL VALIDATION

# WEIGHT CONTROL: A CONCLUDING NOTE

# 9

# BT STRATEGIES FOR
# KICKING THE CIGARETTE HABIT

## GRADUAL SMOKING REDUCTION:
## PINPOINTING THE MOTIVE

## GRADUAL SMOKING REDUCTION:
## PROBLEMS AND SOLUTIONS

# 10
# CONCLUDING NOTES

**BT** BEHAVIOR
THERAPY

# 1

# BEHAVIOR THERAPY (BT) AND YOU

Doing it yourself is a fad in the United States. People build their own garages, change their own oil filters, and venture into more or less complicated terrains to try to solve their own problems. They occasionally try to treat medical disorders by reading books on folk medicine or using miracle diets. There are kits available for filing your own separation or arranging your own divorce.

There are various motivations for these self-initiated ventures. Such as the pride of handling your problems by yourself. Such as saving a fortune.

Of course, doing it yourself can be foolhardy and life-threatening, especially in the cases of medical illnesses or severe psychological problems. If you are severely depressed, seriously questioning whether it is worthwhile to go on living, you should consult a psychologist or psychiatrist. If that is an embarrassing prospect, at least talk thing over with your minister or your family physician. Similarly, if you believe that you are the Messiah and have been having inspiring two-way talks with God about your future activities on our small planet, discuss your plans with a psychologist or psychiatrist. On the other hand, if you really are the Messiah, excuse our impertinence and put in a good word for us in the Right Place.

Some psychological problems, or problems in living, can be dealt with on a do-it-yourself basis, and there is a technology that has matured in the 1960s and 1970s that is at your disposal if you exercise some small cautions that we shall bring to your attention as you read along. The strategies you will learn to use are those of Behavior Therapy. *Behavior* Therapy (BT), as distinct from *Psycho*-therapy.

## Psychotherapy

Psychotherapy is well known, if difficult to define. It usually involves a "warm" client-therapist relationship, some discussion of the client's early life history, efforts to make the client gradually aware of the deep-seated motives for his behavior—and, perhaps, some suggestions for behavioral changes that will permit the client to lead a happier, more productive day-to-day life.

### THE MYSTIQUE OF THE PSYCHOTHERAPIST

Psychotherapists have become magical figures in modern society. Following a lecture to a community group, a well-dressed, articulate engineer approached us and asked sincerely, "Is it true that psychologists can read people's minds?" At cocktail parties, psychologists and psychiatrists are shunned. People are afraid that they may be "analyzed" unwittingly, that the "shrink" may uncover parts of their secret, inner selves from slips of the tongue, body language, or "vibrations." Psychologists and psychiatrists are mystically cloaked as "masters of the mind." And many clients who undertake therapy have the expectation, however unfounded, that the doctor will somehow magically cure them. The client often becomes a mere spectator to his own treatment, as he awaits the psychotherapy "cure."

Many clients are disappointed when they learn that *they* must make changes in the way their lives are run. After spending hundreds or thousands of dollars in therapy, every client must swallow the bitter pill of personal responsibility for changing behaviors. The therapist may direct and guide the client. He may illustrate how the client's problem behaviors relate to psychological factors in his early childhood. But it is the client who must ultimately change the behaviors that cause him distress. It is the client, not the therapist, who must change self-defeating behavioral patterns. It is the client who must shed those extra pounds or stop smoking. It is the client who must confront his fears or meet the world in an assertive rather than an inhibited manner. It is the prematurely ejaculating man or the preorgasmic woman, and not the therapist (we assume), who must climb into bed with his or her sex partner.

## The BT Focus on Problem Behaviors

BT usually begins and ends with focusing on the problem behaviors themselves. Client-therapist discussion of the possible origins of the problem behavior—anxiety, fears, insomnia, nonassertiveness, sexual dysfunction, lack of self-control, and so on—is certainly not forbidden. But such retrospective speculations take a back seat to the construction of BT strategies for directly helping the client change his behavior and thus feel better.

### IS INSIGHT NECESSARY?

Many schools of psychotherapy maintain that unless a client has full "insight" into the causes of his problem behaviors, causes that are usually believed to originate in early childhood, behavioral changes and greater happiness will either be impossible or, at best, temporary. Clients often desire such insights, but it is impossible to reconstruct the personal past with certainty. The BT view is that lasting behavioral changes that lead to greater client happiness can and should be instigated, with or without client "insight." These changes *will* last if they help the client lead a more rewarding life.

- Fear of heights may reflect some deeply rooted unconscious experiences from the first year or two of life. It may take years of psychotherapy to uncover these roots, with no research evidence that such uncovering will reduce the fear. But BT permits you to work immediately to reduce your fear, and research evidence does show that the fear reduction is lasting.

- Nonassertiveness may reflect years of oppression by a tyrannical father, the memory of which has subsequently been forgotten or "repressed." But dredging up painful memories alone may not make you more self-assertive and confident. The BT approach will teach you the *behaviors* necessary to become more assertive—and in a few weeks.

- Women who cannot achieve orgasm, or men who have difficulty achieving or maintaining an erection *may* be responding to parental punishments or injunctions experienced when they began to touch themselves "down there" as early as eight or nine months of age. Even though they "understand" the origins of the problem through psychotherapy, the problem may stubbornly persist. BT provides you with step-by-step programs to learn to overcome sexual difficulties directly.

- Overeating *may* reflect early childhood overdependency, which may be recalled through psychotherapy. Or overeating may reflect being brought up in a house where everyone overate. This may have implications for you in raising *your* children but will not necessarily help you lose weight. BT provides you with strategies for restricting calorie intake *now*.

## The Background of BT

BT is the scientific application of the principles of learning to help clients change problem behaviors. Behavior therapists view problems such as anxiety and fears, nonassertiveness, sexual dysfunction, and lack of self-control as, for the most part, *learned*—and therefore capable of being unlearned. BT strategies help you to replace unwanted, troublesome behaviors with desirable, constructive behaviors.

BT's origins are often traced to the 1920s, when Harold E. Jones and Mary Cover Jones of the Institute of Human Development of the University of California at Berkeley reported using basic learning principles to help a two-year, ten-month-old boy, Peter, overcome fear of a white rabbit.[1] Rather than place Peter on an analytic minicouch to uncover the "deep-rooted reasons" for his learning of the fear, they propped him up in a high chair and directly taught him to *unlearn* the fear by associating food he liked with the gradual introduction of the rabbit. Each day the rabbit was brought progressively closer, while Peter munched away fearlessly on candy or other favorite foods. The joy of eating became associated with the presence of the rabbit, reducing Peter's fear of the rabbit as well as animals and objects similar in appearance. Thus the principle was established that pleasure progressively counterconditions increments of anxiety or fear.

From these simple beginnings, multiple research programs at major universities and clinics have developed, and major leaders in the field have emerged. We shall bring some of these programs and people to your attention in the course of this book.

## Behave Yourself

Some BT techniques are very complex and require years of training and experience to carry out. This book will instruct you in measures that are less complex but equally effective. Among the major schools of therapy, BT is unique in offering strategies that *you* can use to solve your own problems in living.

# 2

# THE BT WAY TO RELAX WITHOUT TRANQUILIZERS

ANXIETY, ANXIETY

## "Nerves" and Anxiety

"My nerves are shot." "My nerves are so bad I'm climbing the walls." "You're getting on my nerves." "I'm a nervous wreck." When you experience thoughts such as these, you may recognize yourself as being anxious.

But if your limbs are shaky, cold, or numb, or if your heart pounds so hard you feel it will leap out of your chest, you may wonder if there is something medically wrong. And there may be. If your physician then examines you and finds no medical reason for these sensations, he may tell you that you have a "good case of nerves" or are suffering from anxiety. Family physicians remark that at least half their patients with physical complaints are actually suffering from anxiety, and that when medical problems are present, their severity is often compounded by anxiety.

## Anxiety: "Body and Soul"

Sometimes you think about problems for which there are no quick or easy solutions. Without awareness, you send

6

messages from your brain to your limbs that cause shakiness or tremors. This process seems related to our evolutionary history: Primitive men had either to fight for their lives or to flee when they were faced with danger. This has been called the "fight or flight" mechanism.[1] In modern-day America, we rarely have to fight to the death or run. But when we receive the month's dental bill, which shows that our children had thirty-two cavities filled at the rate of twenty dollars per cavity, we will probably be transmitting "fight or flight" messages to our bodies—messages that are experienced as anxiety.

## Vicious Cycles

Vicious cycles are common. You are worried or upset about something, perhaps a dental bill, and you transmit messages to your muscles, causing them to shake. You then perceive the shakiness, not recognizing that your thoughts had initiated it, and you begin to say things to yourself like, "I must really be upset!" or "What is wrong with me?" You then become anxious, not only about the initial problem, but also about your bodily reactions to it. Concern about the bodily reactions will then increase the messages from your brain to your limbs, increasing the tremulousness, and, after a while, you may feel that you have "worked yourself up" into a state of panic, that you have lost all control over your emotions, and you may begin to wonder if the feeling will ever end. At such times the first thing you can tell yourself is "Yes! The feelings will subside as time goes on."

Anxiety is not simply a feeling of nervousness, or that "quirky" feeling that something is wrong. Continuing, unrelieved anxiety can lead to muscle-tension headaches, high blood pressure, and a host of other psychophysiological disorders. There are many bodily sensations that are signs of anxiety, and many thoughts or feelings that typify an anxiety picture. In determining how significant a problem anxiety is for you, review the following signs of anxiety. Consider how frequently these bodily sensations, thoughts, and feelings interfere with your day-to-day functioning.

### BODILY SENSATIONS OF ANXIETY[2]

- feeling a tight band around the head
- your heart beating so rapidly that you may wonder if it will leap out of your chest or cause a heart attack

- your heart seemingly skipping beats or beating irregularly
- feeling that your stomach is tied up in knots
- tremulousness in the hands, arms, or legs
- tremulousness in the voice
- dryness in the mouth
- having difficulty in breathing, or feeling that you cannot "catch" your breath
- pains in the chest
- stiffness or tightness in the back of the neck
- stiffness or tightness along the arms or across the back of the shoulders
- coldness in the hands or in the feet
- numbness in the hands, arms, or legs
- weakness in the hands, arms, or legs
- general weakness throughout the body
- having difficulty swallowing
- feeling that you have a "lump" in the throat
- sweating heavily when you have not exerted yourself
- diarrhea or loose or frequent bowel movements
- nausea
- dizziness
- light-headedness or faintness

## THOUGHTS OR FEELINGS THAT ACCOMPANY ANXIETY[3]

Bodily sensations do not occur in a mental vacuum. If you have some of the bodily sensations noted above, you may also experience some of the following thoughts or feelings characteristic of people who are anxious:

- thinking that you cannot cope with your problems
- thinking that you're falling apart
- having your thoughts "jumble up" so that you don't know what to do or what to think about first when you want to tackle your problems
- thinking that there is something that has to be done *right now*, but you're not sure what
- feeling uncomfortable in supermarkets or other crowded places
- feeling that you are often tense
- feeling frightened for no reason that you can put your finger on
- getting upset by "little things" that you think you should not be allowing to "get to" you

- feeling afraid when you are alone
- feeling that you are going to be left all alone, when there is no logical reason for feeling this way
- feeling irritable
- feeling that the room is closing in on you
- forgetting what you were going to do, such as walking into a room and forgetting why, or forgetting major items you were going to buy at the supermarket
- worrying about "every little thing"
- ruminating—that is, having the same worrisome thought over and over, not being able to get a nagging, ugly thought out of your mind
- having nightmares
- feeling that you are under a great deal of pressure to get things done, or that you work under much more pressure than other people in your circumstances
- feeling as if something dreadful is going to happen, though there is no logical reason for this
- feeling that you may lose control of your feelings and hurt someone, even though you don't want to
- feeling as if you are going to die, though your physician tells you there is nothing medically wrong with you
- feeling that the world is caving in around you

By now you will have a clear impression of how significant a problem anxiety is for you. There are many reasons for anxiety. Some of them may be clear to us; others less clear.

## Changing Times: The Age of Anxiety

It has been said many times that we live in an age of anxiety, in times that are restless and changing. There are ongoing international tensions and conflicts, and while the feeling of imminent unclear devastation that caused the bomb shelter craze of the 1950s has to some degree abated, there remains the knowledge that the fabric of our daily lives could be destroyed by international arguments or mistakes. Then, too, we live in a nation in which upward movement has been expected as a matter of course. We continued to expect that our children would be better off than we were. We assumed that college educations would automatically lead to professional positions and material security. We assumed that seniority in blue-collar positions and tenure in teaching positions were rock-solid security. And yet we find that none of these assumptions are necessarily correct. We had assumed that our standards of living and our fringe benefits would improve year by year. These beliefs have not been borne out during the 1970s.

As our basic life assumptions are threatened, we experience a sense of uncertainty or apprehension, which we label anxiety.

## Increased Personal Freedom

The United States is a country in which geographical movement and movement into new vocational and educational areas is relatively free. While this has brought about a sense of personal freedom that may be unique in the history of mankind, it has also led to the uprooting of families and to the placement of individuals and small family groups in strange, unknown communities in which they are not sure whom to turn to for friendship, medical consultation, and the whole gamut of supports and services that had been taken for granted.

With freedom comes the responsibility of choice. No longer is life simply determined from cradle to grave. No generation has had as many opportunities for alternative life styles and careers. Young people are advised to "do their own thing," and often face "decision anxiety" over which course to take in life.

## Crisis in Traditional Values and Beliefs

Our values and beliefs have been thrown into turmoil. In the early 1960s it was assumed that "we" were right and certain foreign points of view were wrong. Now many wonder. We have gone through a series of domestic scandals in high political places and learned that we have plotted assassinations and other acts overseas that we had been raised to believe were un-American. Somehow, the United States is not quite the same.

More personal values and beliefs have also been thrown into turmoil. In the 1930s Americans were shocked when Clark Gable said "Frankly, my dear, I don't give a damn" to

Vivien Leigh at the conclusion of *Gone with the Wind*. The outline of a breast might have been suggested through a screen in a musical extravaganza. In the 1970s four-letter words are a norm in the R-rated movie, as is frontal nudity. In the 1950s male adolescents stole a look at *Playboy* to see a woman's breasts or buttocks. In the 1970s pornography is so prolific that to many it has almost achieved invisibility. Issues such as birth control, abortion, and homosexuality have come out into the open. Legislation and court rulings concerning these matters have taken directions not contemplated in 1950. Some Americans feel that the legal system has failed them and no longer provides morality. Other Americans, as sincere and troubled, believe that the legal system is only beginning to demonstrate morality.

## Interpersonal Conflict

You are likely to feel quite anxious if in your daily work or home environment you must cope with people who hold strongly differing views and are highly argumentative. It may be that your boss treats you like a child, insisting on editing all your written work, or belittling you with lengthy explanations concerning simple procedures that you have already mastered. It may be possible for you to decrease some of these anxieties by becoming more self-assertive, but self-assertion may sometimes lead to the unemployment line.

## Internal Conflict

Internal conflict ensues when you are doing something that you feel you should not be doing, when you are not doing something you feel you ought to be doing, when the things you would like to do have some features that are unpalatable, and when you would like to do more than one thing at the same time but the acts are mutually exclusive. You may like your work enormously but feel that you ought to be earning more money and seeking a new job. You may feel that you should punish your young child for masturbating because you have been raised to believe that masturbation is both sinful and physically and mentally harmful, but you may have read a book that declares that masturbation is only natural and that punishment will make the child sexually inhibited and resentful of you.

When you have mixed feelings about doing something, you are said to be in an approach-avoidance conflict.[4] You want to see a highly recommended movie, but you have already reached the limits of your weekly entertainment budget. You may want to have relations with someone new and exciting at the office, but, oh, how guilty you know you will feel about your spouse. You want to ask someone out but are afraid of being rejected. The French cheesecake looks monumentally divine, but you are counting your calories.

When you want to engage in mutually exclusive acts, you are said to be in an approach-approach conflict.[5] You want to live in the city for the cultural opportunities at your doorstep, but want to live in the country for the peace of mind. You want to live in San Francisco, but you also want to live in New York. You want to marry both Tom and Dick. And Harry.

Internal conflicts also create anxiety and tension. Decision-making will often alleviate the anxiety, but you may worry that your decision will be incorrect. Thus you hesitate to act. Some people make decisions, though they may be admittedly uncertain of the outcome, in order to ameliorate the anxiety that accompanies perpetual "fence riding." Sometimes this works out. Sometimes it does not.

## Anxiety of Unknown Origin

Sometimes you know why you are anxious and upset. Your problems are clearly defined, and you can actually feel your anxiety level changing as you focus on the stress in your life or think of other things. But sometimes you do not know why you are upset. Your anxiety has a "free floating" quality about it, and it does not seem that there is anything you can do, such as making a decision, even a painful decision, to decrease it.

It may be that many "little things" are building up to cause the bodily sensations and ideas that are so discomfiting. Professional counseling may help pinpoint previously unrecognized sources of anxiety and provide you with some strategies for eliminating or reducing these sources of anxiety. But you can also do a great deal on your own before you seek professional consultation.

# YOU CAN TEACH YOURSELF HOW TO RELAX

Regardless of the sources of your anxiety, you can teach yourself to cope more effectively with the bodily sensations and discomfiting thoughts that define anxiety for you.

## Pop-psychology Methods

Various methods for reducing anxiety have recently surfaced in the popular or "pop" literature on psychology. Some of these methods have religious overtones, like Transcendental Meditation (TM). Some appear to be very indirect and "iffy" ways of dealing with anxiety, like special diets and running, the latter having somehow gotten hooked up with "Zen." Some have a mysterious quality or ask you to go into a trance, like self-hypnosis. Some methods with well-demonstrated effectiveness are not readily available for self-use, like biofeedback.[6]

## The Behavior Therapy (BT) Approach

The method you will learn in this chapter has been shown to be effective through a track record of laboratory and clinical successes spanning four decades. BT treats relaxation as a skill that can be learned, like riding a bicycle or playing tennis. You will learn to have your body report messages of relaxation and calmness rather than anxiety and tension to your brain. Thus you will feel less tense and prevent the vicious cycle of distressing bodily sensations and mounting anxious thoughts from developing.

# PROGRESSIVE SELF-RELAXATION (PSR):
# THE BASIC BT STRATEGY FOR HANDLING ANXIETY

Progressive relaxation was first brought to the attention of the helping professions during the 1930s by Dr. Edmund Jacobson of the University of Chicago.[7] Since the 1950s, with the help of Dr. Joseph Wolpe[8] of the Eastern Pennsylvania Psychiatric Institute, it has caught hold as one of the central treatments used by behavior therapists from the disciplines of psychology, psychiatry, and social work.

Through progressive self-relaxation (PSR), an adaptation of this technique, you will learn to relax yourself upon your own command, without resorting to tranquilizers, and without running from a situation in which you feel you ought to remain. Through systematic practice of PSR skills, you will also come to experience less anxiety and tension throughout the course of your daily life. Evidence is also accumulating that many people who engage in deep relaxation for ten to twenty minutes, once or twice daily, experience remission of muscle-tension headaches,[9] show normalization of blood pressure,[10] and are relieved of many other psychophysiological problems.

## Defenses Against Anxiety

The purpose of PSR is to provide you with well-constructed, habitual defenses against anxiety.

### GETTING THE WORD "RELAX" TO WORK FOR YOU

A naïve individual in a tense situation may tell himself to relax. Probably nothing will happen. His self-command will not be effective. If he continues to exhort himself to relax with a virtually meaningless command, he may achieve the "paradoxical" effect of becoming more upset. He is used to being upset when he tells himself to relax. Repetitive pairing of the word "relax" with feelings of anxiety actually make this self-command a *cue* for becoming more anxious. PSR reverses this process by associating the self-command to relax with actual muscular relaxation. The word "relax" thus becomes a cue for inducing feelings of calmness and tranquillity.

## BODILY SENSATIONS OF RELAXATION

Through the use of PSR you will condition yourself so that the word "relax" will have many meanings for many parts of your body. Your muscles will become less tense and shaky, a feeling of calmness will flow through your body, your rate of respiration and your heartbeat will slow down.[11] Your systolic blood pressure will decrease.[12]

## LOWERED ANXIETY—NOT LOWERED AWARENESS

PSR has no mysteries or semireligious qualities about it. It is a skill which, with practice, will show you how to reduce the bodily sensations of anxiety when you are in a stressful situation. Your habitual response to such situations will be different. This does not mean that appropriate vigilance will be reduced to the point where you do not recognize danger. It means that your anxiety level will be lower when you are under stress and that you will be able to think and cope more effectively.

# Developing Relaxation Skills

In PSR you teach your body to relax through self-administered muscular exercises. The bodily sensations that tell your brain you are anxious and tense diminish.

## TENSING AND RELAXING

In PSR you first tighten up or tense selected muscle groups in your body and then relax them, or let them go. The muscle groups that you will focus on are:

1. hands and wrists
2. biceps
3. backs of arms (triceps) and upper forearms
4. forehead
5. middle face region
6. mouth region
7. neck region

8. shoulders
9. abdominal (stomach) region
10. thighs
11. calves

Purposefully tensing each muscle group before relaxing will enhance your ability to feel the contrast between tension and relaxation. This will provide you a stronger frame of reference for feeling the *absence* of tension. Your muscles become more deeply relaxed if they are tensed first.

## HOW TO TENSE EACH MUSCLE GROUP

1. Tense the hands and wrists by clenching your hands into tight fists. Try this slowly at first so that you will determine whether your fingernails are too long for the exercise. If they are, trim them or keep them angled away from your palms as you make tight fists. You should feel the tension in your fingers, along the backs of your hands, and, to a lesser degree, in your wrists.

2. Tense your biceps by bending your arms at the elbows. This is usually what children do in response to the adult request to "make a muscle." However, do *not* also clench your hand into a fist. Focus on the biceps only, keeping the rest of your arm as relaxed as possible.

3. You can see what it feels like to tense your triceps (the backs of your upper arms) and the tops of your forearms by lying on your back on a couch and pressing your hands down flat against the couch. After you have practiced this a couple of times, you will be able to reproduce the tensing sensations in your arms without pressing against an opposing force.

4. Tense your forehead by frowning hard, so that you can place your hand on your forehead and feel wrinkles.

5. Tense the middle of your face by scrunching up your nasal area. Keep your forehead smooth as you do so.

6. Tense your mouth region by pressing your lips together hard. Many practitioners of progressive relaxation instruct their clients to bite their teeth together hard. This can be costly to dental work. Others suggest

that you press your tongue against the roof of your mouth. We note that this can cause discomfort.

7. The feeling you should experience while tensing your neck is the one you obtain when you press your forehead forward against your hands. If you try this sitting, keep your head vertical and do not bend your back. If you try this while lying on your back, keep the back of your head against a pillow or a mat—do not lift it. After you practice this a couple of times and attend to what the tension in your neck feels like, you will be able to reproduce the sensation without using your hands. Practice this a couple of times and then take a brief break. You may be tired.

8. In order to experience tension in your shoulders, stand with your back against the wall and press your shoulders back against the wall. Then reproduce the sensation while sitting or lying down, without actually pressing your shoulders against anything, but just, in effect, stretching them back.

9. Tense your abdominal region by "sucking in your stomach" hard.

10. Tense your thigh muscles by lying down on a couch or a bed, straightening out your legs *hard*, and pushing your legs out from your body. Do not push out your toes or your heels alone. Stretch your legs forward, as if trying to be an inch taller. As you do so, you should be able to feel tightness in the tops of your thighs with your hands. *Do not stretch so hard that you develop a muscle spasm or charley horse.*

11. Tense your calves by drawing your feet back up toward your face while you are lying on your back or reclining. *Again, do not tense so hard that you develop a muscle spasm.*

12. Tense your feet by curling your toes, as you had made a fist with your hands. Be careful: Toes are not as flexible as fingers.

For each muscle group you should experience enough tension so that there is definite work involved, with, perhaps, a slight degree of discomfort, but you should not tense so hard that you feel pain or feel any danger of going into a spasm or "pulling a muscle."

## HOW TO RELAX MUSCLE GROUPS

After you have tensed a muscle group in PSR, hold the contractions for four to eight seconds while you focus your attention on the muscle group. Then just let go. Relax the contraction completely, at once, with no hesitation. Study the difference in feelings in that area of your body. Let the feeling of relaxation in that region go farther and farther. Take from half a minute to a full minute to let the relaxation develop. Study the feeling. The muscle group will feel warmer and a bit heavier. This feeling will spread to adjacent areas. If you just allow that region of your body to become warmer and heavier, you will achieve deeper relaxation.

## BREATHING CONTROL

The first time you practice PSR, begin breathing exercises by the time you reach the ninth muscle group, the abdominal or stomach region. In breathing exercises, you inhale while you are tensing a muscle group and exhale while you are relaxing. Just prior to letting the contractions go and letting your breath out, say the word "relax" or "calm" to yourself.

From the second time you practice PSR onward, take a deep breath as you tense a muscle group, tell yourself to relax, and simultaneously let out your breath and let go of the contractions. This is the pattern:

- Tense a muscle group and take a deep breath.
- Study the tension in the muscle group and hold your breath for four to eight seconds.
- Command yourself to relax or to be calm.
- Immediately and simultaneously let go of the muscle contractions and let out your breath.
- Study the difference in feelings, the relaxation, and allow the relaxation to develop for thirty to sixty seconds.

## A BRIEF REVIEW

This may sound like a good deal of work and memorization. Work, perhaps. It will be valuable for you to practice your PSR skills on a daily basis. But after two weeks you will practice them in an abbreviated form. Memorization? Only to a small degree. Look back at pages 15-16 to the list of muscle groups that you will be alternately tensing and relaxing. Note that they follow a route from the hands to the head and then down through the neck to the feet. You can sub-divide them into four groups, with three steps in each: (1) arms, (2) head, (3) neck to abdomen, and (4) legs.

Right now you may be able to close the book and repro-duce the twelve muscle groups with only one or two errors.

## SETTING THE STAGE FOR PSR

Before initiating PSR, you may wish to consult with your physician if you have experienced any back troubles or muscle sprains. If you have any respiratory problems, use ex-treme caution in the breathing exercises. Any doubts about medical readiness for PSR should be discussed with your physician.

Practice PSR while lying in bed, lying on a couch, or sit-ting in a reclining chair that will maintain a stable position. The proper setting for PSR is a warm, moderately lit, com-fortable room in which there will be few if any distractions. This is not usually a problem in the therapist's office unless the receptionist is trigger-happy with the intercom buzzer or there is an argument about a bill in the waiting room. At home you may require some definitive strategy. You will need either to have your family out of the home or to con-tract with them to avoid distracting you during PSR. Schedule yourself around predictable neighborhood distrac-tions. Some of our clients have lived near flight paths of air-ports or fire stations and have had to choose their times quite judiciously.

## DELIVERY OF INSTRUCTIONS

The following instructions are written as though they were being delivered by another person. Reading them will help you learn what to say to yourself. There are also other possi-bilities. You may wish to tape-record them. If you do, first experiment from memory alone to determine how long the pauses between instructions should be for *you*. Record the breathing instructions to accompany the tensing and relaxing of all twelve muscle groups. Use a firm voice when you in-struct yourself to focus on and tense a muscle group. Make the command to relax or be calm definitive. Use a softer, more fluid tone when you are instructing yourself to allow the feelings of relaxation to develop.

*Use of family or friends.* You may elect to have a family member or close friend help you relax by reading instructions aloud. Experiment to tailor the instructions that will suit you, and begin breathing exercises with the first muscle group during the second PSR session. Select a person who will be able to modulate his or her tone of voice to promote tensing and relaxing. The voice should be strong and direct—though never "unfriendly"—when delivering tensing instructions, and softer when promoting relaxing.

## Full-length PSR Instructions

Settle back and find a comfortable position. Make sure all your clothing is loose. Place your head back and move it around a little, getting it comfortably settled. Get your legs into a comfortable position. Press your head back down to see that it is firmly supported. Do the same with your legs: Press them down to see that they are firmly supported. Take a deep breath, hold it for a few (four to eight) seconds, and then let it out, relaxing as best you can while you do so. Close your eyes.

Focus on your hands. Clench them tightly into a fist for a few (four to eight) seconds and feel the pressure. Now just let them go and note the difference in the feelings. When your fists were clenched, that was tension. When you let them go, they began to relax. Study the difference and allow it to continue (allow thirty to sixty seconds to feel the contrast and let feelings of relaxation develop following each instruction to relax). Now clench your fists again and study the tension. Now relax them. Study the difference in feelings. This is the opposite of pressure and tension. Let the feeling grow. Now focus on your biceps. Allowing your hands to remain relaxed, bend your arms at the elbows and tense your biceps, studying the tensions. Now relax your biceps. Just let your arms relax and feel the difference, the absence of tension. Note the warm feelings in your hands flowing up through your arms. This is relaxation. Let it develop. Now bend your elbows and tense your biceps again, studying the tension. And now relax. Let the tensions go. Let all contractions in your hands and in your biceps go, and study the difference. Note the warm current of relaxation flowing through your hands and arms. Allow this feeling to grow. Now focus on your triceps. Tense your triceps, studying the tensions along the backs of your arms. Now relax. Let the contractions go completely. Let go of all contractions anywhere in your arms. Let the warm current of relaxation flow through your arms. Now tense your triceps again and study the tension. And now relax. Note the warmth flowing through your arms. Let the feelings grow as your arms become heavier. Sense the full comfort of relaxation. Let this feeling grow. Focus on your arms, removing all contractions as you do so, and allow the warm current of relaxation to flow and develop. Allow your arms to continue relaxing, and focus on your forehead. Tense your forehead by frowning, and study the tension as you do so. And now relax. Picture your forehead becoming smoother, and study the growing feelings of relaxation across your forehead. Now tense your forehead again, studying the tension. Relax. Picture your forehead becoming very smooth, and allow the feelings of relaxation to flow across your forehead and your scalp. Now focus on the central area of your face. Scrunch up your nose and study the tension. And now relax. Allow the current of relaxation to flow from your forehead into the central area of your face. Allow your arms to remain relaxed. Now tense your nasal area again, studying the tension. And again relax, noting the difference in your feelings with pleasure. Let the feeling of relaxation develop. Now focus on your mouth region. Keeping the rest of your face as relaxed as possible, press your lips together hard and study the tension as you do so. Now relax. Let all the tensions in your face go. Let relaxation grow. Now press your lips together again, studying the tension. Now relax, noting the opposite of tension—relaxation. Part your lips slightly. Let the warm current of relaxation continue to grow and develop. Just let all contractions in your face go, and note the warm, pleasant feeling of relaxation. Allow it to continue to develop.

Allow your arms to continue relaxing. Allow your facial area to continue relaxing and tense your neck, studying the tension as you do so. And now relax. Allow the warm current of relaxation to flow down from your facial area into your neck. Note the difference between tension and relaxation, and let the relaxation develop. Now tense your neck again. Feel the tension. And now relax. Just let all the tensions go out of your neck and notice the pleasant contrast. Allow the relaxation to continue. Allowing your neck to remain relaxed, focus on your shoulders. Tense your shoulder muscles and study the tension. Now relax. Note the difference. Allow the feeling to grow. Now tense your shoulders again. And now relax. Appreciate the contrast, and allow the feelings of relaxation, the warm, comfortable current of relaxation to grow. Now focus on your stomach region. Allowing the rest of your body to relax, take in a deep breath, and at the same time suck in your stomach hard. Hold the tensions. Now let your breath and your stomach muscles go simultaneously, and note the difference in your feelings. Breathe gently and easily and study the warm feeling of relaxation in your stomach area. Allow the relaxation to develop. This time you will tell yourself to relax just before you let your breath out and your muscles relax. Again, take in a deep breath and suck your stomach in hard. Study the tension. Tell yourself to relax and immediately let go of your breath and your muscles, noticing how much more comfortable you feel when you do so. Continue to breathe deeply, easily, and regularly. As you do so, allow the relaxation to develop all through your stomach region. Allow the warm current of relaxation to flow and develop on its own.

Now focus on the muscles in your thighs. Take a breath and tense your thighs, studying the tension. Tell yourself to relax, and let out your breath and let go of the muscles in your thighs. Study the contrast in your thighs as you allow them to continue to relax. Again, take a breath and tense your thighs. Hold the breath and study the tension. Tell yourself to relax, and immediately expulse the breath and let your muscles go. Breathe easily and calmly, allowing the relaxation in your thighs to develop as they become heavier and are filled with the warm current of relaxation. Allowing your thighs to remain relaxed, focus on your calf muscles. Take a deep breath and draw your toes up toward your face, tensing your calves. Tell yourself to relax, and just let go of your breath and your muscles. Study the contrast in your feelings. Let the warm current of relaxation flow down from your thighs into your calves. Let the feeling develop. Again, take a deep breath and tighten up your calf muscles. Study the tension. Tell yourself to relax, and let go of your breath and your calf muscles at once. Let your muscles go, more and more. Just keep doing the opposite of tension, allowing the warm, heavy, comfortable sensations of relaxation to develop by themselves in your legs. Now focus on your feet. Keeping the rest of your legs as relaxed as possible, take in a breath and clench your toes like a fist. Hold, and study the tension. Tell yourself to relax, and immediately release your breath and your toes. Note the contrast in feelings in your feet. Allow them to relax, and observe the warm current of relaxation flowing down through your legs into your feet. Now once more: Take a deep breath and tense your feet. Study the tension. Tell yourself to relax and just let out your breath with a whoosh as you let go of all contractions in your feet. Let the relaxation develop.

Now let's go back and check for tensions anywhere in your body. Focus on your arms. Take a deep breath, tell yourself to relax, and let go of any contractions in your arms, allowing them to relax even further. Focus on your facial area. and picture your forehead quite smooth and relaxed. Relax your mouth region with your lips slightly parted. Take a deep breath, hold it for a moment, tell yourself to relax, and let your breath out with a whoosh, noting how the relaxation continues to grow and develop on its own. Sense the warm current flowing through your body. Sense how heavy and comfortable your limbs and body feel.

Just go on relaxing like that, enjoying the feelings of warmth and comfort, the absence of tension. By telling yourself to relax as you exhale, you become more and more relaxed. When you wish to get up, simply open your eyes and stretch your body. Move about slowly at first, because you have been in a resting position for several minutes and your muscle tonus has decreased. However, your mind is fully alert, and the warm current of relaxation will remain with you for a while as you begin to go about your business.

Begin the breathing exercises at the outset of the second session. Take a deep breath with the initial clenching of your fists. For a few moments hold your breath and study the muscular tension. Tell yourself to relax and *immediately and simultaneously* relax your hands and let your breath out. From this point forward associate inhaling with tensing of a muscle group, and exhaling with relaxation of the group. Use the self-command to relax or be calm immediately prior to exhaling and relaxing muscle groups.

At the outset of PSR training, use the full-length procedure twice a day for two weeks or once a day for a month, whichever fits in more conveniently with your schedule. Then switch to abbreviated PSR, as outlined below. Eventually, just using the self-command "relax" or "calm" will permit you to achieve the bodily sensations of deep muscular relaxation. A process that had initially required perhaps half an hour will occur in moments. *But as in the formation of any habit or skill, it will be wise to "get back to basics" by using the full-*

*length PSR procedure once every month or so.* This will keep your PSR skills at a strongly operative level.

## Abreviated Progressive Self-relaxation (PSR)

Abbreviated PSR collapses the twelve muscle groups into four areas: arms, face, neck through stomach region, and legs. In PSR, muscle groups in a body area are simultaneously tensed and relaxed. There are only four commands.

- The command to tense the arms means to clench the hands into fists and tense the triceps and upper forearms. Muscle groups one and three are simultaneously tensed.

- The command to tense the face means to wrinkle the forehead and press the lips together. Muscle groups four and six are simultaneously tensed.

- The command to tense the central region means to tense the neck and shoulders and to suck in the stomach hard. Muscle groups seven, eight, and nine are simultaneously tensed.

- The command to tense the legs means to tense the thighs and the calves, drawing the toes back up toward the head. Muscle groups ten and eleven are combined.

Though muscle groups two, five, and twelve are not focused upon specifically, the tension and relaxation from adjacent muscle groups will spread to them.

Before you engage in the abbreviated PSR instructions, try out each component part. Practice tensing muscle groups one and three simultaneously, four and six simultaneously, seven *through* nine simultaneously, and ten and eleven simultaneously. Abbreviated PSR will initially require about ten minutes, but with practice, in a week or so will take about five. Sample instructions follow. As with full-length PSR, you can think the instructions to yourself, tape-record them, or enlist a family member or friend to deliver them.

# Abbreviated PSR Instructions

Settle back comfortably. Loosen your clothing. Stretch your entire body as you take a deep breath; hold the breath for a few moments, let it out with a whoosh, and notice how the warm current of relaxation begins to flow through your body. Close your eyes.

Focus your attention on your arms. Take a deep breath and tense your arms; hold, and study the tension; tell yourself to relax, and let out your breath and let go of your arms. Study the difference in your feelings. Note the warm current of relaxation in your arms. Let the feeling develop. Now take a deep breath and tense your arms again; study the tension; tell yourself to relax and let go of the tensions and of your breath at once. Notice the contrast between tension and relaxation. Notice the heaviness developing in your arms as the warm current of relaxation flows. Release all contractions in your arms, breathe easily and regularly, and note how the relaxation develops.

Now focus your attention on your facial area. Keeping your arms relaxed, tense your face as you take a deep breath; hold and study the tension; tell yourself to relax, and release your breath and the tensions as you do so. Note the current of relaxation flowing across your scalp, your smooth forehead. Let the relaxation grow. Again, take a deep breath and tense your facial area; hold it; tell yourself to relax, and let the tensions and the deep breath go. Notice the difference in your feelings in the facial area, the smoothness of your forehead, the warm, flowing current of relaxation. Part your lips slightly. Let go of any contractions in your facial area and in your arms, and let the relaxation develop.

Now focus your attention on your central region, your neck through your stomach. Take a deep breath, and tense your central region; study the tension; tell yourself to relax, and let your breath and all your muscles go. Just let your entire central region go loose as you enjoy the contrast in your feelings and let the relaxation grow. Once more: Take a deep breath and tense your central region, feeling the tension in your neck, shoulders, and stomach; tell yourself to relax, and let your breath and all the tensions go with a whoosh. Note the contrast, and allow the feelings of relaxation to develop.

Note how you become more relaxed each time you breathe out.

Now focus your attention on your legs. Keeping the rest of your body relaxed, take a deep breath and tense your legs; study the tension from your thighs down to your calves; tell yourself to relax, and let the breath and your tensions go. Just let all the contractions go, and notice the development of warmth and heaviness through your legs. Allow them to become more and more relaxed.

And once more: Take a breath and tense your legs, holding the tension for a few moments; tell yourself to relax, and let the breath and the muscles go. Just let your muscle tensions go completely. Notice the warm current of relaxation growing in your legs and in other areas of your body. Let yourself go, let go of all contractions, and allow the relaxation to go on developing. Notice how much more relaxed you become as you breathe out. Note that your breathing is easy and regular and that the warm current of relaxation develops throughout your body, throughout your legs, up through your central region and your neck, across your face, and through your arms.

You are fully alert though relaxed. When you wish to get up, open your eyes and stretch your body. Move about slowly at first, since you have been resting.

As you continue with PSR day by day, you will notice that you become completely relaxed more readily and that feelings of relaxation remain with you for longer periods of time throughout the day.

After a couple of weeks of abbreviated PSR, you will find that you experience deep relaxation almost immediately upon taking a breath, telling yourself to relax, and then expelling the breath. At this point you will spend almost the entirety of a ten- to twenty-minute PSR session in an enjoyable state of deep muscular relaxation. Clients practicing twice daily report that relaxing in the morning helps them start the day on a calmer footing, and that relaxing in the evening helps them to unwind.

## Alert Relaxation

You will note that you are fully alert when you are relaxed, unless you are specifically using PSR in an effort to help you sleep. Do not think that going jogging, playing tennis, or going for a swim will interfere with your learning how to relax. Athletic activities, with your physician's guidance, are excellent for you. PSR is not directed at inducing muscular weakness or nonresponsiveness. It reduces chronic *useless* muscular tensions, bodily "vigilances" that are in operation constantly because of anxiety even though no enemy is likely to appear on the horizon. PSR addresses itself to disorganized, nonproductive muscular tensions. Muscular activity in athletics is co-ordinated and purposive.

*"Booster shots."* Once a month or so engage in full-length PSR so that all the words used in the abbreviated form of PSR, such as "relax" and "current of relaxation," will retain their meanings. Thus one word or one phrase will continue to induce many pleasurable sensations in your body.

## Outcomes of PSR

### SPREADING OF RELAXATION BEYOND THE PSR SESSION

Clients typically find that the experience of being relaxed appears to "spread automatically" to fill more hours of the day, hours spent on the job, and during household chores and leisure-time activities. Although practiced while lying down or sitting in a reclining chair, the sensations of relaxation would continue while sitting, standing, and walking. The relaxation experienced was not similar to muscular weakness nor inducive of fatigue. It merely reduced unwarranted muscular vigilances.

Some have remarked that they have been able to promote the spread of feelings of relaxation by "recalling" the bodily sensations of relaxation at various times during the day and allowing them to "flow" in. It appears that briefly closing the eyes while "recalling" the feelings of relaxation is more effective than leaving the eyes open.

### USE OF THE SELF-COMMAND TO RELAX

The PSR procedure of pairing the word "relax" or "calm" with relaxation of muscle tensions allows the word itself to become a stimulus or cue that you can use to relax bodily tensions. After several weeks of PSR, saying the word "relax" to yourself while letting out a deep breath should have a relaxing effect on you. Since you require no equipment to relax, you will be able to relax yourself directly in situations that used to make you anxious, whether you are sitting, standing, or walking, whether you are alone or with others. In this manner you will gradually be able to face more stress-producing situations and gain control of the bodily sensations of anxiety as you cope with them.

One forty-two-year-old divorced physicist was able to cope with a "case of the shakes" while driving to pick up a date by taking a deep breath, telling himself to relax, and exhaling. A thirty-eight-year-old mother learned to control tremulousness and "heart palpitations" while "having a talk" with her adolescent daughter about curfew-breaking. The mother reported that bodily relaxation allowed her thought processes to function more clearly so that she could say everything she had wanted to say without "yelling." A twenty-three-year-old graduate student in sociology was able to sit for examinations with less of an urge to eliminate and less difficulty "getting enough air." The student also reported that test material was more readily memorized when he was relaxed, and less likely to get "jumbled up in my head" during the tests themselves.

## HABITUAL, "AUTOMATIC" RELAXATION

One of the more exciting breakthroughs with PSR may come when you unexpectedly find yourself taking and releasing a deep breath. You then examine your situation and discover that it is one in which you *used* to get upset. But now, having engaged in PSR to the point where relaxation skills have become so habitual that the sensing of muscular tension can become an automatic cue for you to begin relaxing, the bodily sensations of anxiety were reduced and replaced with sensations of relaxation even *before you were fully conscious of the import of the situation*. Your habits are now working for you and not against you.

A twenty-seven-year-old teacher with a history of stage fright reported that when she approached her classes she would "almost hear a remnant of the word relax," and the bodily sensations of anxiety would dissipate. She was not consciously attempting to relax—she had practiced PSR so assiduously that the perception of situations that had previously induced anxiety led automatically to sensations of relaxation. Similarly, a twenty-two-year-old graduate student in educational psychology experienced anxiety in which shortness of breath was predominant. Diligent practice of PSR resulted in her "automatically" taking and releasing a deep breath in stressful situations, typically confrontations with a passive father and demanding stepmother. Her exhaling was followed by deep, regular breathing and a quelling of other components of anxiety.

### THE END OF THE VICIOUS CYCLE

PSR can thus help you gain conscious or automatic control over the bodily sensations of anxiety. Without the bodily sensations of anxiety, you are less likely to experience thoughts that accompany anxiety. You are less likely to become caught in the vicious cycle wherein bodily sensations and thoughts interact to stimulate each other until you find yourself in a state of panic.

And when you experience less anxiety, you think more clearly. While decreasing anxiety alone is not the solution to all your life problems, anxiety reduction permits you to make better use of your problem-solving ability.

# ADDITIONAL BT STRATEGIES FOR DEALING WITH ANXIETY

## Self-reward

PSR will permit you to achieve relaxation in situations in which you used to be anxious and upset. When you are thus relaxed, do not hesitate to tell yourself how wonderful you feel. Emphasize how fine *you* have made yourself feel. Vividly imagine important people in your life patting you on the back and telling you how they admire your self-control. Smile and allow yourself to bask in the warmth generated by your accomplishment. Tell yourself how superior you are to the way you were. Emphasize the fact that you successfully taught yourself the skills of relaxing. Tell yourself how much better off you are than people who have not yet learned to master the bodily sensations of anxiety. Don't be falsely modest. Enjoy the idea that you can do something that most others cannot, just as you might enjoy a superior backhand in tennis.

## Fantasizing a Minivacation

The coffee break at work is a time-honored tradition, paying recognition to the difficulty of getting through a day of humdrum activities without some change in stimulation. If you tend to become anxious and tense during work and if the coffee break does not help, it may be that you use your time out to ruminate about your problems. Or perhaps the caffeine in the coffee, a stimulant that helps America get going in the morning, is producing many of the bodily sensations of anxiety—"coffee nerves."

Instead of a coffee break, you may choose to "go" on a fantasized minivacation. You may do this quite comfortably in your own office. If you do not have an office, find a place where you can be undisturbed for ten or fifteen minutes. Place yourself in a comfortable sitting or lying position. Loosen any tight clothing. Close your eyes. Stretch your muscles. Take a deep breath, tell yourself to "relax," and then exhale. As you begin to experience the bodily sensations of relaxation, imagine yourself to be in another place and time, perhaps on a beach during a pleasant vacation. Imagine each of your bodily senses coming alive in the pictured environment. Feel the sand between your toes and beneath your beach blanket. Smell the salt air and the odor of suntan lotion. Listen to the waves as they lap up against the shore, and to the sounds of gulls calling to one another in the air and people laughing on nearby blankets as they drink refreshing beverages from tall glasses in which ice is clinking. Note how the sun is pleasant, hot, and bright, warm against your eyelids, and how there are only one or two faint wisps of white cloud in the sky against a deep vault of blue.

When your preplanned time limit has elapsed, open your eyes and allow yourself a few moments to become completely reoriented to your actual surroundings. Move about slowly at first, because your muscle tonus will have decreased, as will have your blood pressure. Rising too rapidly can occasion light-headedness.

## Controlling What You Say to Yourself

At the outset of this chapter we outlined certain thoughts that are typical in anxiety states and serve to propel people into vicious cycles of anxious thoughts and bodily sensations. When you perceive yourself to be anxious, it is common to wonder if you are going to "lose control" and stand by helplessly as your feelings of tension mount. This need not be the case. You can take a more active and direct approach to coping with the thoughts that accompany anxiety by saying different things to yourself.

Through PSR you have already learned to take a deep breath, tell yourself to "relax," and exhale when you feel yourself becoming anxious. In addition to PSR, you may say things to yourself such as:

- There's no point to getting all upset. In a few moments I'll be feeling fine.

- There was a time when I had no idea what was happening to me or what to do about it. Now I know that I was making things worse for myself by getting more and more upset, and I *can* stop the vicious cycle.

At such times you may briefly go on a minivacation. You have already told yourself to relax and begun to experience the bodily sensations of relaxation. If you have the time and opportunity, you may want to place yourself in a fantasized setting that you have prepared, such as the beach scene, or something more personally suited to your tastes and interests. If someone interrupts you while you are on your fantasized minivacation, you will not become intolerably anxious. Nor need you feel that you have been "discovered." You may merely open your eyes and remark that you were meditating about something for a moment.

Dr. Donald Meichenbaum of the University of Oregon[13] has suggested several statements that can be used to decrease the stress experienced during anxiety-producing situations:

- Telling yourself that your fear of what is going to happen is worse than what actually will happen. Telling yourself that you should not blow things out of proportion.

- Telling yourself that it may not be possible for you to eliminate all the bodily sensations of anxiety, but that you're better off than you were.

- Telling yourself that the situation will soon come to an end.

## Rehearsing an Anxiety-inducing Situation

If you must deal with certain anxiety-inducing situations on a regular basis, you may want to change those factors in your life that make the confrontations necessary. This might mean finding another job or modifying social relationships. But if these solutions are not feasible for you, you can learn to cope more effectively with an anxiety-inducing situation by *practicing* what you might say and do the next time it arises.

Picture that supervisor at work who utters predictably noxious remarks. When these remarks are made, you do not know what to say and feel you cannot cope. But afterward the "right thing" to say usually hits you. Rehearse in your imagination appropriate replies to these situations. Practice them in your imagination, or with a trusted friend or family member, when you are out of the situation and feeling at ease. When you are less anxious, your thought processes function more logically and coherently, so make your plans and refine them beforehand. You may want to look into a mirror and practically snarl when you say the "right thing." When you are back at work and the appropriate occasion arises, you will have a rehearsed response available.

You may also rehearse "branching dialogues." Ask yourself what you would say if your supervisor retorted with five or six different remarks, and rehearse a possible response for each. You will find additional strategies for such confrontations in the chapter on becoming more self-assertive.

## Dealing with Ruminations

Ruminations are a particularly distressing sign of anxiety, and are defined as difficulty in getting persistent, nagging, ugly thoughts out of your head. Thoughts like "I'm falling all to pieces," "I'll never be able to do anything about this," "What am I going to do? What am I going to do?," "I just know I'm going to die," and "My heart is going to burst if it goes on beating like this."

## THOUGHT-STOPPING AND ASSERTIVE THOUGHTS

Dr. David C. Rimm of Old Dominion University[14] has devised a technique for dealing with such repetitive, negativistic, anxiety-inducing thoughts. Dr. Rimm first employs the time-honored method of thought-stopping, or yelling "STOP!" when a client is ruminating about some noxious subject. Doing so disrupts the rumination. Following some repetitions in the office, Dr. Rimm instructs the client to yell the word "STOP!" himself out loud, and, eventually, to make the word "STOP!" a commanding thought.

Dr. Rimm's particular contribution is the *addition* of an assertive thought that the client uses following the self-command "STOP!" The assertive thought is antagonistic to the rumination. If the client ruminates "I'm going to die," he might practice thinking "STOP! I'm in fine health! I'm going to be okay!" If you were out of work and ruminating to the effect that "Everything is hopeless, there's nothing I can do about my life," you might practice thinking "STOP! I'll take things step by step, read the want ads in the paper, and do what I can day by day."

*Using the cassette recorder.* We have found a modification of the Rimm technique to be highly effective with clients who have access to a cassette recorder:

- Outline clearly the content of your ruminative thoughts.

- Construct two or three statements that oppose the helplessness and self-defeating nature of the ruminations. With one client who was convinced he was going to have a heart attack although medical findings showed no physical problems, assertive statements constructed were "My doctor did an EKG and found nothing." "I'm not going to have a heart attack," and "I'm in fine health."

- Record, in your own voice, the strongly stated command "STOP!," followed immediately by the assertive, counterruminative statements, spoken clearly and affirmatively.

- Place yourself in a comfortable sitting or reclining position, with your fingers ready to press the *play* button of the cassette recorder.

- Begin *purposefully* to ruminate the distressing thoughts.

- Press the play button of the recorder. The recording disrupts the ruminations and provides assertive, counter-ruminative statements.

- Rewind the cassette recorder to the beginning.

- Repeat this procedure ten times in a row, three or four times a day for two weeks. After that use the procedure ten times in a row once daily for another couple of weeks.

Clients typically report that their ruminations have ceased by the end of the first two weeks of treatment. Nevertheless, the process is continued to attempt to stamp out the ruminations more permanently. It is not uncommon for ruminations to return after several weeks or months, so keep the tape available, and be ready to repeat the procedure. You will find that the process is more effective the second time around and that you may need to use the method only for a few days. Ultimately you may go through the stamping-out process three or four times before a rumination is finally gone. But the procedure will work and you will know that you have the capacity to control distressing ruminations. You will no longer think of yourself as a helpless victim.

## THE CASE OF ERIKA

Erika was a twenty-year-old licensed practical nurse working the night shift at a nursing home. She was extremely attractive, but because of harsh parental treatment and condemnation during her adolescent years, she viewed herself as barely presentable. Her parents had also accused her of being sluttish shortly following puberty "because I matured early." She rebelled by becoming increasingly active sexually, and labeled herself promiscuous by her middle teens. She escaped her home immediately following high school graduation, became moderately involved in drug abuse and continued to "sleep around," but also managed to acquire nursing skills.

When she presented for therapy, her main complaint was

ruminations that she was worthless and unattractive, accompanied by low self-esteem, tension, insomnia, and a sense of foreboding doom. She felt that the ruminations came from "nowhere," although she readily came to understand that she was experiencing negative ideas that she had internalized from her parents.

Insight was not enough. Thought-stopping and assertive statements using the cassette recorder were undertaken. She made this recording: "STOP! You are attractive! You are worthwhile! A lot of people count on you. You're a fine nurse. You're reliable. You get to work every night. People need you. You're smart. You've done it all on your own, and you're working toward your R.N. You bring home a nice paycheck, and you're paying off a fine car."

Erika lay down on her couch and purposefully brought on the ruminations. After about half a minute she pressed the *play* switch of her recorder, permitting the tape to run its course. She rewound the tape, again initiated the ruminations, and played the tape. She repeated this process ten times in a row, three or four times daily. After two weeks, she reported that she no longer experienced the ruminations. But she was instructed to continue the procedure ten times in a row once daily for another two weeks. Then she used the procedure once weekly for another few months as "booster shots."

Following this BT approach to handling her ruminations, Erika felt full control over her thoughts. The negative thoughts occasionally returned, but they never again held that persistent, ruminative, involuntary quality. The were "like regular thoughts" and could be "turned off" at will. Erika was able to achieve greater satisfaction from her daily work. She lost the feeling of impending doom. She slept better. She continued to work for her R.N. and felt more entitled to say "No" to inappropriate men, providing her the opportunity to develop social relationships in which she felt more appreciated and worthwhile.

## THOUGHT-STOPPING, ASSERTIVE STATEMENTS, AND YOU

Obviously you must select assertive statements that contradict your own negative ruminations and sound right for you. *You may have to use trial and error to get the statements in a proper order and a proper tone of voice.* The "STOP!" must be commanding. Enlisting a "dramatic" family member or friend to make the recording may also prove beneficial.

# 3

---

# BT STRATEGIES FOR REDUCING FEARS

---

Fears differ from anxiety in that the former are negative emotional responses to *specific* situations or objects, such as speaking before a group or receiving an injection, whereas the latter is an emotional state that tends to be prolonged and may be difficult to link to any specific environmental factor. But fears and anxiety are similar in the feelings they arouse: rapid heartbeat, sweating, shakiness, heavy breathing, feeling weak or numb in the limbs, dizziness or faintness, muscular tensions, the need to eliminate, and a sense of dread—the "fight or flight" mechanism.[1] Not all people experience all these signs of fear, but most of you experience some of them.

## Objective Fears

Many fears are useful and necessary. It is logical that we be afraid of:

- touching a hot stove
- falling from a high place
- running into the street without looking for oncoming vehicles
- receiving surgical procedures without benefit of anesthesia
- "egging" larger and more powerful persons into combat

These fears are rational and adaptive.

## Irrational Fears

Other fears are irrational or maladaptive, and this chapter
will help you deal with these fears more effectively. *A fear is
irrational if the objective danger is disproportionate to the
amount of distress experienced.*[2] Such fears are labeled *phobias.* Such fears or phobias include:

- fear of high places, though you are in no objective danger
  of falling (*acrophobia*)
- fear of closed-in, tight places when you are in no objective danger of being smothered or trapped (*claustropho-
  bia*)
- fear of receiving injections—not because of the potential
  minor pain, but because of the "thought" of the procedure
- fear of working with sharp instruments
- fear of dead animals or dead people (*necrophobia*)
- fear of the dark
- fear of crawling insects
- fear of being alone
- fear of observing *others* bleeding or receiving medical
  intervention

Irrational fears or phobias do not necessarily interfere with
our lives. It matters little if you are afraid of heights if your
life style permits you to avoid high places. It matters little if
you fear snakes so long as your only encounter with them is
likely to be a voluntary one in a zoo. But some irrational
fears can be debilitating and interfere greatly with your attempts to lead your daily life. If you have no tolerance for
the sight of blood or being in the neighborhood of medical
procedures, you may find your health or life endangered if
you refrain from seeking treatment of an injury or disease. In
such cases, it is clearly to your benefit to do something about
your fears.

# Why Do Some People Have Irrational Fears?

## THE FREUDIAN OR
## PSYCHOANALYTIC APPROACH

According to Freud and his followers, phobias are *displaced* fears.[3] If you are afraid of closed-in places, Freudians feel this may be symbolic of *unconscious* fear that efforts to control sexual impulses will fail. Fear of knives or sharp instruments may represent unconscious castration anxiety in men, or fear of losing control over unconscious hostile impulses in women. Fear of dirt or of being infected may represent attempts to keep temptation toward anal sexual activity unconscious. Fear of being left alone is equated with concern that one will have the opportunity to masturbate.

Psychoanalytic assumptions remain just that: assumptions. Psychoanalysis as a treatment for phobias has never been proven effective in helping people overcome phobias.[4]

## THE BEHAVIORAL VIEW OF PHOBIAS

The behavioral view of phobias is that the things we fear have at some time in our pasts been associated with pain, or with the strongly perceived and felt threat of pain. If a two-year-old child receives a particularly painful injection, he may develop fear of medical procedures even if he cannot consciously recall what occurred in infancy. As you will see in the chapter on asserting yourself, it was shown in a landmark experiment more than fifty years ago[5] that an eleven-month-old child would develop fear of a white rat through pairing sight of the rat with repeated pain-inducing experiences—in this case the loud clanging of two iron bars behind the infant's head.

But not every person with acrophobia has had painful experience with heights. Not every person afraid of crawling insects and spiders has had early painful interactions with insects and spiders. Most people who fear the presence of snakes or touching snakes have never been bitten, strangled, nor even casually insulted by a snake. We would be hard pressed to demonstrate that every adolescent or adult who fears being left alone was subject to terrible consequences from being left alone early in life.

## OBSERVATIONAL LEARNING

But the behavioral view also allows for a type of learning called *vicarious learning*,[6] or learning through observing others. A child can learn that spiders are something to fear by observing his mother or a friend yell "Yuck!" in the presence of a spider. A child may observe an adult squirm or show facial indications of disgust when a snake is shown on television. If a mother happens across a statue of a nude in the company of her young daughter, shudders visibly, and labels the work disgusting, this is likely to have an effect on the child's conception of nudity. Children learn which words are acceptable and which words are "disgusting" not only through being hit for using "bad" words, but also through observation of how the important big people in their lives react to these words. This type of learning can occur on an automatic "gut" level, without the child later recalling the learning process.

## FEAR OF EXCESSIVE NOVELTY

People are known to react with interest to objects that are slightly different from the norm, or novel.[7] But excessively novel objects are usually avoided.[8] Many may fear spiders and snakes because their methods of locomotion—in fact, their entire physical makeup—are so foreign to humans. These animals may be viewed as "weird." They represent the unknown. We are intrigued by people who differ slightly in their habits, such as movie stars or the rich. But we shun cannibals or cultures where female infants are left to die.

People who fear the dark develop this fear, as children, only after they are capable of comprehending the threatening but undetectable things that might occur. Again, fear of the unknown.

We could try to make the case that fear of the unknown develops as a logical consequence of the fact that the less we know about a thing, the more susceptible we are to its potential harm. But we are still left with the problem of explaining why some are more afraid of spiders and the dark than others, why some fear spiders but not the dark, and so on. In many cases we shall just have to do without ultimate satisfying explanations for irrational fears and get on with dealing with them.

### DEALING WITH FEARS

This chapter will show you four methods for reducing or eliminating fears, and provide you with guidelines for choosing the methods that are right for you.

*The threshold method.* This method involves gradually approaching the feared stimulus object or situation by dealing with a hierarchy of gradually more fearful stimuli. You begin at a comfortable stage by exposing yourself to a stimulus that is similar to the "target" situation—the dreaded stimulus object itself—getting used to that stimulus, and then tackling stimuli progressively closer to the "target."

*Systematic self-desensitization (SSD).* With this method you combine progressive self-relaxation (PSR) with a hierarchy of *imagined* or fantasized fearful stimuli.

*Gradually prolonging exposure.* In this method, you expose yourself to the actual feared situation or object for as long as possible. When your discomfort becomes intolerable, you remove yourself from the situation. Once you have calmed down, you again expose yourself, thus gradually building up the amount of time during which you can tolerate the fear-inducing stimulus.

*Sink or swim (SOS) method.* Referred to as "stimulus flooding" in the technical psychological literature,[9] you expose yourself without relief to the feared stimulus with this method, until the bodily sensations of fear subside or are "fatigued."

## Strategy 1: The Threshold Method

With the threshold method, you gradually approach the feared object, situation, or activity. You establish the actual fearful situation as the "target" situation and create a series of graduated steps that build toward the target. You approach these steps one by one, and remain with each until all discomfort or concern vanishes. A few cases will clarify the procedure.

## KATE: FEAR OF DRIVING

Kate, a woman in her forties, had developed fear of driving her automobile, making her dependent upon family members and friends, and creating general inconvenience. The identified target situation was driving a round trip of thirty miles to work and back. The series of graduated steps were:

1. sitting behind the wheel of her automobile with an "understanding" friend who would keep her company
2. driving around the block in the company of her friend
3. driving a few miles back and forth with her friend
4. driving the route to work and back with her friend present
5. sitting alone behind the wheel of her automobile
6. driving around the block alone
7. driving a few miles back and forth alone
8. driving the route to work and back alone on a non-working day
9. driving back and forth to work alone

She was instructed not to go beyond any step in the hierarchy until she could engage in it totally without fear.

Treatment was completed in a few weeks. She remarked, in retrospect, that she would have preferred to carry out each step first with her friend, then alone, in the order 1, 5, 2, 6, 3, 7, 4, 8, 9. She felt this would have been more effective. We shall never know. This raises the following point: *Sometimes the series of graduated steps chosen is not the best series, but any logical sequence of steps can work.*

## RAYMOND: FEAR OF HEIGHTS

Raymond was a forty-seven-year-old office worker with fear of heights (acrophobia). He had worked on the second floor of an older office building for several years. Then his company moved—to the twentieth floor of a new building. At first Raymond panicked, but upon reflection he felt that he would be all right if he avoided working near a window. Since window space was highly desirable, this would be his option. His surrender of seniority in this matter was seized upon by someone his junior.

His first day of work in the new setting was on a Thursday. Raymond first became uncomfortable on the elevator, but then lost some of his concerns with unpacking chores, carving out his own workspace, and settling into his new desk. The offices had glass partitions. Late in the day he noticed the light shifting in his room as the sun moved west. His attention was increasingly drawn to the windows, a couple of offices away. He began to experience discomfort shortly before the workday came to an end. He ruminated about his fears that night, obtaining little sleep. Friday he felt "wrecked" at the outset. Panic gripped him in the elevator, but he forced himself to his desk. He began to sweat profusely and found his eyes drawn to the windows against his will. He soon felt nauseated and went to the bathroom. He eliminated and almost threw up. Another employee found him in the bathroom, and Raymond asked him to inform their supervisor that he was ill and leaving for the day.

Over the weekend Raymond seriously entertained the notion of quitting his job. Instead, he phoned his family physician and was referred to the clinic. At his initial interview Monday morning, Raymond needed to ventilate his frustrations and wanted to know why *he* must have this fear. He was gently informed that years of psychoanalysis might not provide the *whys*, but that a few days of graduated effort through the threshold method—with the target behavior defined as being able to sustain himself comfortably on the twentieth floor of his company's new building—might reduce the fear.

In Raymond's case, the graduated series of steps was obvious. Beginning at the first floor at which he could comfortably look out the window, he would work his way up from there, waiting at each level until he was perfectly comfortable before he would move on to the next.

He arranged a combination of personal days and sick leave to take the remainder of the week off, and undertook the threshold method program with the companionship of his wife. He chose a building near his own so that the views would be similar, but he would not have to explain his program to coworkers. A note from his therapist helped clear his purpose with the building's security personnel.

Raymond was in a rush to complete the program. Several times he tried to skip a floor or two, but then learned to return to the lower floor and become fully acclimated to that elevation before proceeding, as he had been directed. He phoned the clinic to express his disappointment at not being able to skip floors and to express fear that he might not complete the program before his authorized leave ran out. It was pointed out that he was responding to self-defeating, anxiety-producing thoughts and not realities.

He stuck to his task four hours a day, and by Thursday afternoon he had successfully climbed to the twenty-*fifth* story of the practice building. He asked his wife to leave him alone at that elevation. He phoned the clinic to boast that he had been able to skip a couple of floors at the higher elevations—this was predictable, since at the higher elevations one story would produce a less noticeable difference than at the lower elevations—and to state that he would return to work on Friday. It was suggested that he use Friday to continue in the practice building, and then use the weekend to "transfer" his fear reduction into his own building, since he would not then run into coworkers.

He returned to work on Monday. At first he was anxious because "Things are different when all your staff is there," but he purposefully walked over to the windows, looked out and down, and patted himself on the back for not becoming overwhelmed by bodily sensations of fear. He ate his lunch on a floor several stories above his office, and this practice became habitual.

Raymond's case points out other factors that will help you cope with your own fears. *Do not attempt to accelerate your self-pacing so that you become overwhelmed by fear in the situation in which you are attempting to reduce fear gradually. Go beyond your target behavior in practice sessions if you can.*

## ADRIA: FEAR OF DOGS

Adria was a fashion designer in her late twenties who was "simply petrified" by dogs. This was not a meaningful problem until a close friend inherited an adult German shepherd, and Adria had to limit their meetings to places other than the friend's apartment. This prompted her to seek therapy. Adria had had therapy before. She remarked that she could have continued to avoid dogs, but felt that she may as well try to do something about it, "other than take a stiff shot," so long as she did not have to undergo "years of psychoanalysis" to find out why she was afraid of dogs. She was asked how she felt about puppies. Puppies were "not so bad," but still "a bit unnerving because they're so frisky."

The series of graduated steps employed was as follows:

1. Handle puppies three or four weeks old. Adria knew persons who bred dogs and could arrange this.
2. Handle and play with puppies at the age at which they are commonly sold, six to eight weeks. Adria visited numerous pet shops. She was more comfortable with smaller puppies at first, and graduated to larger puppies.
3. Handle and play with small adult dogs owned by friends, with the friends present.
4. Take the small adult dogs out for walks by herself.
5. Play with her friend's German shepherd with her friend present.
6. Take the German shepherd out for walks by herself.

Adria "became friends" with the German shepherd within a month, and remarked that she would have done so more rapidly if she had not had so many things to do besides playing with dogs.

## RICK AND MARCY: FEAR OF FEMALE SEX ORGANS

Fear of women's sex organs does not imply homosexuality, but our case deals with a man and woman, both of whom had a same-sex orientation. Rick was a twenty-five-year-old gay male who had moved in with Marcy, a twenty-five-year-old Lesbian, for purposes of sharing rent, an "air of legitimacy," and companionship. They fell in love. Unfortunately, Rick was intensely afraid of Marcy's genitalia. He found her to be attractive "in the abstract" and "a wonderful person." She had also brought him to climax on a number of occasions through manual or oral ministrations. He could not reciprocate nor contemplate intercourse.

They presented themselves at the clinic as a couple with a sex problem. Rick acknowledged that he could kiss Marcy and fondle her breasts without distress. He received her manual and oral stimulation with as much pleasure as he had received from any man. Her vaginal region terrified him. Compounding the problem, both had naïvely assumed an "all or nothing at all" expectation concerning intercourse. The threshold method was employed to allow Rick to become gradually more comfortable with Marcy's genitalia. Rick was to proceed in the following sexual activities, progressing at his own pace:

1. During the first week, Rick and Marcy were simply to massage each other. Rick was to feel no pressure to stimulate Marcy's genitalia, although she was to feel free to stimulate his penis. Thus he would learn to associate her nudity and the general feel of her body with his own sexual arousal.
2. Rick would manually stimulate Marcy's genitalia as they were engaged in mutual massage.
3. Rick would rub his penis against Marcy's pubic hair.
4. Rick would rub his penis against the outer lips of Marcy's vagina.
5. Rick would insert his penis an inch or so into Marcy's vagina with up-and-down rather than in-and-out movements.
6. Intercourse.

Marcy was advised that she must not become progressively more demanding as Rick engaged in these behaviors. This would serve to make him more fearful by creating "performance anxiety"—anxiety about the adequacy of his ability to please her. It was acknowledged that treatment would be temporarily frustrating for Marcy. She must focus on the long-term payoff potential.

In step one of treatment, Rick "jumped the gun" by a couple of days and fondled Marcy's genitalia. He reported he was shocked to find how wet and soft she was. Though she was surprised, Marcy did not overreact. Nor did she show disappointment when Rick pulled his hand away. He paused in their mutual caressing and concentrated on breathing deeply and regularly. He replaced Marcy's hand on his penis, and sexual arousal helped further quell the bodily sensations of fear. Shortly thereafter he continued his manual stimulation of Marcy's vaginal region and, after several pauses, was fondling her without distress.

Rick decided to skip step two and the next day immediately began to rub his penis against the outer lips of Marcy's vagina. The first time he shuddered and lost his erection. But they had been forewarned that fear can cause loss of erection. After a while he returned to mutual manual stimulation, regained his erection, and returned to the step-by-step program. Within a few days, proceeding at a pace that was comfortable for Rick, the couple were having intercourse.

Later they returned to the clinic because it appeared that Rick was manifesting premature ejaculation. This problem was handled straightforwardly as outlined in the section of this book on men's sex problems.

Rick was able to employ the threshold method because he was living with a woman who was fully co-operative with his treatment. Many men who fear female nudity do not have this advantage. We have been told by some clients of frightening experiences with pornographic films, from which they had practically run, breaking out into sweats. Pornography is certainly too explicit for men with such fears.

If you fear women's sex organs but do not have a partner available to help you with the threshold method, you would be wise to employ systematic self-desensitization (SSD), described in the next section, which permits the use of photographs or fantasized images of feared objects on a graduated basis. This will be illustrated in the case of Marie, a young woman who feared male nudity and for whom "real life" exposure to the feared stimuli would have been impractical.

# Strategy 2: Systematic Self-desensitization (SSD)

Systematic desensitization is a technique for replacing fear with relaxation in usually fear-arousing situations. It is perhaps the most widely used BT technique, and to some clinicians it is what BT is "all about." Invented by Dr. Joseph Wolpe of the Eastern Pennsylvania Psychiatric Institute,[10] it combines progressive relaxation with gradually increased exposure to frightening *imagined* stimuli. The client does not actually approach the fear-inducing stimulus, object, or situation. In imagination, or through the use of photographs or slides, he pictures himself gradually moving closer through space or time. Research has shown that if a client can be desensitized to fear-arousing stimuli in imagination, he can usually transfer these gains to real-life situations.[11] Systematic desensitization has powerful advantages.

- The client always feels as relaxed as possible while he is exposed to symbolic (photographs or imagined scenes) fear-arousing stimuli.
- The client fully controls the pace of approach to the imagined "target" situation, as in the threshold method.
- As in the threshold method, small, distinct steps leading toward the imagined target are used, with each step

being only slightly more fear-arousing than the one preceding it.

- Thus the client never experiences more than a few seconds of slight discomfort and does not move a step closer to the imagined target until *all* felt discomfort at the present step has vanished.

Though systematic desensitization has traditionally been administered by a therapist, recent research studies[12] have shown good results with *self-administered* systematic desensitization, which we label systematic self-desensitization, or SSD. SSD entails the following steps:

1. Master progressive self-relaxation (PSR), as described in the chapter on anxiety.
2. Construct a hierarchy of fear-inducing objects or situations that logically lead toward the target situation. There may be few or many steps. We recommend ten to twenty.
3. Relax yourself using the abbreviated PSR procedure. This will take you five minutes once you have mastered PSR.
4. Expose yourself to the first fear-inducing stimulus in the hierarchy. Allow yourself to experience only a few seconds of discomfort. Then stop imagining the scene or remove the photograph.
5. Regain full relaxation. Concentrating on a pleasant "safe scene" that has been prepared beforehand, such as the beach scene in the fantasized minivacation in Chapter 1, will help.
6. Re-expose yourself to the fear-inducing stimulus. You will be able to imagine or view it longer without discomfort.
7. When the fear-inducing stimulus no longer interferes with your state of full relaxation, move on to the next stimulus in the hierarchy. Repeat steps four through seven fo reach stimulus in the hierarchy.

Some of the elements of SSD will be elaborated in detail.

## PROGRESSIVE SELF-RELAXATION (PSR)

Follow the complete PSR procedure as outlined in Chapter 2. Make no effort to expose yourself to fear-inducing stimuli until you have mastered PSR. This will typically occur after you have practiced PSR for a month: two weeks of the full-length procedure and two weeks of the abbreviated procedure. More concretely, practice the full-length procedure twice a day for two weeks, and the abbreviated procedure once a day for two weeks. If you can only practice once a day, wait until six weeks have passed, and practice the full-length procedure for the first four weeks. By adequately building your PSR skills, you will both help give SSD every opportunity to be effective for you and acquire relaxation skills that will make you a more relaxed person throughout the course of your daily life.

## CONSTRUCTION OF THE HIERARCHY

The hierarchy you construct for SSD will depend on the nature of the target stimulus and the limits of your imagination. Let us construct a hierarchy for a biology student who fears rodents but will have to handle live mice. Handling live mice independently is defined as the target behavior. We can use photographs of mice or vividly imagine mice. The student selects to imagine the mouse. Then we manipulate other factors, such as the distance between the mouse and the student, whether or not the student is alone or with a friend, whether or not the mouse is caged, and whether or not the student is merely watching or actually touching the mouse. *Each hierarchy item considered for use should be written on a separate index card, and the cards should be ordered and reordered until the student is fully satisfied that the order progresses from the least fear-inducing stimulus to the target.* In the sample hierarchy the student might imagine:

1. seeing the mouse in a cage fifteen feet away
2. seeing the mouse in a cage ten feet away
3. seeing the mouse in a cage five feet away
4. seeing the mouse held by another student fifteen feet away (note that the "uncaged stimulus" is more frightening than the caged stimulus, so once more the distance is increased)
5. seeing the mouse held by another student ten feet away
6. seeing the mouse held by another student five feet away
7. standing next to the student who is holding and stroking the mouse
8. stroking the back of the mouse while the other student

holds it (he finds the mouse to be soft, warm, furry, and somewhat "squirmy")

9. holding the mouse with the "model student" while he—the fearful student—strokes it
10. holding the mouse and stroking it while the other student is present
11. briefly holding the mouse and stroking it in the absence of the other student
12. returning the mouse to its cage
13. standing nearby while the model student removes the mouse from the cage and hands it to the fearful student, who is then left alone with the mouse, strokes it, and replaces it in the cage
14. removing the mouse from the cage in the company of the model student, stroking it, and replacing it in the cage
15. removing the mouse from the cage without companionship, stroking it, and replacing it in the cage

This hierarchy *was* used by one of our clients who was given the basic principles of SSD. She also wanted to know if she had been fearful of the mouse because the mouse was "a phallic symbol." We confessed ignorance in these esoteric matters and told her to settle for patting herself on the back for her accomplishment.

## VIVID IMAGINING

Produce a vivid image of each item in the hierarchy. Imagine yourself directly in the scene. If you do not do so, SSD may not work for you.[18] Close your eyes as you imagine. Attend to all the sensory impressions you might experience in the presence of the imagined stimulus: visual, tactile, auditory. Imagine appropriate smells and tastes. Attend not only to the feared stimulus, but also to its common surroundings. If the feared object is the laboratory mouse, also clearly visualize the physical configuration of the laboratory, its other objects, and its smells.

## EXPOSURE TO THE
## LEAST-FEAR-INDUCING STIMULUS

Attain deep muscular relaxation through the abbreviated PSR procedure. Expose yourself to the least-fear-inducing stimulus in imagination or by pictorial representation, as with photos or slides. The first stimulus in the hierarchy must oc-

casion some fear, but only a slight amount. Nothing is gained
by desensitizing yourself to a stimulus that causes no discomfort. On the other hand, more than slight discomfort could
cause SSD to backfire. Too fearful a stimulus could panic
you and temporarily interfere with your capacity to relax.

By analogy, lying on a beach with the sun warming you
and the sound of the surf lulling you may be quite pleasant.
But if your last several visits to the beach were terminated by
a plague of sand crabs biting your toes, the beach would lose
its calming value. So, too, relaxation can lose its calming effects if the stimuli with which you pair relaxation are overwhelming. *At every step in a hierarchy, each progressive
stimulus must only be slightly discomforting.*

Remain with the first fear-inducing stimulus until you begin to feel discomfort. Then focus your attention elsewhere.
This may mean making your mind "blank" or imagining
something else. If the stimulus becomes markedly discomforting after only a few seconds, initially select a stimulus even
farther from the target.

## REGAINING COMPLETE RELAXATION

After removing your attention from the hierarchy stimulus,
you may focus completely on a pleasant scene that you have
constructed for this purpose and practiced visualizing beforehand. *In SSD it is essential to follow each hierarchy stimulus
with complete relaxation.* As you focus on the pleasant scene,
attend to any muscle contractions that might have occurred.
You may simply try to "let go" of contractions you find in
any particular muscle group. If tension remains, keep the rest
of your body as relaxed as possible, take a dcep breath and
tense the muscle group purposefully, hold the tension and
your breath for four to eight seconds, tell yourself to relax,
then simultaneously let go of your breath and the muscle
contractions. Allow the relaxation in that muscle group to develop and grow for thirty to sixty seconds.

## RE-EXPOSURE TO THE
## FEAR-INDUCING STIMULUS

After you have reachieved complete relaxation, re-expose
yourself to the stimulus. You will be able to expose yourself
gradually to a stimulus for longer periods of time before you
experience discomfort. After a certain number of exposures,
you will be able to tolerate the stimulus indefinitely. If you
can expose yourself, in imagination, to the item three times

without discomfort, move on to the next higher fear-inducing stimulus in the hierarchy. Repeat the process for each stimulus in the hierarchy until none of the items occasions any fear or discomfort.

## QUESTIONS AND ANSWERS

*How much time do you spend relaxing yourself before you expose yourself to the first item in the hierarchy?*

Since you will be at the point in PSR training at which you are using the abbreviated procedure, this will take approximately five minutes. Some people require one or two minutes; others, ten.

*How many times will you have to expose yourself to a specific item in the hierarchy before you are desensitized to it?*

This depends on how many steps you have chosen and on whether each step induces only a slight amount of fear as it is approached. We have found that ten to twenty exposures to an item are usually sufficient. Some items move surprisingly rapidly. Others seem to pose a stumbling block. If an item becomes a stumbling block, break it down into three items, with the first two less fear-inducing than the problem item.

*Then how much time will it take to become desensitized to an item in the hierarchy?*

Let us assume that SSD to a particular item requires eight exposures. The first exposure lasts half a minute, and it takes a minute to reachieve complete relaxation. But the next exposures are longer, since you are becoming habituated to the stimulus. It could take easily forty minutes to determine that three successive exposures evoked no discomfort.

*Then if a hierarchy has twenty steps and each step takes the better part of an hour, SSD could take up to twenty hours?*

Yes. And since we would not recommend more than an hour of SSD a day, this could require three weeks. We presume that you will not be undertaking SSD unless the fear-inducing stimulus or event seriously interferes with your life.

*How do I know if things are going wrong?*

Things are going wrong if you cannot increase the amount of time during which you expose yourself to a hierarchy item.

*As an occasional event this is normal, but as a habit there is something wrong with your approach.* Ask yourself whether you have spent all the time required to develop PSR skills. Have you used index cards in constructing your hierarchy and, by comparing every grouping of two or three cards, placed them in the proper order? Have you reachieved complete relaxation between exposures? Are you allowing yourself to experience *some* tolerable discomfort when you expose yourself to a hierarchy item? Did you expose yourself three times without distress before moving on? Are you clearly imagining the hierarchy items?

If your answer to all these questions is "Yes," you may wish to consult a behavior therapist for more personalized attention in receiving training in systematic desensitization. Names of practitioners across the country are available from the Association for the Advancement of Behavior Therapy, 420 Lexington Avenue, New York, NY 10017. In the New York area, consultation may be arranged through the Institute for Cognitive Behavior Therapy, in Hempstead and Manhattan.

Some cases will further clarify the use of SSD.

## DAVID: FEAR OF TEACHING

David, a twenty-five-year-old art teacher, was scheduled to begin his first full-time teaching job in a month and a half. During the prior few weeks he had begun to ruminate about his shaky and difficult student-teaching experience the spring before. He was becoming increasingly fearful of placing himself before his classes. He had thought of resigning before he began. He had developed light-headedness, shakiness and coldness in the hands, loose bowel movements, and "spells" during which he forgot what he was going to do. A friend who had finished a few courses in psychology told David that he, David, was really afraid that by becoming a competent teacher he would run out of excuses for continuing to live with his mother. Unfortunately, neither this "insight" nor David's haphazard attempts at self-medication with beer were very useful.

David was taught the principles of SSD and constructed a hierarchy of fear-inducing stimuli along two dimensions: time left to go before teaching, and number of students involved in teaching situations. He listed all hierarchy items on index cards and sorted them until he was satisfied that they were in a gradually ascending order. In a couple of cases, an item from one "dimension" was as fear-inducing as an item from the other "dimension," and the order was randomized. The resultant listing:

1. imagining it is four weeks before classes begin
2. it is three weeks before classes begin
3. talking after school with one student who has dropped by to discuss the possibility of a career in art
4. it is two weeks before classes begin
5. supervising one student after class on an individual art project
6. it is ten days before classes begin
7. supervising one student on a project during class while other students are working independently elsewhere in the class
8. it is one week before classes begin
9. supervising a group of two students working on a project while other students work independently elsewhere in the class
10. supervising a group of three students working on a project while other students work independently elsewhere in the class
11. it is five days before classes begin
12. asking a class that is already involved in individual projects if there are any questions
13. it is three days before classes begin
14. it is the night before classes begin
15. driving to work on the morning classes begin
16. greeting a new class, talking about the course, and fielding questions

David was given two weeks of intensive relaxation training, and SSD began four weeks prior to the beginning of classes. He practiced SSD on his own.

So that he would not be wondering how to greet his classes, he was instructed to prepare specific, concrete initial talks for his students. He practiced them until they felt quite automatic. Some clinical session time was spent in behavior rehearsal, with David delivering parts of his talks to the therapist. The therapist occasionally asked a difficult question or made a sarcastic, adolescent remark, providing David with the opportunity to respond in a nonthreatening situation. Specific responses to sarcastic remarks were rehearsed.

When David did appear before his classes, he experienced mild fear. He found himself automatically taking a deep breath, telling himself to relax, and expelling the breath. The effect was calming. By the time David introduced himself to his last class, he was enjoying his first day as a teacher. He had known what to say and his manner, stiff in the morning, had become increasingly loose and casual. He was especially pleased that he had been relaxed with his last class, which had been somewhat restless nearing the end of the school day.

## MARIE: FEAR OF MALE SEX ORGANS

Marie, a twenty-one-year-old college junior, was attracted to men but "scared to death" of them. Her personal history showed some plausible reasons for her fears, but was not particularly unusual. Her religious background had emphasized that sex prior to marriage was sinful. Her mother had implied that when she married she would have to do her "duty" for her husband. She had run into an exhibitionist who asked her directions from a car when she was in her early teens. She did not clearly recall the incident, but the thought of further male nudity was frightful. She had shuddered when college friends had shown her photographs of nude men in popular magazines like *Playgirl* and *Viva*. She would not attend an "R rated" film unless a trusted friend had informed her beforehand that there was no male nudity. She had done some dating, but had been quite nervous. She enjoyed dancing with young men, but recently a partner had achieved erection during bodily contact. When she became cognizant of it she was overwhelmed by sensations of fear and threw up in a nearby bathroom.

When she presented herself for therapy, Marie had been dating a "nice" boy for two months. She thought she might love him. While he was not pressuring her into petting, Marie felt that petting and intercourse were activities she ought to be able to tolerate and enjoy if she felt the desire. But her thoughts and her "gut-level reactions" viewed the prospect differently.

SSD was undertaken with the therapist's guidance. Marie was presented with several photographic slides concerning themes of heterosexual contact and male nudity, and she interspersed these with imagined scenes in constructing her stimulus hierarchy:

1. imagining being at the beach and observing men in swimsuits
2. imagining necking with her boyfriend as their bodies, fully clothed, touch
3. looking at slides of men in swimsuits
4. imagining lying next to her boyfriend at the beach, both dressed in swimsuits
5. imagining that her boyfriend kisses her on the beach, both dressed in swimsuits
6. looking at slides of nude men in the distance, back view
7. looking at slides of nude men in the foreground, back view
8. looking at slides of nude men in the distance, front view
9. looking at slides of nude men in the foreground, front view
10. looking at slides of penises
11. imagining that her boyfriend achieves an erection while they are dancing, fully clothed
12. imagining that her boyfriend achieves an erection while they are kissing on the beach, dressed in swimsuits
13. looking at slides of nude couples kissing
14. looking at slides of nude couples petting
15. looking at slides of nude couples having intercourse

After Marie had mastered PSR skills, the entire SSD sequence took only sixteen hour-long sessions in the privacy of her own room, allowing ten minutes at the outset of each session to become completely relaxed, and allowing another five to ten minutes at the conclusion of each session to simply enjoy the bodily sensations of deep muscular relaxation.

Marie became much less anxious about her dating and readily engaged in graduated petting. During her last "talk session," she had not decided whether she was going to have intercourse with her boyfriend, but she felt confident that any decision would be made on grounds other than fear.

# Strategy 3: Gradually Prolonging Exposure

## CONTACT WITH FEARED SITUATIONS OR OBJECTS

One of the central facts concerning irrational fears is that the amount of fear experienced by the person who perceives the dreaded situation or object is greater than the amount of pain or distress actual contact with the situation would entail. As a result, phobic people usually do their best to avoid contact with that which they fear. But if they were to allow themselves to maintain contact with the fear-inducing situation or object, their fear might eventually diminish or extinguish entirely. In order to reduce a phobia, some contact with the dreaded stimulus—even imagined, as in SSD—must be endured.

This principle is employed in both the threshold method and SSD. In both techniques the feared stimulus or "target" stimulus is gradually approached, actually or symbolically.

## GRADUALLY PROLONGED EXPOSURE[14]

With gradually prolonged exposure, you expose yourself initially to the "target" stimulus. You also vary the *amount of time* during which you expose yourself.

Gradually prolonged exposure is particularly effective in situations in which you (1) can tolerate exposure to the phobic "target" situation or object at least briefly, and (2) have complete control over the amount of time during which you expose yourself to the dreadful target.

Gradually prolonged exposure would not have been a practical procedure for Raymond, who needed to learn to maintain himself on the twentieth story of the office building in which he worked. Once he had outworn his visceral welcome on the twentieth floor, time would have passed while he (1) waited for the down elevator and (2) was in transit to a lower level. All this time he would have ruminated self-defeating thoughts such as "My God, I've got to get out of here!," and his discomfort might have mounted to fear of panic proportions.

## STEPS IN GRADUALLY PROLONGING EXPOSURE

1. Be certain that the target situation or object meets two requirements: (a) you can tolerate brief exposure to the target, and (b) you have complete control over the duration of exposure to the target. Examples of fears amenable to these conditions include: fear of being in a small room, fear of viewing a removable small animal, fear of being with someone who has an intravenous feeding tube in the back of his hand or arm, or fear of handling sharp tools.

2. Create a situation in which you can readily expose yourself to the target and then readily remove yourself. *A ready exit and opportunity to make use of the exit are musts.* It is of little use to sit near a door in a frighteningly crowded room if social pressures will prevent you from *using* the door.

3. Place yourself in the target situation until you begin to feel discomfort. Maintain yourself in the situation for *only* a few moments longer.

4. Leave the situation and relax. Breathe deeply and regularly. If you have mastered PSR skills as outlined in Chapter 2, take a deep breath, tell yourself to relax, and exhale. Focus on a pleasant scene.

5. After you have reachieved relaxation, return to the fear-inducing situation until you again begin to experience discomfort. Remain a few moments longer, then leave.

Through gradually prolonging exposure to a fear-inducing situation, and then allowing the bodily sensations of fear to dissipate or be replaced by sensations of relaxation, you will be able to remain in the situation longer and longer.

Gradually prolonging exposure is by definition a gradual procedure. Do not torture yourself, going for a rapid "cure." This may have the reverse effect of increasing your sensitivity to the fear-inducing stimuli. Be satisfied with small, gradual gains. You may hit "plateaus" in which you do not make gains. Do not allow this to discourage you. Follow the technique precisely, and you will find yourself gradually increasing the amount of time you can spend in the fear-arousing situation. *Eventually this situation will no longer induce fear.*

Some cases will illustrate the procedure.

## TONY: FEAR OF VISITING HOSPITAL ROOMS

Tony, a thirty-one-year-old architect, was disturbed by his inability to tolerate visits to friends and relatives in hospitals when they were receiving dextrose solutions or other fluids intravenously. Typically his face became hot and flushed, he would begin to sweat heavily, he would become dizzy, and the "only thought in my head would be, 'I've got to get out of here, I've got to get out of here!' " He would rush from the room, send someone back to the patient with an excuse, leave the hospital, and tell himself what an awful person he was.

Upon clinical interview it was noted that it took a couple of minutes for these sensations of fear to build to the point where they propelled Tony from the sickroom. His motivation to overcome this fear was high. He feared that "someday" he would require similar procedures. His father had been scheduled for an operation that would be followed by intravenous feeding to reduce the probabilities of dehydration and shock.

A treatment plan was worked out in which Tony first candidly discussed his fear with his father prior to the surgical procedure. Tony would use his father's postoperative situation in order to "get used to" the "IV" tube. This would permit Tony to spend time with his father in the hospital, though his visiting pattern would be unusual. Tony's mother also had to co-operate with the procedure since she would be with his father continually and witness Tony's comings and goings. Occasional visitors would be less likely to notice a pattern to Tony's excusing himself for a moment. The following were also specified:

1. When visiting his father, Tony would pay particular attention to the IV tubes.
2. When leaving the room, Tony would simply say, "Excuse me." No other explanation would be required.
3. Tony would stay in the room as he was beginning to experience bodily signs of fear, but would limit the building up of these sensations to a period that was clearly tolerable for him—no longer than half a minute.
4. When the bodily sensations of fear were building, Tony

would not ruminate, "I've got to get out of here." Instead, he would say to himself, "You will be able to remain here longer and longer as time goes on."

5. Tony would go to a preplanned waiting area where he would sit and relax. As he relaxed he would fantasize preplanned enjoyable imagery, breathe deeply and regularly, and tell himself, "Good, you managed to stay there without getting ill."

6. When the bodily sensations of fear had dissipated completely, he would return to the sickroom and repeat the process.

It was essential to the plan that Tony gradually prolong exposure *at his own pace*, without concern about the social consequences of leaving the room when he felt he must. Had his parents not co-operated fully, the plan would have been impractical.

During the first evening of visiting his father, Tony was able to increase his tolerance of the IV tubes from about two and a half to eleven or twelve minutes. This occurred within a four-hour period. On the second evening, Tony could not initially return to the full eleven or twelve minutes, but felt comfortable for more than five. It took less than an hour to build back to the twelve-minute mark, and by the end of the evening Tony had been able to stay in the room a full half hour, leaving only because visiting hours had ended. On the third evening, Tony left the sickroom only once because of bodily sensations of fear. He found that he was able to examine closely the structure of the IV materials and to touch them.

Approximately two months later, Tony phoned the clinic to report that he had just visited the wife of a friend, who had given birth, and that she, too, had had an IV. After five or six minutes into the visit, he began to experience some bodily sensations of fear, but they were not nearly so extreme as they had been prior to treatment. Furthermore, he was not ruminating thoughts about the necessity of leaving, but rather telling himself to reinitiate the treatment plan on an abbreviated basis. Thus he waited until the sensations built some more, and excused himself for a moment so that he could practice his relaxation regimen. He returned to the room a few minutes later and remained for more than an hour without further discomfort. Note that *treated fears may return if you are not exposed to fear-inducing stimuli for a long period of time. But reducing them and eliminating them the second time is a relatively brief and easy process.*

## NANCY: FEAR OF CROWDED PUBLIC PLACES

Nancy was a thirty-two-year-old divorcee who could not tolerate crowds in stores and at concerts. She would be "all right" for a few minutes, but would then develop the feeling that "things" were closing in on her. Her heart would begin to pound. She would perspire, although her hands became "cold as ice." She would become dizzy from hyperventilation. And she would "get this awful feeling as if I were going to die. My heart would be racing so rapidly, I wouldn't believe that I could survive." She would typically fight off these sensations as long as possible and then almost literally run to the nearest exit. That would signal the end of her shopping or the end of the concert.

The situation she chose for gradually prolonged exposure was a crowded department store at one end of a shopping mall. The store had several direct exits to parking areas, and near one exit were benches and trees. Nancy undertook gradually prolonged exposure on consecutive Thursday and Friday evenings, and the Saturday following. On Thursday evening she began to browse in the department store. Perhaps because of her heightened expectation of the bodily sensations of fear, she became uncomfortable after only a couple of minutes, whereas she typically "lasted" several minutes, perhaps half an hour. She waited only a few more moments, as instructed, and then left the store through the planned exit. She relaxed on the benches, breathing deeply and regularly, focusing on a preplanned romantic scene involving a Caribbean cruise.

After a few minutes she felt completely relaxed and then did something she had never done before: returned to the store on the same day she had been forced to leave by feelings of fear. This time she was able to browse for fifteen minutes until the noise of the crowd and the felt narrowness of the aisles began to "get to" her. She bore the discomfort for another half minute and then, with a deliberate but unhurried pace, returned to the benches outside the store. On the way out, she told herself, "Everything *will* be fine" rather than "If I don't get out of here, I'm going to die!" She relaxed and entered the store four more times that evening, ending the night's browsing by remaining in the store for more than a half hour prior to closing time.

On Friday evening, Nancy returned. She was not so expectant of experiencing negative bodily sensations as she had been the evening before, but she was able to tolerate the store for not quite a full half hour on her first visit. As with Tony, after a pause in treatment, some of the prior day's gains were temporarily lost. By closing time, Nancy had remained in the store for a full hour, noting that boredom was the predominant feeling she was aware of as she left. Saturday she arrived at ten in the morning and remained for an hour and a half without distress. She wondered whether she might dare to have lunch in the store. She ordered a sandwich and coffee in a take-out cup, in case she might feel the urge to leave. As she ate, distress began to build. But it was completely tolerable, and she remained in the lunchroom as it grew more crowded. After eating she took a respite at the benches. She returned and remained for another few hours, visiting other stores in the mall, thus venturing knowingly farther away from her "safe spot." She tried on clothing, recognizing that this would further impede exit from the mall should she desire to leave. At one point in a dressing room she did begin to feel "the need for air." But she cut off the rumination that she might die and repeated to herself, "You're only getting upset because you convinced yourself you would." She sat and relaxed in the dressing room, maintaining regular and deep breathing, and vividly imagining her Caribbean scene. In a couple of minutes she felt capable of leisurely dressing and unhurriedly leaving the mall through the department store. But once she had dressed, the urge to leave had passed, and she spent more time shopping. She made a point of congratulating herself for her success.

Several months later, Nancy would still experience intermittent discomfort in crowded places, but she no longer felt she must leave. She replaced self-defeating ruminations with the thought that her distress would be temporary and that she was *not* going to die. She focused on breathing deeply and calmly, visualized her Caribbean scene, and soon the need to leave would pass.

## Strategy 4: The Sink or Swim (SOS) Method

The "sink or swim" (SOS) method assumes that your body can experience the sensations of fear for just so long without these sensations terminating. The analogy is that just as you can run without rest for just so long, so too can you shake and shiver with fear for just so long without these bodily activities coming to an end. Thus if you exposed yourself unceasingly to fear-inducing stimulation, you would eventually stop experiencing the bodily sensations of fear, and the stimulus would lose its phobic quality.

The SOS method is like "baptism under fire." If you are afraid of mice, lock yourself into a cage of mice and stay there until your fear is gone. If you are afraid of the dark, remain in the dark until your shakes have played themselves out and your brain is no longer expecting "things that go bump in the night." If you are afraid of the water, sling on your water wings and jump right in and stay there until being blue with cold has replaced any vestiges of fear. If you faint while facing the phobic stimulus, focus on it again as soon as you awaken. If staring down the stimulus causes you to throw up or go to the bathroom to eliminate your solid waste, go right back to the stimulus after you wash your hands. Eventually the bodily sensations of fear must fatigue and cease. You will no longer be afraid. Unfortunately, this is only *sometimes true*. People who are deeply depressed and low in spirits or who are very highly agitated may experience seemingly endless bodily sensations of fear.

We recommend that you *not* use the SOS method for dealing with fears unless you must. The SOS method would be indicated for medical students who initially cannot tolerate the sight of blood and do not know of methods available such as SSD. The SOS method is required of soldiers in their first battle, although for soldiers in battle, fear can hardly be considered inappropriate. Certainly, if you are ill and require medical attention, yet dread doctors, we recommend the SOS method as an alternative to possible death. But if any alternative method is available, such as initially taking your physical illness to an understanding phychiatrist, use it. Still, if you sense an emergency, the proper place for you is the emergency room of your hospital no matter what your fears may be.

*Why suffer?* We see no moral value in forcing yourself to suffer. This book is oriented toward helping you learn to do the things you feel you ought to be doing with the least stress possible. The only significant "benefit" we see to the SOS method is that for most people it can work, despite the suffering it requires. So take heart if you find yourself in a situation in which you must confront your phobias without recourse to any of the time-absorbing methods outlined in this chapter. As time passes, the odds are with you that you will be increasingly able to tolerate the situation in which you are forced to remain.

# A Specic Group of Fears:
# Fear of Social Incompetence and Social Criticism

Some of you may not be prey to fear of animals, fear of blood, fear of heights, fear of tight places, and some of the more common phobias. Instead you may be deathly afraid of social situations in which you feel that you may be ignored, that you will not say or do the right thing, that someone may disapprove of you, that others will not accept you, or that people may think that you are silly. The prospect of being left alone with a member of the opposite sex may frighten you. You may be afraid of striking up a conversation with coworkers or strangers. You may become tremulous at the prospect of speaking before a group.

## USE OF SYSTEMATIC
## SELF-DESENSITIZATION (SSD)

It is certainly possible for you to deal with some of these situations through SSD. You read how David was able to engage in a SSD program that made it easier for him to introduce himself to his classes and work with students.

## USE OF ASSERTIVE BEHAVIORS

But if these fears are not extreme and debilitating, it might be possible for you to try to tackle them "head on," by planning to carry out many of the things that frighten you about social situations. If you feel that your own needs and life situation may allow for such experimentation, we direct you to the chapter on asserting yourself. Assertiveness is not synonymous with aggressiveness or boorishness. Assertiveness is rather the expression of your feelings through appropriate social remarks and behavior.

## SELF-ASSERTION REDUCES FEAR

Dr. Andrew Salter[15] of New York City and Dr. Joseph Wolpe[16] of the Eastern Pennsylvania Psychiatric Institute have noted that encouraging clients to be more assertive appears to have the effect of reducing fear or anxiety in the social milieu. Both therapists have theorized that there are neurological explanations as to why a person behaving assertively would be less likely to experience social discomfort. Their explanations remain quite controversial and we shall not go into them here, but it seems self-evident that if you go into a usually frightening social situation knowing what to do and say, and feeling that it is your right to speak up, you are less likely to experience fear and helplessness. Assertive responses to such situations seem incompatible with anxiety and fear, just as deep muscular relaxation is incompatible with the bodily sensations of anxiety and fear. The person who is socially gregarious is not the person who sits in the corner, trying to blend in with the wallpaper because of social fears.

## SSD AND ASSERTIVE BEHAVIORS

When fear is strong and debilitating, you may wish to try a combination of SSD and assertive behavior in reference to social situations. An eighteen-year-old female client held views that differed markedly with those of her traditionalist mother. Through therapy, the daughter became more "in touch" with her own feelings and developed a concrete list of things she would like to be able to say to her mother. But the daughter simply could not tolerate the anger her mother was likely to express. Thus the daughter underwent a program of systematic desensitization, with the "target" in the stimulus hierarchy being "imagining my mother screaming away at her worst" before the daughter employed her assertive behaviors. The daughter did not alter her mother's points of view, but this was not a realistic goal for her. The daughter nonetheless felt that she had managed to establish her identity as separate from her mother.

# 4

## BT STRATEGIES FOR GETTING TO SLEEP WITHOUT DRUGS

### In Search of that "Sweet Oblivious Antidote . . ."

Stanford University professor William Dement,[1] whose pioneering work in the 1950s led to many of our present theories on the nature of sleep and dreaming, links man's need for sleep with his primitive ancestors' need to avoid the psychic terrors of darkness. Consider, for a moment, the sheer terror we experience when robbed of all our light-producing sources: fire, electricity, or the light of the sun. Dement suggests that before there was fire, man used sleep to blot out his consciousness of the night's complete darkness. Perhaps family life developed as people huddled together for mutual protection during the night's repose. Because of his lack of consciousness, sleeping man was vulnerable to the vagaries of the night. Places of refuge in caves or huts were sought where sleeping man could be protected, and feel secure in his "home."

This speculation underscores our approach to treating many clients who have difficulty falling asleep. We have found that fears of losing conscious control, of surrendering oneself to the inner darkness are common among people for whom getting to sleep is a nightly and often losing battle.

Sleep, that sweet oblivion, requires a change in level of consciousness from our daytime logical reasoning to disorganization, chaos, and flux. It requires a trusting attitude toward losing consciousness, toward being off-guard and vulnerable.

## Sleep: Who Needs It?

Although extensive research continues, scientists have not yet completely solved the mysteries of sleep. Questions such as why we need sleep, how much sleep we need, and why we dream are as yet unanswered. Still, much is known about sleeping patterns. Normal sleep patterns vary among individuals. Newborn babies sleep about sixteen hours, sixteen-year-olds sleep between ten and eleven hours, and college students sleep about eight hours on the average. We dream in color, we dream approximately every ninety minutes, and although our first dreams may last but a few minutes, later dreams, like feature movies, may last upward of one hour.[2]

## Do You Have a Problem Falling Asleep?

It has been estimated that about 20 per cent of young, healthy people complain of chronic difficulty falling asleep. Studies have shown that more women than men complain of difficulty falling asleep.[3]

While many people fall asleep seemingly in an instant, many others normally require fifteen to forty-five minutes of preparatory time. We consider the person's report of difficulty falling asleep *and* a typical sleep latency period of more than forty-five minutes as the joint criteria in determining the presence of a sleep-onset problem. If these criteria apply to you, study this chapter to design behavioral strategies to fall asleep more readily and remain restful through the night.

# FALLING ASLEEP NATURALLY THE BT WAY

contact your physician for a thorough physical examination to determine whether there is a physical basis for your sleep If you've identified a persistent difficulty with falling asleep, problem. Discuss the potential benefits and liabilities of sleep-inducing medications. One common liability is that withdrawal from certain sleeping pills produces temporary "rebound" effects, such as insomnia and terrifying nightmares.[4] If your doctor has been denying your requests for sleeping pills, this may be the reason why. Many patients who claim that if they miss their pill, they just can't get to sleep, are often using their pills to avoid the symptoms of withdrawal. The initial sleep disturbance is thus compounded by these drug-induced effects. After consulting your physician, begin to adopt the following behavioral strategies to achieve restful sleep.

## Strategy 1: Progressive Self-relaxation (PSR) Exercises

Several recent studies have shown that anxiety and tension are among the most significant characteristics of poor sleepers.[5] Other studies have documented the effectiveness of relaxation training in the treatment of insomnia.[6]

In treating the insomnia of an eleven-year-old girl, researchers at Bar-Ilan University[7] used relaxation exercises. Susan was referred for treatment by a school nurse who was concerned about the child's apparent fatigue. It was determined that although Susan was regularly put to bed at nine, it would routinely take her two hours to fall asleep. The treatment plan attempted to relax Susan where it really counted—in her own bed. The researchers first used a tensing and relaxing procedure to relax Susan at home. Then a thirty-minute tape recording was made of the researchers' instructions, which Susan played back to herself to help her relax in bed upon retiring. Susan's sleeping improved rapidly. Within two weeks Susan was falling asleep either halfway through or immediately following the tape. After two weeks a new tape was made, eliminating the tensing instructions and providing instructions for relaxing specific muscle groups only. Several weeks later, the tape-recorded relaxation instructions were discontinued, and Susan was simply told to relax herself when going to bed. A six-month checkup revealed no recurrence of the sleeping problem. Susan's mother spontaneously commented: "It's another Susan. It's as if she matured three years in one year."

## USING PSR TO SET THE STAGE FOR SLEEP

First follow the full-length PSR instructions in Chapter 2 for two weeks to acquire relaxation skills. Practice the full-length instructions twice daily, if possible including once before sleep. During these first two weeks you will be learning how to relax. *Do not expect immediate gains in your sleeping habits, though these may occur naturally.* Then familiarize yourself with the abbreviated PSR instructions (pages 25–26) before proceeding to tape-record or memorize the following specific abbreviated PSR instructions for helping you get to sleep:

First lie down and close your eyes. This relaxation exercise will help you erase tension and anxiety throughout your body through having you tense and then relax selected muscle groups. You may find yourself falling asleep during the tape. That's perfectly all right; the machine will stop itself. Now let's begin. Begin by relaxing your entire body. Take in a deep breath, and on the outbreath imagine that all your anxiety is being expelled (pause). Now, once again (pause).

Focus your attention on your arms. Take a deep breath and tense your arms; hold, and study the tension (four to eight seconds); tell yourself to relax, and let out your breath and let go of your arms. Study the difference in your feelings. Note the warm current of relaxation in your arms. Let the feeling develop (fifteen-to-thirty-second pause). Now take a deep breath and tense your arms again; study the tension; tell yourself to relax, and let go of the tensions and of your breath at once. Notice the contrast between tension and relaxation. Notice the heaviness developing in your arms as the warm current of relaxation flows. Release all contractions in your arms, breathe easily and regularly, and note how the relaxation develops (allow feelings of relaxation to develop after each instruction to relax).

Now focus your attention on your facial area. Keeping your arms relaxed, tense your face as you take a deep breath; hold and study the tension; tell yourself to relax, and release your breath and the tensions as you do. Note the current of relaxation flowing across your scalp, your smooth forehead. Let the relaxation grow. Again, take a deep breath and tense your facial area; hold it; tell yourself to relax, and let the tensions and the deep breath go. Notice the difference in your feelings in the facial area—the smoothness of your forehead, the warm, flowing current of relaxation. Part your lips slightly. Let go of any contractions in your facial area and in your arms, and let the relaxation develop.

Now focus your attention on your central region, your neck through your stomach. Take a deep breath and tense your central region; study the tension; tell yourself to relax, and let your breath and all your muscles go. Just let your entire central region go loose as you enjoy the contrast in your feelings and let the relaxation grow. Once more: Take a deep breath and tense your central region, feeling the tension in your neck, shoulders, and stomach; tell yourself to relax, and let your breath and all the tensions go with a whoosh. Note the contrast, and allow the feelings of relaxation to develop. Note how you become more relaxed each time you breathe out.

Now focus your attention on your legs. Keeping the rest of your body relaxed, take a deep breath and tense your legs; study the tension from your thighs down to your calves; tell yourself to relax, and let the breath and your tensions go. Just let all the contractions go, and notice the development of warmth and heaviness through your legs. Allow them to become more and more relaxed. And once more: You take a breath and tense your legs, holding the tension for a few moments; tell yourself to relax, and let the breath and the muscles go. Just let your muscle tensions go completely. Notice the warm current of relaxation growing in your legs and in other areas of your body. Let yourself go, let go of all contractions, and allow the relaxation to go on developing. Notice how much more relaxed you become as you breathe out. Note that your breathing is easy and regular and the warm current of relaxation develops throughout your body, throughout your legs, up through your central region and your neck, across your face, and through your arms. Just let the warm and heavy feelings of deep relaxation grow. Accept the drowsiness that comes with the feelings of deep relaxation. Breathe calmly, and notice the anxiety just leaving your body. Now take a deep breath and say "relax" softly to yourself on your outbreath. Let your mind wander to a peaceful, calm image. Just picture in your mind's eye a relaxing scene—that day on the beach, or a walk through the clean, cool forest. Continue to grow calmer, warmer, and more relaxed. Let your mind settle on that peaceful, calm image. Just continue to let the warm, heavy current of relaxation spread through your body. Good.

Many people find that by memorizing the PSR instructions they are able to achieve deep relaxation without a tape recorder. Others find that the calming attributes of the recorded human voice increase the relaxation effect. Experiment for yourself to determine which method suits you best. Use this tape for two weeks and then switch to a more abbreviated, relaxation-only tape, such as:

Lie down, close your eyes, and relax to the best of your ability. Take in a deep breath, tell yourself to "relax," and just let the walls of your chest whoosh out the breath. Recall the warm, heavy feelings of relaxation and allow them to flow into your body. Part your lips slightly and breathe easily in and out, and each time you breathe out say "relax" softly to yourself. Focus on your hands and arms, and allow the warm current of relaxation to flow. Let all the tension go from your arms and hands. Good. Now concentrate on releasing the tension in your face and head region. Relax your eyes and your eyelids. Remember to keep your lips slightly parted. Let all the tension out from your jaw, and relax your mouth and your whole facial area. Allow the warm, heavy current of deep relaxation to flow and develop on its own.

When you feel all the tension gone from your eyes, your forehead, your eyelids, your jaw, and your mouth, begin to relax the muscles in the rest of your body. Remember to let your mind just flow with the calming feeling of deep relaxation. Relax your neck and shoulder muscles. Just let the tension go. Allow the warm current of relaxation to flow through your neck and shoulders. Good. Now feel the relaxation spread to your chest and stomach muscles. Relax your chest and stomach muscles. Let all the tension in your midsection just pass right through you. Allow the warm, heavy current of relaxation to spread down your body. Good. Now feel the relaxation spread the feelings of heaviness down to your thighs, calves, and feet. Let the tension in your lower body just disappear.

Notice that each time you breathe, you feel warmer and heavier and more comfortable. Good. Now search your body for any remaining tensions and let them go. Let the warm and heavy current of deep relaxation flow and develop on its own. Let your body completely relax as your mind wanders to that pleasant, serene image. Find that calming image in your mind's eye and enjoy the peacefulness of the scene. Allow your body to remain completely at ease as your mind continues to enjoy that peaceful, calming scene. Just let your mind and body take you to deepening relaxation.

Make PSR a routine part of your sleep preparation. After practicing the instructions given above for several weeks, you may be able to achieve deep relaxation by simply taking several deep breaths and saying "relax" to yourself softly on each outbreath. Or you may continue with the taped instructions. Whatever method you choose to become fully relaxed, you should, each month or so, practice the full-length PSR instructions in Chapter 2 to maintain effective relaxation skills.

## Strategy 2: The Use of Imagery

In the PSR procedure, we suggested using pleasant mental imagery or fantasy in order to bridge the transition between progressive relaxation and sleep. At the end of the muscle-relaxing instructions, picture a pleasant mental image, particularly a scene you've associated with peace and quiet. Use several different scenes, to be alternated night to night. Use images such as

1. walking through a pristine forest, clear and clean, on a crisp spring day
2. sitting by a bubbling, clean brook, listening to birds chirping
3. picturing that beautiful family picnic in the park last June
4. lying on a sun-warmed beach, as in the fantasized mini-vacation in Chapter 2, listening to the rhythm of the waves

Scenes of water in particular appear to be most relaxing to many people. Imagine these scenes with your eyes closed, and allow the image to develop and take form. Smell the flowers, and listen to the sounds of the forest. Accentuate your involvement with all your senses. Re-create the scene so that you can almost feel yourself there.

As you become familiar with the use of progressive self-relaxation and mental imagery, you should find that your mind may wander, on occasion, as your muscles unwind. Mental pictures may come into your awareness during or after the relaxation procedure. We suggest that you allow your mind to take you wherever it goes. Allow your mind to paint pictures for you. The use of mental imagery may help set the stage for the unconscious mental imagery we call dreaming, and ease you into sleep.

Many people express fears of such mind wanderings. Perhaps they are afraid of "losing control." Yale psychologist Jerome Singer[8] suggests that the person inexperienced in using mental imagery or fantasy may be frightened by these vivid, seemingly alien mental images. But he also notes that visual imagery is man's predominant modality for engaging in fantasy, and that it is an almost universal occurrence. These mental images, often called daydreams, occur most frequently in the period before sleep, and least frequently upon awakening in the morning or during periods of eating. If nighttime imagining initially frightens you, begin to desensitize yourself through practicing daydreaming or creation of mental images during the day, while fully awake and in control. Begin to enjoy the rich inner life available to you. One note of caution: Don't begin to enjoy it at the expense of carrying out your daily responsibilities.

One young man who was treated for insomnia complained that each time he tried to sleep he found his mind wandering. His belief was that in order to sleep his mind had to be "blank." Hence, each time his mind wandered, he cut it short and forced himself to think of nothing. He'd lie awake for hours waiting for his mind to clear. His sleeping quickly improved with the simple suggestion that he allow his mind to travel its own course.

However, many people do report success in falling asleep through turning their minds blank or by engaging in repetitive mental tasks, such as counting sheep. We have our clients investigate various sleep-inducing techniques to find strategies that work best for them.

Though nightly mind wanderings often lead to mental imagery conducive to sleep, do attempt to avoid mind wanderings that center on daily troubles and anxieties. Use thought-stopping (page 33) to prevent ruminating thoughts. Then return to muscle relaxing or creation of mental imagery. Pay particular attention to the section later in the chapter on controlling ruminating thoughts. In addition, to keep your mind wanderings on sleep-inducing images, you may wish to employ the following directed-imaginings method.

## "TELL ME A STORY, DADDY"

Many of us remember being lulled to sleep by stories of fantastic heroes and beautiful princesses. As we mature, the "bedtime story" is replaced by "Police Story" and other reminders of daily anxieties, like the eleven-o'clock news. We neglect the closest link to our childhood fairy tales: our inner fantasy life. But we can learn from our children to induce sleep through using directed fantasies or imaginings. As the poet Wordsworth wrote, "The child is father to the man."

Dr. Jerome Singer of Yale University describes his personal use of directed imagery to prepare himself for sleep. His many daily responsibilities—as family member, therapist, university professor—do provide him with many occasions for ruminating while in bed. To avoid the traps of rumination and the consequent bodily sensations of anxiety, Dr. Singer has used a continuing or serial fantasy method to induce sleep. His particular fantasy involves an imaginary football team starring the legendary though imaginary player, Poppy Ott:

Now as I compose myself for slumber I begin the sequence of one of the famous games in which Poppy Ott starred. I start running through the sequence of plays and within a short time I awaken in the morning to realize that I left Poppy Ott and his teammates with third down and five to go on the opposition's ten-yard line. This use of fantasy as a means of getting to sleep is now so effective . . . that once I start the sequence I rarely get more than a few plays run before I fall asleep. . . .[9]

A serial fantasy like a TV soap opera can run forever. Use your imagination to create your own masterpieces of personalized fiction. Here are some suggestions:

1. How would I live as the world's richest person?
2. How would I decorate the house with unlimited funds available?
3. How would I command an interstellar spaceship whose missions was colonization of Earth-type planets in other solar systems?

## Strategy 3: Establish a Regular Routine

With many insomniacs, disruptive patterns of waking and sleeping time may compound their original sleeping problem. We have found that many insomniacs report that they rise at different times during the morning, depending on when they managed to fall asleep the night before. Thus the actual time spent during the waking day, the time spent before trying to fall asleep again, may vary between twelve and sixteen hours. Their nighttime sleeping efforts are hindered by these fluctuations in daily waking times.

If these patterns describe your sleeping and waking habits, begin to establish strict limits for your sleeping and waking cycles. Allow your body to adjust to a regular fifteen- or sixteen-hour waking cycle. Upon retiring for the night, set the alarm for eight or nine hours later and get yourself up, no matter how many hours you slept. Go to bed at a regular time during the week, and avoid napping during the day. Doubtless you may feel tired and deprived of sleep during the first few days of changing your routine. Consider it payment due for your past irregularity. Use this system for two to three weeks and see if your sleeping patterns become more regular. In addition, avoid caffeinated drinks, particularly in the evening.

## Strategy 4: Avoid Ruminating: Don't Bring Your Troubles to Bed

Investigate the thoughts you have while tossing and turning. Are you concerned about financial pressures, school problems, interpersonal problems? Very often we leave the unfinished business of the day to be resolved in those twilight minutes, or, unhappily, hours before falling asleep. Excessive rumination often raises the level of anxiety and maintains brain-wave patterns associated with critical thinking, rather than sleep.

Instead of endless rumination, schedule for yourself five or ten minutes of "thinking time." Lie with your eyes open and put pressing problems in their proper context during this time. Don't use this time to solve problems, but rather to sort them out for the next day's deliberations. It is not constructive, for the sake of your sleeping habits, to ruminate endlessly about your job problems or your daughter's latest relationship. It is better to acknowledge these concerns but postpone any further deliberation. Think, "I hope I can get that account . . . ," but stop it there with, "Oh, well, I'll work on it tomorrow." Use the technique of thought-stopping (see page 33 for details) coupled with an assertive thought (for example, "Worrying about this isn't doing any good. I'll work it out in the morning.") to prevent further rumination. End this sleep-preparation period abruptly after a five or ten minute interval, and begin to engage in the progressive self-relaxation and/or imagery techniques for sleep induction.

If the next day's uncertain schedule compounds your efforts to relax, use part of your thinking time to sketch the day's itinerary briefly, to prepare yourself for the morning's awakening. But then call it quits!

## Strategy 5 : Reduce Performance Anxiety

The belief "I must sleep tonight" often creates such demands on your sleeping "performance" that you become increasingly anxious and unable to sleep. You try to force yourself to sleep, and wind up feeling more anxious and self-defeated. *Sleep, like the female orgasm and the male erection, cannot be willed. We merely can set the stage for these natural functions and allow nature to take its course.* To avoid this source of anxiety, avoid making demands on your sleep performance.

Simply lie down, reduce external distractions, and use the PSR and/or imagery suggestions to allow feelings of relaxation and drowsiness to grow. Do not try to force sleep, for 'tis a contest worthy of a fool. If you do fall asleep, fine. If you can't sleep, that's okay too. Remember that unlearning poor sleeping habits takes time, and you should expect some initial periods of sleeplessness. However, you've gone without sleep before and have survived unscarred. It would not be such a terrible thing not to sleep well tonight. The *belief* that it would be a catastrophe not to sleep well *tonight* creates performance anxiety that destroys the psychological setting for sleep. Don't fall victim to these self-destructive traps. Your only task is to relax yourself and to allow feelings of relaxation to spread, without trying to force yourself to sleep.

There need be nothing so terrible about not sleeping well. Reduce this source of anxiety and you're halfway home.

Peter, a sophomore psychology major, experienced near sleeplessness on nights he had to drive home or back to school, a distance of two hundred miles. His overriding concern that he must sleep well in order to drive safely created such performance anxiety that he was kept awake for hours worrying that he would not be able to sleep. However, after several experiences driving successfully and easily after a poor night's sleep, his concern with needing his eight hours diminished, as did his performance anxiety and insomnia. Peter remarked, "Sleeping or not sleeping didn't seem to make a difference, so I stopped worrying about it and began to sleep more easily."

If you remain awake tossing and turning for an extended period of time, get up. Each toss or turn raises your anxiety level, making it more difficult to fall asleep. Break this spiraling anxiety by taking a relaxation break. Take in the night air, use PSR exercises, read, or have a glass of milk. Return to bed when you're feeling more relaxed, and help ease yourself into sleep by using PSR and imagery instructions. Do not feel depressed or discouraged, since your only responsibility is to begin learning the adaptive habit of relaxing yourself. Rest assured (pun intended) that should you succeed in relaxing yourself deeply, sleep will be a most accommodating companion.

## Strategy 6: Sleep: Comfort or Loss of Control?

In our approach to sleep problems, we have stressed that many insomniacs implicitly fear sleep itself for its association with loss of conscious control. In his contest with Cyclops, Odysseus was overpowered until "all-conquering sleep held hold" on his adversary. While Cyclops slept, Odysseus blinded him with a spear. With Cyclops blinded, Odysseus was able to escape. Though sleep may have helped primitive man avoid the terror of outer darkness, the unconsciousness of sleeping man left him, like Cyclops, vulnerable and unprepared.

In what kind of rituals do you engage to secure your home before retiring to the oblivion of sleep? Do you recheck the locked doors, the windows, the gas jets, and the children? Do you lie awake unable to sleep, wondering if the back door is secure? Do you have problems sleeping in motels or in other people's homes? How well do you sleep when your son or daughter is not yet home from a date or when one of the children is sick? If these questions hit home, then we suspect it may be difficult to turn off that watchful, guardian attitude and accept loss of conscious control.

We have also noted the relationship between fears of being a passenger and fears of losing control. Many persons relate their phobia to their need to be "in the driver's seat." A young woman whom we were treating for insomnia had developed her chronic sleeping problem shortly after an attack of viral encephalitis ten years earlier. She had described the muscular symptoms of her illness as follows: "I had no control over my movements. I felt helpless, unco-ordinated. I was scared to death." This attack on her self-control left her with psychological scars: fear of losing control and persistent insomnia.

People for whom the guardian attitude predominates often implicitly hold the following irrational beliefs:

1. Something might happen to me at night and I wouldn't be prepared.
2. I've got to keep a tight grip on things, or else watch out!
3. I've got to make sure that everything that could possibly go wrong is accounted for before falling asleep.
4. I can't allow myself to lose conscious control.
5. Sleep is confusion, chaos, and I'm afraid I won't be able to control it. I'll be swept away.

The Greek philosopher Epictetus stated that "What disturbs men's minds is not events but their judgments on events."[10] *The insomniac's anxiety about falling asleep generally does not stem from any actual physical danger, but rather from the irrational belief that the unconsciousness of sleep is a dangerous state and should be resisted.* The paradox is this: He feels he must have sleep, but fears he mustn't sleep. Deep relaxation is feared as the prelude to loss of control. The insomniac may not be consciously aware of these fears, but they become known through his withdrawal, however unwittingly, from deeper relaxation.

The insomniac maintains his vigilant attitude throughout the night, but at what cost? In addition, his expectation that he won't be able to sleep, and his belief that he must sleep, create performance anxiety and result in the self-fulfilling prophecy of continued insomnia. These factors interact to create cyclical patterns of sleeplessness. If these self-defeating patterns seem to describe you, attempt to reduce your fears of deep relaxation by using the following procedure.

## NONSLEEP-DEMANDING SELF-RELAXATION

Begin to desensitize your fears of deep relaxation by using the PSR exercises in Chapter 2 *during the day only*, when you should feel protected and safe in your easy chair. Use daytime relaxation not to induce an afternoon nap, but to allow your fears of relaxation to weaken through gradually experiencing the phenomenon in a supportive atmosphere. Relax yourself in the presence of others, or with your eyes fully open, if these suggestions are additionally supportive for you. Train yourself to let go of the bodily vigilances or tensions that restrict deep relaxation.

Learn to allow the experience of relaxation to develop gradually. When you've learned to relax deeply during the day, begin to use the sleep-relaxation and imagery procedures described earlier upon retiring for the night. *However, do not make demands on yourself to sleep.* Remember that your responsibility is to become more accepting of the feelings of deep relaxation in order to set the stage for sleep. Avoid development of performance anxiety. Simply relax. If you find yourself withdrawing from deepening relaxation, recognize your old demon, fear of losing control, and tell yourself assertively, "There's nothing to fear—everything's all right. Everything's fine." Then return to your use of self-relaxation and personal imagery to help ease you into sleep.

# 5

# ASSERT YOURSELF

## The Pains of Being Nonassertive

Many people experience vague anxieties, tensions, and physical aches and pains because of lack of assertiveness. They permit others to take advantage of them. They cannot say "No." They avoid arguments at any cost because they get shaky and upset when they confront others. At work they feel nauseated or as if they have "a lump in the throat" whenever their supervisors ask if they can speak with them for a moment. At home they let their families "walk all over" them. They continually do what their friends and acquaintances want them to do. They rarely speak up. If someone tells them that they happen to look particularly nice on a given day, they blush and say something ineffectual like, "Oh, you must be kidding." They may work harder than coworkers but fail to obtain the salaries they deserve because they are reluctant to ask for raises.

Some nonassertive individuals cannot raise their voices. When we can hardly hear the complaints of our clients on an initial visit, we automatically think: assertiveness training! Upon request, nonassertive individuals may embarrassedly raise their voices, but they quickly revert to their soft-spoken manner. They may avoid direct eye contact. They may go so far as to cross the street to avoid meeting someone they know because they are too shy to say "Hello." Because of this avoidance, some nonassertive people get a reputation for being "stuck up" or snobbish, though they may hunger for more social contact.

Some recognize their nonassertiveness and present it as a straightforward problem when they seek professional help. They may say that they sought therapy because they never seem to say or do the right thing. They are confused about proper social behavior. A spouse or parent continually asks favors, all of which are granted. They may be afraid to try new things. Their bosses abuse them or their coworkers poke fun at them. They let things ride. They haven't the courage to reply, and if they did they would not know what to say. Others readily make conversation with new acquaintances. They get tongue-tied. Other people "have a way" with the opposite sex. Nonassertive people take furtive glances and then look abruptly away for fear of being discovered. Or it may be that since the breaking up of their last relationship—a marriage or another type of union—they haven't been able to "get going" again.

Dr. Andrew Salter, one of the pioneers of assertiveness training, thought most problems were due to fear of self-expression.[1] He felt that clients were rarely in touch with their needs. They knew that they felt bad, but they would not own up to their behavioral shortcomings. In his landmark book of 1949, *Conditioned Reflex Therapy*, he wrote that most clients had handy excuses for their lack of assertive behavior, such as claims of being concerned for others, or putting others first. A hint of altruism certainly makes this little planet a nicer place to live in, but sometimes "selfishness" is required for one's own well-being. We have also found that many clients confuse assertive behavior with aggressive behavior.

# WHAT IS ASSERTIVE BEHAVIOR?

## Assertive vs. Aggressive Behavior

Popular conceptions of the term "assertiveness" have not helped clarify its meaning. In a recent issue of a magazine popularizing psychology,[2] an experiment in assertiveness training was illustrated with a cartoon of a man kicking his foot through a door in order to help him escape "nagging fears." Assertiveness is not to be confused with belligerence or antagonism. Self-assertion does not demand continual confrontation. An assertive person does not have a "chip on his shoulder."

Assertive behavior is rather the expression of oneself in a manner that is consistent with the way he feels. As pointed out by Dr. Herbert Fensterheim[3] of Cornell University and Jean Baer, who recently wrote the popular *Don't Say Yes When You Want to Say No,* the assertive individual takes an active rather than a passive approach to life. He directly expresses his thoughts and his feelings. He communicates who he is as a person.

While assertive behavior may sometimes include verbally aggressive acts, as in the case of an argument necessary for self-defense, it also includes smiling at other people and engaging in small talk about the weather. It involves walking with your head held straight, not looking down and appearing "in a mood," or looking up and appearing snobbish.

## Assertive vs. Inhibited Behavior

Assertive behavior may be best understood as the opposite of inhibited or anxious behavior. While the inhibited person may avoid direct eye contact because of low self-esteem, the assertive individual seeks appropriate eye contact. He neither avoids the gaze of others nor stares in an attempt to hide feelings of inadequacy. While an inhibited or nonassertive person may avoid commenting that a waiter has incorrectly totaled his check, claiming that there is no point to "making a scene," the assertive person mentions the error briefly and without anger. Thus he rectifies the situation. He has not made a "fuss," and he has not allowed others to take advantage. An assertive individual may insist upon saying or doing what he feels is right, but if he is shown that he is wrong, he can confess to error just as he can accept success. An assertive person is outgoing, but he is not overbearing or boorish. He talks easily to others at parties and get-togethers. He neither retires to corners nor plays the buffoon. When an assertive person feels that someone is taking advantage of him, he says what he must in order to correct the situation. But he leaves it at that. He does not become involved in physical violence, and he does not argue for the sake of arguing. He does not seize the occasion as an opportunity to "let it all hang out," to express anger and hostilities that have been accumulating.[4]

A person acting assertively can say "No" when he wishes to decline a request. He may be preoccupied or tired. But a truly assertive person has nothing to prove in such cases, and he may at times allow himself to be inconvenienced if someone asking a favor is in need and the inconvenience is not overwhelming. Assertive people *can* say "No." They do not feel that they *must* say "No."

# WHY ARE SOME PEOPLE ASSERTIVE AND OTHERS NONASSERTIVE?

## Assertiveness Is Learned

Most theorists in psychology tend to be in general agreement concerning the types of early-life experiences that may lead to assertiveness or nonassertiveness. Assertiveness is not viewed as a characteristic that springs up in adolescence or early adulthood by chance. Assertiveness and nonassertiveness are largely learned patterns of responding in social situations, not "accidents of nature."

### THE ROLE OF "BIG" PEOPLE IN OUR LIVES

Assertiveness probably develops gradually over the years as a result of the types of interactions a child has with his parents and other significant "big" people in his life. If a child is punished every time he raises his voice, "plays around," or does something that interferes with the convenience of his parents, he may tend to become withdrawn and nonadventurous, or, at the other extreme, angry and aggressive.[5] Children and adults who behave aggressively have usually observed their parents or other important models for behavior act aggressively when they are under stress. Fears and beliefs may also interfere with self-expressive, assertive behavior.

## CONDITIONED FEAR

Learned or conditioned fear may impede assertive behavior. If a child is punished for what others label misbehavior, such as raising his voice or saying "No," he will come to experience fear when he again feels impelled to raise his voice or say "No." The old adage, "Children should be seen and not heard," suggests that physical and social punishments may often be applied to children's normal self-assertive behaviors. A child punished for "speaking his mind" or other assertive behavior will come to associate pain with acting assertively. He may learn that to be good is to be quiet and unobtrusive. His parents may confuse healthy assertiveness with undesirable aggressiveness, and the child himself may come to label his healthy expressive urges as aggressive and bad.

*"Little Albert": The learning and spreading of fear.* As early as 1919, James Watson, considered by many to be the father of behavioral psychology, demonstrated the conditioning of fear with an eleven-month-old child named Albert. Albert enjoyed playing with a white laboratory rat. But Dr. Watson arranged for steel bars to be clanged together loudly behind Albert's head each time Albert reached for or saw the animal. After several repetitions, Albert showed a strong aversion to the rat. The typically phlegmatic infant whined and cried in its presence. Fear also generalized to objects similar in appearance to the rat, including a white rabbit and Albert's mother's fur collar. It was no longer necessary to clang the bars together when Albert saw the rat in future demonstrations, even though the experience was no longer overtly painful. Fear of the rat had been learned or conditioned.

*The body remembers.* . . . The concept of conditioned fear suggest that a child can learn to be fearful or anxious in a situation in which he has been punished in the past, even if he was too young to recall, when older, the events of the conditioning process. Who among us can recall the rewards or punishments we received at the age of one or two? We may not be able to recall images of what occurred, or be able to explain it in words, but the bodily sensations of fear tell us that *something* painful may have occurred. If an infant was struck consistently for howling in his crib, as an adult he may feel fear in social situations that call for raising his voice. But he has no other memory of what happened in his crib.

*Adaptive vs. maladaptive fear.* As noted in Chapter 3, many conditioned fears are extremely useful and have helped us develop habits that keep us alive and well. Being slapped on the behind for running into traffic may have conditioned a useful trepidation that prevents us from walking into the street without reflection. Having our hands slapped for reaching toward a hot burner may prevent many burns. But some conditioned fears, such as fear of ever raising our voices or of ever becoming involved in arguments, are maladaptive, although the mechanism for learning is quite the same.

## BELIEFS

Dr. Albert Ellis, the originator of Rational Emotive Therapy, has isolated many common beliefs that cause us to behave irrationally and nonassertively.[7] These include:

*The belief that it is essential that we be approved of or loved for everything we do.*[8] We have seen why a child may legitimately fear the disapproval of "big" people in his life, but adults may sometimes have to risk or purposefully incur the disapproval or anger of others if they are to be true to their own feelings. You can't please all the people all of the time. Why feel that you must?

*The belief that we must be fully competent and adequate in all that we undertake.*[9] Many of us have had a perfectionistic parent who gave us unrealistically high standards for our own performances. Thus we avoid many social activities that might bring us pleasure for fear of falling short. Just as we need not be tennis professionals to enjoy competing with our peers, we need not be perfect conversationalists in order to attend social gatherings. We can act assertively even if we occasionally fall short or are "shot down."

*Human happiness results from the way we are treated by others, and we are relatively powerless when it comes to trying to eliminate fears and sorrows.*[10] We all can act to make a difference in our lives. We must adopt the attitude that it is possible for us to change ourselves and our relationships, or else our negative beliefs may become self-fulfilling prophecies."

*We can be happiest doing as little as possible, effortlessly floating through life and enjoying whatever we can.*[11] No, we have the capacity to be creative with our lives, to try new things, to achieve greater happiness than we currently know or imagine if we allow ourselves to take reasonable risks. Believing that we must accept our lives as they are is antithetical to self-assertive, socially effective behavior.

## MODELING EFFECTS

One of the more intriguing developments in the psychological literature of the 1960s and 1970s has been the demonstration by researchers such as Dr. Albert Bandura of Stanford University of the powerful influences of "models" on children.[12] Some of this research was undertaken to see whether TV violence had harmful effects on children. It has been shown that children who observe aggressive people in real life, or on film, or cartoons of aggressive people or animals tend to act more aggressively, especially in situations similar to those portrayed.[13] Boys and girls who watch people behaving aggressively gain knowledge about how to imitate aggressive behavior and also develop the notion that aggressive behavior is more legitimate, especially if they view the aggressor being rewarded.

*Modeling assertive behavior.* But aggressive behavior is not assertive behavior. Still, we may reasonably generalize that many people behave nonassertively because they did not have the opportunity to observe assertive role models as they developed, or because assertive and aggressive behaviors were confused by the "big" people in their lives and punished equivalently. A young girl may have observed her mother "suffer quietly" for years in bearing the demands of a sexist father, and thus never have developed the knowledge that assertive behavior is an option for wives. Or she may have observed her mother punished by her father whenever her mother expressed an opinion or attempted to refuse a request. Many believe that women, like children, are to be "seen and not heard." A young girl in such a household may develop the expectation that one cannot expect men to accept assertive behaviors from a woman.

### ARE ASSERTIVE WOMEN BRA BURNERS?

We may assume that most young adults are part of the "television generation" and have consequently had the opportunity to observe a wide variety of models displaying different types of behaviors. It is thus unlikely that people in their twenties or thirties would never have observed assertive behavior as they grew. But "filtering effects" occur. Their home situations might have taught them to feel that behaving assertively in a given situation was not right for *them.* The young girl with the nonassertive mother may have learned from television and schoolmates that women as well as men can behave assertively, but home influences may have placed her in conflict by leading her to believe that assertive women are "women's libbers," "bra burners," "commies," or "sluts." Thus home influences interact with other influences, providing guidelines we use to determine which behaviors we witness might be appropriate for us. The young girl may mistakenly label assertive women as aggressive and masculine and adopt a passive mode of interrelating with others, repeating the folly of her mother.

*The professional woman.* Young women who enter college or the work world have also tended to incorporate sex-role stereotypes from mass media. Business executives are usually male and their secretaries female. Women are shown decorating offices, flirting with office visitors, bringing their bosses coffee, or protecting them from unwanted callers in a stern, "motherly" fashion. Physicians, too, are typically depicted as men, and nurses as women. In the business world as in the home, women have been ubiquitously portrayed as handmaidens to men.

The women drawn to medicine may automatically think of nursing, whereas nursing is an occupation that has only recently been considered by men. In cases where business executives or physicians are portrayed by women in the media, the story typically involves the conflicts encountered as she tries to be both aggressive physician and housewife, or aggressive executive and mother. The policewoman who is not a meter maid is a curiosity in the media, dangerously juggling femininity and toughness, vulnerability and muscle. We are used to watching the television businesswoman—dressed in tweeds, moving stiffly, barking orders to subordinates—alienating her teen-aged daughter, with the result that the daughter becomes pregnant, involved in drugs, or attempts suicide. The woman physician on television is forever delaying plans for doing things with her family, caught up in the brisk, demanding world of the hospital, again alienating family members and running the risk of loneliness. If the story ends happily it is because she learns through suffering to balance her professional and her family life.

Somehow this is rarely required of male characters. Male professionals seem to have relatively less difficulty finding a little time for their families. *Never* is it suggested that the man might be better off staying home and tending to the house. Only minuscule compromises are required.

Thus the woman who becomes professional may confound assertive, self-fulfilling behavior with aggressive, insensitive prototypes. She may learn to feel that by "striving to get ahead" she is in danger of "sacrificing" her femininity.

## ARE ASSERTIVE MEN JOCKS?

Given certain home attitudes, boys may also learn to confound aggressive and assertive behaviors. But whereas the girl will probably be taught to be passive, the boy will probably find that older males and his peers will reward him for behaving aggressively. For many boys, positive values are placed on uninhibited tackling in football, checking the skater in hockey, guarding the area around the hoop in basketball, and running right through the catcher if the catcher is doing what his coach and peers want him to do—standing in the path of the runner trying to get "home" in baseball. The popular song lyric expresses the value, "If a man's going to make it, he's got to be tough." Such expectations have placed enormous pressures on boys and young men who would prefer to avoid contact sports but wish to please their fathers, coaches, and peer groups. Many young men do not wish to feel that accomplishment and self-aggrandizement require kicking someone else down. For many men it would be highly assertive to affirm, "I will not be aggressive."

**I HAVE DIFFICULTY:**

|  | Requesting favors from | Denying requests from | Disagreeing with | Conversing with | Saying what I really think to | Giving compliments to | Receiving compliments from | Making complaints to | Receiving complaints from | Maintaining eye contact with |
|---|---|---|---|---|---|---|---|---|---|---|
| Spouse (boy/girlfriend) | | | | | | | | | | |
| Parent(s) | | | | | | | | | | |
| Older people | | | | | | | | | | |
| Relatives | | | | | | | | | | |
| In-laws | | | | | | | | | | |
| Children | | | | | | | | | | |
| Friends | | | | | | | | | | |
| Casual acquaintances | | | | | | | | | | |
| Neighbors | | | | | | | | | | |
| Roommates | | | | | | | | | | |
| Attractive men | | | | | | | | | | |
| Attractive women | | | | | | | | | | |
| Employers/supervisors | | | | | | | | | | |
| Coworkers | | | | | | | | | | |
| Teachers | | | | | | | | | | |
| Students | | | | | | | | | | |
| Religious leaders | | | | | | | | | | |
| Sales clerks | | | | | | | | | | |
| Waiters/waitresses | | | | | | | | | | |
| Repairmen | | | | | | | | | | |
| Doctors/dentists | | | | | | | | | | |
| Lawyers | | | | | | | | | | |
| Job/college interviewers | | | | | | | | | | |
| Charity collectors | | | | | | | | | | |
| Others (specify) | | | | | | | | | | |
| Others (specify) | | | | | | | | | | |

ASSERTIVENESS GRID

# HOW ABOUT YOU?
# DO YOU NEED TO BECOME
# MORE ASSERTIVE?

You have probably already answered that question for yourself. You may have bought this book because you wanted to become more assertive, or you may have thought that you were reading about yourself when we described nonassertive people and the burdens that they cause themselves to carry.

*The assertiveness grid.* Fill out the assertiveness "grid" on page 88 in order to help you find specific areas in which you feel you have difficulty acting assertively. The grid will help you develop a program for behaving more assertively that meets your individualized, special needs.

## Learn More About Yourself

Increasing your assertiveness is a matter of deciding what types of behaviors you need to substitute for the ones currently causing you stress, and then systematically practicing the new behaviors. Sometimes your new behaviors will immediately "feel right" to you. But sometimes you may feel that you are doing something "wrong" and you will find yourself examining the beliefs that may cause you to cling to old, unsuccessful behaviors.

### BEHAVIORAL TRACKING

You already have some idea about the areas in which you tend to be nonassertive from studying the assertiveness grid. But it is important for you to invest some time in examining just how accurate your impressions are. You can do this through self-observation or "behavioral tracking" for a period of a week. Begin on any day and, for the next seven, keep a record of your assertive and nonassertive behaviors. Drs. Stephen Johnson and Geoffry White of the University of Oregon[14] ran an experiment in which they found that students who were merely asked to pay closer attention to their study habits spent mere time studying and earned higher grades than students who did not pay particular attention to their study habits.

*A small experiment in increasing assertiveness.* You can find out if behavioral tracking for a week will help you become more assertive. Before you begin to observe your own behavior systematically, take the Rathus Assertiveness Schedule (RAS) on pages 137–39. Score the RAS as directed, then write your score down here:—. Now erase the answers to each of the thirty RAS items. At the end of your week of behavioral tracking, take the RAS again and write your score down here:—. Did your score go up or down? If it went up, it may mean that you have tried to become more actively assertive during the week of behavioral tracking. If it went down, perhaps you have become more self-critical as you have become more in touch with your own behaviors in social situations.

## PINPOINTING NONASSERTIVE AREAS

Self-observation of your assertive and nonassertive behaviors will highlight certain problem areas you might not have expected. It will also help motivate you to become more assertive. You will typically find that when you have behaved assertively, you feel good about it. If assertive behavior is habitual in some areas, you will notice that you have fewer life problems in these areas. On the other hand, you will notice that you tend to feel bad when you behave nonassertively. How many times have we regretted not saying something we feel we should have said?

You will also get in touch with some of the bodily sensations of fear or anxiety that may be preventing you from behaving more assertively. You will notice if there are times when you choke up, have a lump in your throat, feel a tight knot in your stomach region, or become shaky.

Also pay attention to what you say to yourself when you are behaving nonassertively. Is the nonassertive behavior so habitual that you hardly attend to it and say nothing at all to yourself? Do you justify your nonassertive behavior to yourself by saying things that do not hold up to rigorous examination? If your supervisor called you in for a talk when you were in the middle of doing something important to you, did you drop what you were doing and tell yourself that your job might be at stake or that by not "jumping" you might fail to show proper respect for your supervisor? If so, was your job really at stake? Did you really think that a moment's delay would be a sign of disrespect? Or were you experiencing bodily sensations of fear? Were you reluctant to say something like, "I'll be there in five or ten minutes if that is all right with you"? If someone pushed ahead of you in line, did you hold back and say nothing, rationalizing your nonassertiveness by saying something to yourself like, "Just because this jerk is uncivilized doesn't mean that I have to be." We are not suggesting that you physically tackle someone who cuts in front in a line. But some people can be inconsiderate, and you may wish to avoid self-condemnation by saying something like, "Excuse me, but the end of the line is over there."

Perhaps there is a coworker you commonly pass in a hallway or meet in an elevator. Have you failed to take the initiative in introducing yourself or saying "Hello" and found the meetings to be uncomfortable? Perhaps you have been saying something to yourself like, "Why should I bother with this person?" or "Why should I have to take the initiative with someone I hardly know?" You may have been rationalizing away your shyness. You may feel better by doing something like smiling and saying, "Hi, how are you today?" Do you sometimes avoid saying hello to people because you think they are too good-looking to be interested in talking to you? Do you automatically assume that they will put you down? If you do think this way, how is your self-esteem holding up? Many clients who used to kick themselves for letting opportunities with attractive persons of the opposite sex slip by have been surprised to find that when they take the initiative, they stimulate the attractive person into expressing more interest in them.

## RECORD-KEEPING

We recommend use of a notebook in self-observation. As soon as possible after a notable social encounter, jot down (1) the situation you were in, (2) what you felt and did, (3) what happened as a result of your behavior, and (4) how you felt about the outcome. Note some examples from a record kept by Jane, a twenty-one-year-old office worker:

MONDAY, APRIL 6

9:00 A.M.     Passed Artie in the hall. Ignored him. No result. I felt disgusted with myself.

NOON          The girls asked me to join them for lunch. I felt shaky inside and told them I still had work to do.

They said all right, but I think they were fed up with me. I felt miserable, very tight in my stomach.

7:30 P.M.   Kathy called and asked me to go shopping for clothes with her. I was feeling down and said I was busy. She said she was sorry. I don't believe she was sorry—I think she knows I was lying. I hate myself, I feel awful. I wish I were dead.

Jane was painfully shy and socially nonassertive, but had not realized the extent of her problem prior to behavioral tracking. Below are some notes kept by Michael, a twenty-six-year-old mathematics teacher:

WEDNESDAY, DECEMBER 17

8:30 A.M.   Kids noisy in homeroom. I got very angry and screamed my head off at them. They quieted down but looked at each other as if I were crazy. My face felt red and hot, and my stomach was in a knot. I found myself wondering what I was doing.

4:00 P.M.   Driving home from school. Some guy cut me off. I followed him closely for two blocks, leaning on my horn, but praying he wouldn't stop and get out of his car. He didn't. I felt shaky as hell and thought that someday I was going to get myself killed. I had to pull over and wait for the shakiness to pass before I could start driving again.

8:00 P.M.   Writing lesson plans for tomorrow. My mother comes into my room and starts crying that her husband has gone out to drink again. I yell that it's her problem. If she can't stand the bastard's drinking, she should divorce him. She cries harder and leaves the room. I feel pain all through my chest. I feel drained.

Michael was behaving aggressively rather than assertively. His aggressiveness was causing him as much anguish as Jane's passive avoidance was causing her.

Michael is currently undergoing lengthy insight-oriented therapy involving his difficulties in extricating himself from a triangle involving him and his parents. But he was quickly shown that much of his behavior was inappropriate and dangerous, and in many instances appropriate assertive responses were substituted for habitual aggressive responses during the first few weeks of therapy. At times it was necessary for him to be able to relax before he could engage in an appropriate assertive response. Thus he was taught deep muscular relaxation, as outlined in Chapter 2. Often he would take a deep breath, tell himself "relax," and exhale before responding to social situations in which he had been typically aggressive. He remarked that this technique "helped me clear my head so that I could think of a better way to handle things."

Leslie was a strikingly attractive twenty-four-year-old third-year medical student whose husband was a professor of art and archaeology. She was not socially withdrawn or shy, as was Jane, but was nevertheless experiencing interpersonal problems at school and at home with her husband, Tom. She was asked to track her behavior for a week, as had Jane and Michael, and the following events were abstracted from that record.

TUESDAY, OCTOBER 5

10:00 A.M. Discussing specialization interests with classmates. I mentioned my interest in surgery, and Paul smirked and said, "Shouldn't you be going into pediatrics or family practice?" I said nothing, playing the game of ignoring him, but I felt sick and weak inside. I was wondering if I would ever be able to get through a residency in surgery if every physician who supervised me or worked with me thought I should go into a less-pressured or "more feminine" branch of medicine.

THURSDAY, OCTOBER 7

7:30 P.M. I had studying to get to but was, as per usual, doing the dinner dishes. Tom was reading the paper. I wanted to scream that there was no reason that I should be doing the dishes just because I was a woman. I wanted to say that I had worked harder that day than Tom had, that my career was just as serious as his, that I had homework to get to, but I said nothing. I felt "symptoms" of anxiety or anger. I don't know which. My face was hot and flushed, there was rapid heartbeat and sweating.

Leslie's record highlighted the fact that although she was striving and competing successfully with male peers, many men did not consider her accomplishments as meaningful as their own. Though women are admitted to medical schools, their talents are commonly questioned, and they may be expected to limit themselves to certain less-threatening or "less-powerful" areas of specialization. Tom recognized that he and Leslie were at least equally occupied during the day and that they were both burdened with homework—she studying and having to be prepared for the possibility of going out on call, he preparing lessons or writing professional articles—but it never occurred to him that she should be given some relief in carrying out the myriad household chores that fit the sex-role stereotyping he had observed during his own growth process.

Leslie's nonassertiveness was attributable to her own ambivalent feelings toward her roles as physician-to-be and housewife. She also literally did not know what she should expect from others. Through clarification of her own self-defeating doubts and behavior rehearsal with assertive statements, she soon learned to counter male classmates' sarcasms with comments to the effect that perhaps *their* specialties should be limited to male urology. To her initial surprise, she found Tom to be quite receptive to her suggestion that they share housework: "I was shocked. It had simply never occurred to either of us that housework was something to be talked about or negotiated."

## ANALYSIS OF THE RECORD

Analyze your one-week record. Look for commonalities, trends that may emerge. Review the assertiveness grid and try to clarify a list of statements that describe your problem areas in behaving nonassertively. Examples of such statements for Jane were: I have difficulty requesting favors from everyone. I have difficulty denying requests from supervisors. I have difficulty disagreeing with everyone but my immediate family. I have difficulty beginning conversations and knowing what to say with coworkers, guys, and friends. I have difficulty saying what I really think with everybody. I have difficulty receiving compliments from coworkers and attractive persons of the opposite sex.

Michael noted that he had difficulty telling his parents, supervisors, and students what he really thought. He had difficulty making complaints, feeling threatened that he might explode rather than complain more tactfully. He experienced difficulty denying his mother's requests, again leading to intermittent aggressive outbursts that he had initially found inexplicable. He, as Jane, had difficulty knowing what to say to persons of the opposite sex.

*Looking for excuses.* As you examine your record, recall the excuses you might have found for your nonassertive behavior. Michael had not sought excuses. He did not pride himself on being "tough." The pain he experienced when he behaved aggressively precluded delusions of toughness. Jane was another matter. She had almost completely convinced herself that she did not want to be more outgoing. She admitted to being "nervous" and low in spirits, but for a long time she clung to the idea that the superior solution to her social problems was to withdraw totally from everyone around her. She was clinging to three of the beliefs noted by Ellis: She should be perfectly competent in all endeavors, especially social endeavors, or else not try at all. She felt she had little or no ability to deal with her own feelings. She felt that if a pathway to happiness existed for her, it was through "inertia and inaction."

If you have engaged in self-observation for a week and clarified the rationalizations that you are using to avoid acting more assertively, you have already begun an effective self-change program.

# THE EIGHT-WEEK PROGRAM FOR GREATER ASSERTIVENESS

Clinical experience and research evidence[15] have suggested that assertive behavior can be effectively developed through an assertiveness-training program of eight weeks. Set yourself the following goal: During the next eight weeks make specific assertive behaviors part of your daily routine. Review your responses to the assertiveness grid and the Rathus Assertiveness Schedule (RAS). Which areas and items strike home? Plan on learning to behave more assertively in these situations.

## Increase Assertive Behavior on a Graduated Schedule

Set yourself behavioral homework assignments, specific assertive behaviors that you will try out each week. At first adopt relatively easier tasks, such as complimenting someone, smiling and saying "Hi," initiating small talk with non-threatening people, or asking someone close for a small favor.

*Self-reward.* Reward yourself with special favors or gifts when you complete your behavioral homework assignments. You may establish a special luxury fund and add a reasonable amount of money to it every time you complete an assignment. Then, as the money mounts, go out and treat yourself to something you might normally do without. Or make going to an acclaimed film or a concert contingent upon your carrying out a certain number of assertive homework assignments the week before.

In the later weeks of the program, progress to more demanding homework assignments, such as asking someone for a date, saying what you really think to someone who has intimidated you, denying requests, or disagreeing with persons who seem to have a certain prestige. Reward yourself for completing these assignments. Buy yourself something. Tell yourself what a great job you're doing.

## Continue to Track Your Behavior

During the eight-week program it is again important to observe yourself or track your behavior. Keep track of your successes and failures. In the case of successes, you will wish to refer back to the incident to study the conditions and behavior that made it a rewarding experience, and to recall how good you felt as a result of behaving more assertively. Allow yourself to feel good. Compliment yourself. Accept the compliment graciously. When assertive behavior has failed, you will wish to isolate the elements of the situation that led to failure. This will permit you to modify your behavior or your expectations so that you will learn as much from your failures as from your successes. Much successful behavior results from careful preplanning. But not all planning leads to success. Learning also occurs from trial and error. Do not catastrophize errors. Learn from them.

## Invent Yourself

Use your problem-solving abilities. Outline behaviors that will be more assertive and rewarding for you in your daily encounters. We have noted that to a large degree people *invent* themselves. Often during adolescence, when peer pressures and peer comparisons are so important, we find "heroes" among our friends, adults we know, and in the media, and we try to pattern our behavior after theirs.

People are imitators and problem-solvers. We look around, determine who seems to be getting more out of life than we, and try to analyze why. Use these abilities. Search out models, not necessarily heroes. Note how friends, acquaintances, family members, coworkers, employers, and characters on television, in movies, and in books behave when they are in situations similar to yours: If their behaviors are more successful than yours, consider whether it is possible to adapt some of these behaviors in such a way that they feel natural or become you.

*Nibble. Don't swallow whole.* Do not attempt to incorporate a whole other person inside yourself. Look around you, and select and choose *behaviors*. Take one adaptive rewarding behavior from a coworker, another from a friend, another from a character on television. Find adaptive behaviors that fit your problem areas. Do not imitate these behaviors precisely. Reshape them so that they are more in keeping with your own style.

## Behavior Rehearsal

In therapist-aided assertiveness training, behavior rehearsal—or practicing the assertive behavior in the office of the warm and accepting therapist—is commonly part of the training procedure. Rehearsing a particular assertive response several times prior to application in your actual life situation can help to remove some of the "rough edges."

Adopt some of the benefits of behavior rehearsal to your own home setting. Use a mirror and talk into it as if you were talking to another person. Pay attention to the expression in your eyes, the expression in your face, your bodily posture. If you are rehearsing greeting someone, does your smile seem sincere?

## SOCIAL FEEDBACK

The therapist provides the client with "feedback" concerning the appropriateness of the rehearsed behavior. In self-directed assertiveness training, you may wish to tap the resources of friends, confidants, and family members in rehearsing assertive behaviors. Ask those you choose to provide you with social feedback whether your behavior looks and sounds "right." Are you "coming on too strong"? Are you maintaining effective eye contact? Does your choice of words sound like *you?*

## CHECK OUT YOUR TONE OF VOICE

Listen to your tone of voice as you rehearse assertive comments. Does your voice waver? Is it too loud? Too soft? If your voice is too soft and it is difficult to raise it, you can engage in exercises that will increase your volume. The first of these is growling.[16] Yes, that's right—growling. Look in the mirror and growl argumentatively at yourself. At first you will probably be quite amused and laugh. But our clients typically "get into growling" more and more when they imagine themselves expressing negative feelings toward some of their more prominent social antagonists. They sometimes wind up snarling, and feeling great about it.

Another technique for raising volume employs muscular relaxation. Follow the instructions in the chapter on anxiety to develop Progressive Self-relaxation (PSR) skills. When you practice PSR, double or triple the number of instructions you employ to relax in the mouth, neck, and abdominal regions. Prior to behavior rehearsal, take a deep breath, tell yourself to "relax," focusing particularly on these regions, and let your breath out. You will find yourself speaking up more effectively. You will have decreased the pertinent bodily sensations of anxiety and fear that make it difficult for you to raise your voice.

## PRACTICE MAY MAKE PERFECT, BUT . . .

Do not overdo behavior rehearsal. There is the old saying that practice makes perfect. But like many old sayings, this one is only partially correct. *Accurate* practice will increase your assertive behavioral skills. Apply your assertive behaviors to "real life" situations as soon as is reasonably possible so that you begin to get social feedback from the intended recipients of your behaviors. Their response to your behavior will help you to refine it. Then rehearse the refined behavior for a reasonable period and try it out again.

Practice can also be fatiguing. Too much practice may teach you to associate fatigue and a desire to stop doing what you are doing with your use of assertive behavior in actual social situations. Use your judgment. Use moderation.

# ATTACKING
# SPECIFIC PROBLEM AREAS

Now let us return to the format of the assertiveness grid to explore ways in which assertive behaviors may be substituted for inhibited or aggressive behaviors in specific problem areas.

## Requesting Favors

Nonassertive people typically have difficulty enlisting the aid of others. Often they do not feel that they have the right to ask others to go out of their way for them. Or, if they do ask for favors, they make infinite apologies and go out of their way, to the point of nausea, to promise the person granting the favor that he will be paid back manyfold for his troubles.

First tell yourself that it is natural for people to do reasonable favors for one another—even for you! Unless you have notions of an aristocracy, you are no less inherently worthy of the favors and attentions of others than is anyone else. Insist upon this to yourself.

When you ask others for favors, do not begin by underscoring the fact that you are requesting favors. Do not say, "Jim, may I ask you to do me a favor?" Phrasing questions in this way requests two favors: first, that Jim grant you permission to ask the favor, and second, that he grant the favor. Don't ask people to say yes twice when once will suffice. Rather, say, "Jim, will you give me a ride to the office in the morning?" Be direct.

If possible, include a brief word of explanation. But do not overdo it. For example, add, "I have to drop off my car tonight so that they can tune it up tomorrow." Don't say, "I have to drop my car off at the garage tonight for a tuneup. My wife is going to meet me there and drive me home. I would have asked her to drive me to work in the morning and then pick me up at five, but in the morning she'll have to take the kids to school, which means leaving the house before I do and going off in the opposite direction. Do you see what I mean?" This is confusing and burdening, even though true. Putting someone through this verbal maze is asking a third favor—that he not shut you off in the middle. It also demonstrates that you are unsure of yourself and doubt the validity of your own request.

When Jim says that he will drive you to work, say something like, "Thanks, I appreciate it." Don't go on to say, "It's really nice of you." Assume that others will treat you nicely if you give them the opportunity. Don't say, "You know, I'll do the same for you if I can." This is clumsy. Let Jim assume that you would do the same for him.

To review: In asking people to do you favors,

1. Stop telling yourself that you are unworthy of favors!
2. Do not begin by asking permission to ask the favor.
3. Include a *brief* word of explanation, if convenient.
4. Do not go on forever about how wonderful the recipient of your request is for granting your favor.
5. Do not go on forever about how you will reciprocate.

## Denying Requests

Stop being a doormat. Nonassertive people tend to get talked into doing many things that they do not really want to do. The belief that you must make everybody happy at all times is irrational! We are not suggesting that you never go out of your way for others, but you must have some time *for yourself* and not get into the habit of doing things for others that they can very well do for themselves.

Do not be overapologetic when you deny requests. It is customary and almost automatic for people to say they are "sorry" when they cannot act on a request. This is acceptable so long as you keep the statement brief. If you are asked to give someone a ride to work in the morning and you cannot do it, or it is too much of an inconvenience, say something like, "Sorry, I can't." Don't go on endlessly about how you would have really liked to grant the request. Let this be assumed. You need not be overapologetic in a relationship that is basically secure. If it is not secure, overapologizing will not make it secure. Overapologizing does not sound sincere.

Do offer a brief explanation for denying the request. But do not overdo it. You will sound silly, insecure, or insincere. Simply say, "Sorry, I can't. I have to go by —— in the morning and drop Betsy off." Don't go on about how *tomorrow* morning is the one bad morning, or about how Betsy is the one deserving person.

Nor should you go on and on about how in the future you would be pleased to grant the favor. Don't say, "Gee, if tomorrow were only Friday . . ." or "If only the second car were in better shape . . ." A simple statement will suffice: "You asked on the wrong day."

It would be decent of you to suggest another way in which your coworker can meet his needs, if you happen to know of one. You may say, "Why don't you ask Arnie? He lives near you." But don't say this if your coworker knows very well that Arnie lives near him. And don't stand there all day trying to come up with alternatives because of your feelings of guilt. You will burden not only yourself with your guilty ruminations, but also everybody within a radius of fifty feet. Don't make unnecessary, guilt-evoked comments. Let your coworker get on with solving his problems in another way.

To review: When you have to turn down requests,

1. Stop thinking that your prime duty on Earth is to make everybody else happy all of the time!
2. Offer a brief apology only.
3. Offer a brief explanation only.
4. Do not endlessly reassure the party making the request that you would have been genuinely pleased to do the favor if only . . .
5. If you can think of another way the party making the request can meet his needs, offer a brief suggestion.

These five principles will help guide you through most situations in which you cannot or choose not to meet the needs of others, but they may be insufficient for those who have gotten used to having you do favors for them. In the cases of relatives who have come to use you on a regular schedule, your refusal will be something of a shock, and you may find your guilt being played upon.

## MICHELLE: SAYING "NO" TO MOTHER

Michelle, a twenty-eight-year-old single physician whose father had recently died, was in continual conflict with her mother because the widow insisted that Michelle return to the family home to keep her company. Though in conflict, Michelle continued to assert herself and deny this request. She felt that she was entitled to her own life style, and, with some therapy, recognized that her mother, a relatively young widow, must reconstruct her own life. For several months Michelle's mother went into crying episodes and guilt-provoking recriminations. Michelle was counseled to give up trying to convince her mother that she was right, but simply to continue to deny her mother's request with the same brief explanation that her decision was best for both women in the long run.

Two techniques that you can use in denying requests from extremely persistent people are the "broken-record" technique and "fogging."[17]

## BROKEN RECORD

The broken-record technique, put most simply, is repeating yourself, self, self, self. The purpose is to wear down the person making the request. Obviously it is not necessary to use the broken-record technique with someone who fits your definition of being reasonable, someone who is "willing to take a simple 'No' for an answer." With persistent, nagging people you often must be firm and unyielding. Here the broken record comes in. You repeat your refusal ad infinitum, ad nauseam. Keep your tone of voice constant. Do not get upset. Do not raise your voice. Do not waver. Such fluctuations will give your opponent the feeling that he is "getting to you" and encourage him to ask the favor again or continue the argument.

In using the broken-record technique, it is usually best to find and stick to one statement that you repeat such as "I don't want to subscribe to any magazines now." Regardless of how your antagonist repeats himself or rephrases the request, you simply repeat your statement of refusal. If your antagonist should ask if you would be interested in any magazines at some time in the future—seizing on the "in" that you said you were not interested "now"—simply repeat your broken-record statement exactly. Do not feel the need to defend the word "now" or to modify it. Change your *conception* of the situation. Don't think of it in terms of how inconvenienced you are and worry that your antagonist may break through. Look upon it as a game in exploring human nature. Wonder amusedly how long your antagonist is going to bang his head pointlessly against a brick wall. A few or a dozen repetitions and your antagonist will resign himself. If you become defensive about a word or two, you may only encourage an altered approach.

## FOGGING

Fogging is a method for denying requests or disagreeing with someone in which you show that you recognize the possible validity of the request but still say "No." *Use fogging when you care sincerely about the feelings of the other person.*

In fogging, it is most effective to paraphrase the other person's point of view or request, thus showing that you understand it clearly and are paying attention, but then you still deny the request, either because you cannot or choose not to comply. If, for example, your husband is warm and asks to turn down the heat, but you are freezing, you may say something like, "I know what it feels like to be too warm and I'm really sorry you feel warm, but I've already got a sweater on and I'm still freezing. Why don't you dress more lightly or go for a walk for a few minutes?"

Fogging has three advantages:

1. You cannot be accused of failing to listen to the other person's point of view.
2. You cannot be accused of failing to understand the other person's point of view.
3. You still deny the request or disagree.

Some cases will show that you can use either of these techniques independently or combine them.

## SUSAN: FOGGING OFF SEX

Susan, a twenty-year-old college junior, was very much in love with her boyfriend, but she did not feel that she was ready for intercourse, for which he was pressing. He would constantly tell her how frustrating it was for them to "go so far" and then be "left high and dry." Susan, feeling guilty and sexually frustrated herself, found her thoughts becoming confused, and would sometimes wind up crying or yelling that her boyfriend did not care for her—which was apparently untrue.

Following one session at the clinic in which many possible avenues for dealing with this problem were explored, Susan learned to use fogging effectively and also find a behavioral compromise. The next time she and her boyfriend had been petting for a while and he began to pressure her, she said, "Believe it or not, I know how frustrating this must be for you because of something I've never told you—I get awfully frustrated myself. But I'm just not ready to go all the way. But I do have another idea . . ." They were able to settle comfortably for mutual caressing to orgasm.

## BROKEN RECORD FOR A GOOD CAUSE

The broken-record technique is especially helpful for assertiveness-training clients who have difficulty denying requests for contributions to charities, sometimes because they have not personally believed in the value of the particular charity, sometimes because funds have been tight. We have suggested that they use the same exact refusal again and again, despite persistent rephrasings of the request for a donation and further explanations of the potential benefits of the donation: "Sorry, but I would rather not make a donation at this time."

Clients have told us that saying that they would *rather* not make a donation has often lifted their self-images by giving them the satisfaction of saying what they really wanted to say. On the other hand, if you literally cannot afford a donation, say so. And stick to it.

## JOAN: BROKEN RECORD AND
## FOGGING WITH MOTHER

Joan's case was the mirror image of Michelle's. A recently divorced twenty-nine-year-old secretary, Joan had returned home to live with her parents for financial reasons and emotional support. Six months later her father died from a heart attack, and her mother, fifty, after an initial period of mourning and sullenness, came to be dependent on Joan for doing errands and driving her about, though she was fully capable of driving herself. Joan at first acceded to her mother's requests, responding both to her own sorrow at the passing of her father and her mother's learned helplessness.

As time passed, Joan felt increasingly inconvenienced and

confused and sought therapy. She quickly came to realize that acquiescing to her mother's requests, though well motivated, was not only personally painful but effectively denied her mother the opportunity to regain independent functioning.

Joan was first helped to realize that she could not be expected to replace her father in her mother's life. Then she was instructed in the use of the broken-record technique and fogging. With the broken-record technique, she repeated her denial of her mother's requests without raising her voice or becoming angry. Through fogging, she acknowledged her mother's feelings, going so far as to paraphrase her mother's statements, but then said "No." Joan reported a conversation that went something like this:

MOTHER: Dear, would you take me over to the A&P?

JOAN: Sorry, Mom, I'm tired. Why don't you drive?

MOTHER: You know that I haven't been able to get behind the wheel of that car since Dad passed away.

JOAN: I know how hard it's been for you to get started doing things again [fogging], but I've had a long day and I'm tired [broken record].

MOTHER: You know that if I could do things by myself I would.

JOAN: I know that you feel you can't do this by yourself right now and that it may be very hard for you to start doing things for yourself [fogging], but you'll have to start sometime.

MOTHER: I don't think you understand how I feel. [At this point Joan's mother begins to cry].

JOAN: I know that it's hard for you to believe, but I do understand how you feel [fogging], but I'm thinking of your welfare as much as my own. I'm very tired and I don't feel like driving [broken record].

MOTHER: But we need something.

JOAN: I'm tired, Mother [broken record], and you are capable of driving yourself over to the A&P.

MOTHER: Well, perhaps we'll go tomorrow evening.

JOAN: Mother, I'll be working all day tomorrow and there's a perfectly good car here. I think it would be a good idea for you to get out on your own [broken record].

MOTHER: Does that mean you don't want to help?

JOAN: I think it would be a good idea for you to get out on your own [broken record].

This one conversation did not change the dependency that
Joan's mother had been developing on Joan, but it was one
of many which, with persistence, led to Joan's fostering her
mother into increasingly self-reliant behavior. A year later,
Joan phoned the clinic to report that her mother finally understood that Joan had in fact been acting with her mother's
best interests in mind.

# Disagreeing with Others

Nonassertive people often find themselves agreeing with
others in order to "keep the peace." Some nonassertive people
shiver at the prospect of disagreeing with those who appear
to be socially dominant. But by continually feigning agreement they progressively lower their own sense of self-esteem
and integrity. They also find themselves fostering causes and
beliefs that they abhor.

## STOP FEELING EVERYONE MUST
## APPROVE OF YOU ALL THE TIME!

The first task in learning to disagree with others is to allow
yourself to experience the disapproval of others. Disapproval
is not equal to destruction. It may be that you fantasize that
some of the people you deal with are more formidable than
they really are. You may sometimes forgo disagreement with
a senile or prejudiced family member because you would
only by getting each of you more aroused. But you need not
remain in such situations. If you continually agree with others at work and at play, especially with your supervisors, you
run the change of losing respect. "Yes men" may be occasionally soothing to have around. But one never seeks their
counsel in making pivotal decisions.

## WITHHOLDING AGREEMENT

Disagreeing is not a uniform type of behavior. At a mini-
mal level, it can simply mean the withholding of agreement.
When someone goes on about some issue with which you disagree and then pause, sort of waiting for your approval, you
may simply say nothing or change the subject. Pay attention
to the messages you deliver with your body! Note whether
you encourage others to go on by nodding yes even though
you disagree with them. Become conscious of your body language and stop agreeing nonverbally.

## DON'T NOD "YES" WHEN YOU MEAN "NO"

Nodding yes also rewards someone for speaking in his current vein[18] and compounds your task in getting across your desired message, that you disagree. We have found it effective to ask assertiveness-training clients to imagine themselves holding their heads, one hand on the scalp and the other beneath the chin, preventing vertical rhythmic movement. The image is sometimes humorous for them and removes some of the threat or sting of showing disagreement—humor is incompatible wtih anxiety or fear.

## ACTIVE DISAGREEMENT

At a more confronting level, disagreement is active and vocalized. Depending upon your relationship with the person with whom you disagree, you may wish to be voluble and forceful, or you may choose to be subtle. If you have no positive feelings for the other person, no fear of the situation, and find that your patience is being taxed, you may choose to be nasty. Dr. Andrew Slater suggested that all disagreement be highly emotional and forceful,[19] but some clients report this to be a counterproductive "overkill." You may make enemies when there is no need to do this. You may be overreacting to relatively minor situations.

In disagreeing you can employ the fogging and broken-record techniques. In fogging, first paraphrase what your antagonist has said so that he will know he has been understood. Then disagree.

## NICK: FOGGING FOR WELFARE

Nick, a nineteen-year-old college sophomore, complained that he was being driven "up the wall" by his "fascist" roommate. His roommate was constantly complaining about "welfare chiselers." Nick was encouraged to say something like "I can understand how frustrating it is to see your parents work hard for a living and have to struggle to put you through college, and then see that they are hardly better off than some people who collect welfare and that there are some educational-opportunity students who actually get paid for going to school here. It makes you wonder why your parents go on working their asses off to make a living when they can never seem to get ahead. I guess there must be a lot of people who take advantage of welfare, and it sure hurts when you see kids who aren't as well qualified as you being paid to go here.

But I also understand that most welfare recipients are children, or disabled people, or older people, or mothers who are trying to get day care for their kids so they can find jobs. It's a very complicated thing, but I think it would do more harm than good to dump the entire program."

Nick went through his routine three times. His roommate never brought up the subject again.

## GAYE: FOGGING FOR THE BOSS

Gaye, a registered nurse in her middle twenties, was tired of hearing one of her coworkers continually elaborating on the horrors of their head nurse, complaining that she was overly rigid, with no consideration for the feelings of her supervisees. With some assertiveness training Gaye said, "I've seen her act that way at times, and I know that a lot of the nurses and aides get aggravated with her. But I also know that she's working under a lot of pressure here and is having a hard time dealing with the director. Try to catch her at a time when she's not feeling so pressed. She's a very different person. She can be fun to talk to."

Fogging helps to convince by demonstrating that you are not automatically shrugging off the other person's point of view.

## HANDLING PEOPLE WHO ARGUE FOR THE SAKE OF ARGUING

Some people love to argue for the sake of arguing. They are always ready to get into verbal confrontations. They seem more concerned in eliciting emotional reactions from their audiences than in honestly searching for truth or maintaining two-way discussions. With such people, the broken-record technique may be in order. You may say something like, "I really don't feel like talking about it" despite all efforts to engage you in conversation. When your antagonist changes his line of patter and appears ready to engage in legitimate conversation, you may reward this change by responding with interest. But retain some initial skepticism and be ready to return to the broken record if you have been duped back into a worthless argument.

*Is personal attack ever legitimate?* With people who are habitually disputatious, you may consider the ad hominem argument that is frowned upon in legitimate debate. You may make remarks like, "At times you can be an awful boor,"

"Doesn't it ever get back to you that you impress people as being awfully pigheaded?," "Why do you have this constant need to bicker about every unimportant issue that comes along?," or "Are you afraid that if you kept your mouth shut for a minute you might actually learn something from someone else?" Do not employ such remarks during the first week or two of your eight-week program. First gain confidence through the use of less combative techniques. Use these remarks with discretion. Weigh the benefits to yourself of being so candid against the possible injury to your social antagonists. As Drs. Joseph Wolpe and Arnold Lazarus have noted,[20] new assertiveness-training clients may temporarily become social monsters until they level off with the gaining of self-confidence and some months of appropriately assertive, nonaggressive social interaction. We all know some people who are deserving of ad hominem remarks. But perhaps we should not turn our impulses to attack completely loose.

## Beginning Conversations and Knowing What to Say

Nonassertive people are usually quite introverted. They keep to themselves. They tell us at the clinic that the extroversion of others is a natural gift they lack. Despite the Irish saying, no one is born with the "gift of gab." We are born with the gift of babbling, which some of us retain till our twilight years, but conversational skills are learned.

### STOP CONVINCING YOURSELF THAT YOU ARE NATURALLY SHY!

Nonassertive individuals are notoriously shy, and tend to justify their social withdrawal by saying things like "Other people just aren't worth it" or by reminding themselves of one or two attempts at being gregarious that did not work out. This is especially common in attitudes toward approaching members of the opposite sex. One or two bad experiences and the nonassertive person has gotten himself convinced that he will be forever "shot down." The fact is that all of us have been shot down, many times.

Many people seek therapy following the breakup of a marriage or another type of union. They complain they cannot get going again. They ruminate about their appearance. They don't know where to go to meet people. They don't know

what they would say or do if they met someone who attracted them.

## GRADUATED ASSERTIVE BEHAVIOR

We recommend a graduated, step-by-step approach to becoming more assertive and outgoing. Accumulate little
successes one by one. Your social and conversational skills
will gradually increase.

## STEPS IN BUILDING GENERAL
## CONVERSATIONAL SKILLS

1. Think of someone at work, at school, or in the supermarket with whom you do not communicate but whom
you pass or see on a regular basis. If you have any
feeling at all that this is a person you might wish to get
to know better, smile sincerely and say "Hi, how are
you today?" during the next few encounters.
2. Think of someone you know "by face" but not by name
and come across regularly. The next time you encounter
this person, say something like, "We seem to see a lot of
each other. My name is ———. I work in the ———
Department." If you sound sincere, the other person is
practically obligated to introduce himself and tell you
where he works. It is then an easy matter for you to say
something like, "How are things over there?" or "Has
the ——— policy affected your department?" This
commonly opens conversations in which experiences are
shared. If the other person is shy and disdains to continue the conversation in depth, continue to greet him in
a friendly manner. Other opportunities for conversation
will arise, and people can have their resistances worn
down to your *mutual* satisfaction.
3. Select someone with whom you have a talking relationship of a superficial, nonpersonal nature. The next time
you have lunch together, bring up a more personal topic. Talk about how you feel about something, whether it
pleases, saddens, or confuses you.
4. Invite someone with whom you have a comfortable,
talking relationship at school, at work, or across the
backyard fence to do something together. Suggest skat-
ing, going for a drive to a shop where you might find
an article of common interest, or going to a movie
about which you have heard good things.
5. Get to know somebody you know more deeply. Ask

him something like, "What turns you on?," "What do you like to do when you can get away from it all?," "How do you feel about what's happening in the country these days?," or "How is the financial/international/racial/educational/vocational/medical crisis affecting your family?" *Talk about yourself.* Let this person get to know you more deeply. You may not be convinced that you are an interesting person, but much of the time the people who appear more "interesting" have simply acquired the ability to talk about themselves more easily. *It is usually the way people present themselves rather than what they say that is of continuing interest.* Most people care about the feelings and experiences of others—even yours! Give them a chance to exercise their interest in you. Talk about yourself for your fair share of the conversation. Report something that happened over the weekend, or at work, or at school. Talk about your tennis backhand or your bellydancing lessons. Offer your reaction to some item in the news. Give others the opportunity to respond to you, and let a conversation develop into a "give and take."

*Express your feelings.* Take a risk and get out of your shell. Allow people to get below the surface with you.

*You can live with being shot down!* Remember that it is irrational to expect that everybody will like you or that you can please everybody. From time to time in developing conversational skills, you will be "shot down." We all have. Being shot down is unpleasant, but the sky will not cave in.

We now examine two specific types of situations in which you can learn to increase your assertive, conversational skills in a step-by-step manner: seeking a job and seeking a date.[21]

## Job-seeking Skills

*Easy practice level.* Read through the advertisements in newspapers. Select several positions in which you have *no* interest. Call the prospective employer, introduce youself by name, indicate how you learned of the opening, request a fuller job description than the one offered in the paper, and ask for a fuller description of the qualifications desired in applicants. Thank the employer for his time, and indicate that you will get in touch if you wish to pursue application. You may also wish to ask why the position has become available, through expansion, reshuffling of personnel, or employee resignation, and for information about the criteria used to determine raises and promotions.

Contact a number of friends and ask them if they are aware of any openings in your field.

Make a list of the assets and liabilities *you* would bring to a new job. List reliability and concern that a job gets done properly among your assets! Nonassertive people commonly have a blind spot for the value of these qualities in themselves.

Answer a newspaper advertisement for a job in which you might be interested by letter (unless telephoning is required).

*Medium practice level.* Go to your state employment office or list yourself with personnel agencies. Inform these agencies of your assets and of your preferred working conditions.

Use *behavior rehearsal* to practice an interview with a prospective employer. Write down a list of questions that you are likely to be asked. Include challenging questions such as why you are contemplating leaving your present position or why you are out of work. Expect to be asked what special talents or qualifications you can bring to the job. Look in the mirror and answer these questions. Maintain direct eye contact with yourself. Rehearse several statements that you will probably be able to use intact, attending to your tone of voice and bodily posture. Have a family member or confidant provide you with social feedback. Use someone who can be constructively critical, not someone who thinks that all your behavior is either perfect or beyond salvation.

Go to local businesses in person, ask for application forms, fill them out, and return them.

Write or, if possible, phone employers advertising openings in which you do have interest. Request a fuller job description by saying something like, "I wonder if you can tell me more about the opening." Indicate that you will send a résumé, as required, and that you will look forward to the prospect of an interview.

*Target behavior level.* After you have sent in a résumé in response to an advertisement and waited a reasonable period of time, phone the prospective employer and say, "I wonder if there is anything you can share with me about the recruitment process."

During interviews, be certain that you have had an opportunity to point out your assets for the position. Maintain direct eye contact with the interviewer. Admit freely and openly to liabilities that would become evident with the passage of time—such as lack of administrative experience in a given area. But also emphasize your capacity and interest in learning about new phases of your work. Point out your desire to "grow."

During interviews, be certain to ask what would be expected of you on a day-to-day basis. Inquire about the firm's policies for advancement and raises. Do not be afraid to inquire about the fiscal solvency of the firm. Have a few specific questions prepared that will show that you have knowledge of your field and are aware enough to wish to alert yourself to potential pitfalls in the new position. You must ask why the position has become open. If someone was unhappy with the job, you must inquire why. This inquiry need not be negativistic in tone, but failure to ask will make you appear very "hungry" for the position.

At the conclusion of an interview, thank the interviewer for his time. You may write a one- or two-line note of thanks. Indicate that you look forward to hearing from the firm. Keep it brief so that you will not appear overly anxious.

*During interviews it is normal to be nervous.* If your voice cracks at some point, or if your thoughts get momentarily jumbled, say straightforwardly that you are "somewhat nervous." This *is* assertive behavior. You are expressing an honest feeling.

## Date-seeking Skills

*Easy practice level.* Select a person of the opposite sex with whom you are friendly but have no desire to date. Practice making small talk about the weather, about new films that have come into town, television shows, concerts, museum shows, political events, and personal hobbies.

Select a person you might have some interest in dating. Smile when you pass this person at work, school, or elsewhere and say "Hi." Engage in this activity with other people of both sexes to increase your conversational and social-approach skills.

Speak into your mirror, using behavior rehearsal and role playing. Pretend you are sitting down next to the person you would like to date, say, at lunch. Say "Hello" with a broad smile and introduce yourself. Make some comment about the food, or the setting in which you both find yourselves—school, work, the laundry room, etc. Use a family member or confidant to obtain social feedback about the effectiveness of your smile, tone of voice, posture, and choice of words.

*Medium practice level.* Sit down next to the person you want to date and engage him or her in small talk. If you are in a classroom, talk about a homework assignment, the difficulties involved in doing a certain type of problem, or the pleasures of carrying out a certain procedure. If you are at work, talk about the building or some recent interesting occurrence at the place of work or in the neighborhood. Ask your intended date how he or she feels about the situation. If you are at some group like Parents Without Partners, tell the person who attracts you that you are there for the first time and ask for help in learning how to get along with the group.

Engage in small talk about the weather and local events. Channel the conversation into an exchange of personal information, such as your likes and dislikes, how you came to the school or company or group, and ask the prospective date how he or she feels about these things.

Behaviorally rehearse asking the person out, using your mirror, a family member, or a confidant. If you are male, you may wish to ask the woman out "for a cup of coffee" or to a film. If you are female, you may initially feel more comfortable inviting the man to a gathering at which "some of us will be getting together." Or you may ask the man to accompany you to a cultural event, such as an exhibition at a museum or a concert. These do not quite have the character of asking the man out on a "regular" date, and women who are nonassertive may be more comfortable with a borderline-date invitation.

*Target behavior level.* Ask the person you have selected out on a date, according to the behavior rehearsal you have used. If the person cannot accept the invitation, you may wish to say, "That's too bad" or "I'm sorry you can't make it," and add, "Perhaps another time." You should be able to "feel," during the remainder of the conversation, whether the person you asked out was seeking an excuse or does have a genuine interest in you and was, as claimed, unable to accept the specific invitation at that time. Before asking the person out again, pay attention to his or her apparent comfort level when you return to "small talk" on a couple of occasions. If you are turned down twice, do not ask a third time. Do not catastrophize the date refusal. Look up. Notice that the roof has not fallen in. The birds are still chirping in the trees. You are still paying taxes. Then go and find someone else.

## Saying What You Really Think

We have all heard the saying, "If you can't think of anything nice to say, say nothing at all." Some of us have been taught to be overly polite. Such training is not totally harmful. Perhaps there is such a thing as being civilized, and if we were to spend all our time assaulting others with our hostile feelings we might not be overburdened by the quantity of our friendships.

But there is danger if what we say is too unfaithful to our actual feelings. We may eventually "lose touch" with how we feel about things. In extreme cases, there may be little relationship between what we feel and what we say. Some people complain bitterly while they giggle, or make sweet talk as they frown. In less severe cases, we may find our talk taking on a superficial tone. We may begin to wonder if we dare express any feelings to others.

There is a step-by-step approach to making necessary but negativistic remarks. First,

### STOP SAYING THINGS THAT YOU DON'T MEAN

Do not compliment others on their appearance when they look awful. Rather, say nothing at all.

When asked for an opinion, do not say what you think the other fellow wants to hear. If you are reluctant to express your negative feelings because you do not wish to hurt the person asking for your opinion, say something neutral. A twenty-one-year-old college student remarked in an assertiveness-training group that she had developed the practice of telling her friends that an item in clothing "fits you well" when she hated it. Other assertiveness-training-group members have used the ploy joked about when people are asked their opinion of a contemporary work of art that is beyond their comprehension. They say, "Interesting." But sometimes saying that something dull impresses you as interesting is also contrary to the way you feel. You can say something like, "It doesn't turn *me* on," which suggests that you are not casting an ultimate judgment but expressing your opinion.

Second, begin to express your honest feelings. If someone or something is unbearable or disgusting, speak up. Make a remark that is congruent with your feelings. Do not be gratuitously nasty, seizing every opportunity to ventilate hostilities and excusing yourself by calling yourself assertive. Unsolicited nastiness is more likely to be a response to your inner frustrations than to what others are doing and saying.

### "I FEEL . . ."

Talk about how you feel about things—not only what you think about things, but also how you *feel*. Each day begin several sentences with "I feel . . ."[22] As you begin to express your feelings to others, they will begin to share theirs with you.

### BE POSITIVE!

Don't share only negative feelings. Share your positive, optimistic thoughts as well. When something enthuses you, say so! When something goes right, tell the world. When you have accomplished something, pat yourself on the back and let others know. When you are feeling cheerful, be absolutely infectious with your feelings. If you feel bubbly, bubble!

## Giving Compliments

Giving compliments is one of the easier and more pleasurable assertive behaviors. Be certain that the compliment fits exactly the way you feel. But do not extend yourself to the point of finding daily compliments for others. You may become labeled a flatterer.

### BE SPECIFIC

Compliments not only serve the purpose of making the recipient feel good, they also show the recipient what *you* like. If your spouse has bought a new article of clothing that you find attractive, your compliment will indicate what type of clothing you like to have him or her wear. If your spouse does something in the bedroom that turns you on, be sure to make an appreciative sound or say something about it. Your spouse becomes more likely to repeat the behavior.

If a coworker has had his or her hair styled and looks more attractive, do not simply say "Your hair looks marvelous." The coworker will perhaps feel that looking good is a matter of chance, or might wonder if you had made your remark out of a sense of obligation. Rather say something like "I much prefer your hair parted on the side. It makes your face look wider. And the length makes you look more mature, but not old."

## Receiving Compliments

Nonassertive clients usually possess low self-esteem and have difficulty believing and responding to compliments. Often they become embarrassed and flushed when complimented, and make some self-deprecating remark like, "Oh, really?" A nonassertive office worker in one of our assertiveness-training groups reported that he had been complimented on a report he had written and said, "Oh, it's just something I hammered out." Another group member joined in, talking about a dinner she had taken all day to prepare for her family the night before. When her husband had complimented her, she said, "I just threw some things together."

Such self-deprecation creates a vicious cycle. You continue to reinforce your feelings of low self-esteem and, because of this low self-esteem, continue to make self-deprecating remarks.

### DENYING COMPLIMENTS PUNISHES!

Self-deprecation in response to a compliment also has the effect of *punishing* the person delivering the compliment. This decreases the likelihood that you will be complimented in the future. Thus your refusal to accept compliments can lead to a "self-fulfilling prophecy" in which your belief that you do not deserve compliments leads to reluctance of others to compliment you.

The first step in receiving compliments centers around what you say to yourself. Stop telling yourself that you are unworthy of compliments! Nobody does everything perfectly all the time. On the other hand, we have never met a client who did not do something worthwhile at least occasionally! Stop being your own worst enemy.

Tell the person offering the compliment one of three things:

1. Say a simple but sincere "Thank you." Saying "Thank you" is the easiest assertive method of accepting a compliment. Smile when you say "Thank you" and look the complimenter in the eye. This briefly rewards the complimenter, increasing the likelihood of receiving further compliments, and effectively breaks the habit of self-deprecation.

2. Offer a more prolonged statement of appreciation. Once you have learned to say "Thank you" without anxiety, extend your responses somewhat. Say something like, "Well, thank you, that's a very nice thing to say," or "Thank you, I really appreciate that." This will permit you to dwell longer on the process of receiving the compliment and further build your self-esteem.

3. Agree with the compliment. Dr. Andrew Salter[23] suggested that inhibited people should get into the practice of agreeing with and extending compliments. If you were complimented for cooking a savory repast, you might say, "Thank you. I was delighted with the way it turned out myself. The sauce had just that right hint of orange." If you were told that your sweater was attractive, you might reply, "Yes, I'm glad you think so. I had a difficult time finding it, but the search was worth it. It's also very warm and comfortable."

Clients in assertiveness-training groups and in individual sessions have told us they find that this type of response usually feels inappropriate. "I felt phony." "I really felt like I was overdoing it." We have come to appreciate this point. If extending the compliment seems phony to you, stick with a simple "Thank you," or with a slightly longer, "Thank you, I really appreciate it." *Any phony response is by definition nonassertive.* Assertive people avoid false modesty. Perhaps they also avoid haughtiness.

# Making Complaints

When it comes to making complaints there is usually not much that can be done to approach the situation step by step. You usually either say something or do not.

## BEHAVIOR REHEARSAL

In situations that are ongoing and predictable, however, you can employ the principles of behavior rehearsal to check out your facial expression and tone of voice, and practice "getting the words out of your throat." Again, you can use your mirror, or perhaps obtain social feedback from a family member or close friend or confidant.

*Easy targets.* Our assertiveness-training clients often report an analogue to the step-by-step approach in making complaints. This usually involves the selection of "easy targets." A registered nurse in an assertiveness-training group reported that she practiced making (appropriate) complaints to her coworkers and peers before she tackled her head nurse and some of the physicians with whom she worked. Thus she managed to "get in touch" with what it felt like for her to have complaints emanating from her own throat in relatively nonthreatening situations. Similarly, a college woman tackled her roommate before she tackled her mother. We have also found it useful to approach a given individual on an "easy" topic before getting to "the meat of things." Thus you get used to the idea of dealing with that person in a novel way before you have to "bring out the big guns."

## BE SPECIFIC

In making complaints be as specific and concrete as possible. Saying "I would appreciate your keeping the stereo down after 10 P.M." is better than "Your stereo is too loud." "You didn't fix my car right" is less effective than "On December 4 you adjusted my carburetor and replaced the points, but the loss of power returned by the seventh." Being specific gives you more credibility and also gives the person receiving the complaint more information that can be used to meet your needs.

## FOGGING AND THE BROKEN RECORD

Fogging and the broken-record technique may be profitably employed in making complaints. Kevin, a thirty-year-old assertiveness-training-group member, would get into arguments that sometimes led to physical violence because of his angry outbursts. Typically, he would ascertain that waiters and waitresses dealt with him justly by inappropriately shouting "I was here first!" if, by error, someone who had been seated after him was waited upon first. The group encouraged him to say things like, "Sir, I can see that you are very busy in here and are having a difficult time keeping track of everything, but I came in before the gentlemen seated at that booth." His fogging showed that he understood the plight of the waiter. He received service, not anger.

## ALISON: BROKEN RECORD ON DELIVERY

Alison, a twenty-eight-year-old saleswoman, expected delivery of a new living-room set in the morning, but it did not arrive until dinnertime. She reported the following conversation to her assertiveness-training group:

ALISON: You're arriving rather late.

DELIVERYMAN: We had a very busy day.

ALISON: I've been waiting here all day. If you had phoned to let me know when you were going to arrive, I could have taken care of other things.

DELIVERYMAN: We were out on the road all day.

ALISON: If you had bothered to use a phone to let me know when you were going to get here, I could have taken care of other things [broken record].

DELIVERYMAN: You know, lady, we can't really guarantee what time we're going to make a delivery.

ALISON: My name is not "Lady." If you had phoned to let me know when you were going to get here, I would not have been tied down all day and I could have taken care of other things [broken record].

DELIVERYMAN: Well, what would you like us to do?

ALISON: I would like to have you understand that if you phoned people to let them know you were going to be late, you would not tie them up all day and they could take care of other things [broken record].

DELIVERYMAN: Well, I'm sorry we kept you tied up.

ALISON: So am I, but I'm glad you see that you prevent people from doing other things by keeping them prisoner all day long [broken record].

The group applauded Alison. They, and their therapist, had been inconvenienced waiting for the delivery of furniture.

Complaints are goal-oriented modes of behavior intended to modify the behavior of others so that injustices will be rectified or less likely to be repeated. Be concrete and specific. Sometimes demonstrating that you understand the other person's plight through fogging helps. At other times you may have to use the broken-record technique to have your points sink in. Avoid insults or personal statements. Insults are inappropriate unless you have been intentionally injured. Insults also cause others to erect defenses so that they respond to the insult and not to the complaint. You may also get punched in the nose.

## Receiving Complaints

Receiving complaints is a touchy business. You often deal with the complainant's anger as well as the substance of the complaint. A nonassertive, inhibited individual indiscriminately accepts complaints and apologizes. An assertive individual will admit when he has been wrong, but will not accept an unjust complaint to "keep the peace." *Assertiveness is congruence between what you feel and what you say and do about it.* If you have erred and feel guilty, own up to it. But not endlessly. And people who become highly aroused and livid when they receive complaints are behaving aggressively, not assertively. They wear their insecurity on their sleeves.

### SEPARATING THE WHEAT FROM THE CHAFE

An assertive individual will accept the substance of a just and proper complaint, but not the vindictiveness of a complainant. If a complainant is overly bitter or insulting, say something like "If you stick to the subject without getting personal, we can continue to talk," or "I'll discuss the problem, but I will not take abuse." If you have been unacceptably insulted, terminate the discussion on the spot.

### TERRY: "WOMANING" THE COMPLAINT COUNTER

One assertiveness-training client in her thirties worked at the return counter of a department store. She presented herself at the clinic as "being on edge," feeling as though she constantly had "a tight band around my head" and being "blue." It took little time to unravel the fact that Terry absorbed the continual wrath of people dissatisfied with their merchandise as well as going through the required motions of her job. She was encouraged to discuss the problem with her supervisors, something she had never had the courage to do, and was pleased to find that they did not expect her to take abuse—only merchandise.

Terry employed behavior rehearsal with a couple of statements: "We regret that you were inconvenienced" for reasonable customers, and "We shall have nothing to do with you unless you are very polite with your language" in the case of nasty customers. She reported "getting a kick" from using the latter comment in the flattest possible monotone, emotionless, with direct eye contact. She also found herself becoming "entertained" by customers' rudeness since it provided her an opportunity to practice her role.

### FOGGING

Fogging is of use in receiving complaints. Paraphrase the complainant's remarks to show empathy. This often reduces the sting of the complaint. If you are repairing an appliance and are behind schedule, say something like, "I know how painful it must be for you to go without your TV set. Ours is like a member of the family. But we can't go any farther until that part comes in."

### BROKEN RECORD

Use the broken-record technique if a discussion has passed the point of usefulness. Repeat a relevant phrase calmly despite the impassioned contentions of your antagonist. Do not budge from your position. Anchor yourself with a statement like, "There is nothing we can do about it," "We are doing what we can," or "We do regret that you have been inconvenienced." Your antagonist will either leave or come to understand your point of view.

Fortunately, not one of our assertiveness-training clients has used the broken-record technique in making or receiving a complaint and confronted an antagonist who was *also* using the broken-record technique. We are waiting. . . .

# Maintaining Eye Contact

Male adolescents often engage in a game of "staring down," the object of which is to see who will give up and look away first. The "winner" is silently awarded the benefits of being recognized as the more aggressive, or potentially aggressive, of the two. This practice is reminiscent of male-dominance rituals in other species. Male robins display their red breasts to warn off other male robins from a given territory, not to provide James Audubon with models for painting.[24] Similarly, the three-spined stickleback male (a fish, gentle reader) will go into a headstand and display his magnificent belly to any other male stickleback impetuous enough to trespass on the family estate.[25] The interloper will usually see the error of his ways and back off. Fights to the death are rare.

## NONVERBAL SIGNALS

Forgive this extrahuman digression as a method of highlighting the fact that when people encounter one another they emit nonverbal as well as verbal signals of confidence and capability. Any mental health professional will tell you that a particularly significant sign of adjustment is the capacity to look you squarely in the eye, without fear, without hostility. The expression "shifty-eyed" means dishonest. Lowering ones eyes suggests coyness. Looking others in the eye communicates the desire to be believed, understood, listened to, respected.

Nonassertive clients are forever avoiding the gaze of their peers and their therapists. When this is pointed out to them, they typically say that they don't want to "stare." Appropriate eye contact is not staring. Or they say they can look into others' eyes for a moment but not longer.

*Counting.* If maintaining eye contact is difficult for you, we have found a technique that will help you gradually prolong your gaze and give eye contact a gamelike nonthreatening quality. For the first week of assertive training, count to two before you look away. For the second week, count to four, and so on. After a few weeks you will have little if any difficulty looking people squarely in the eye. You will appear more self-confident, and you will feel much happier with yourself.

# ASSESSING GAINS IN ASSERTIVE BEHAVIOR

## The BT Transformation

After you have systematically applied these assertive behaviors in your own life for an eight-week period you will find that many of them have become habitual. You will also note that you look upon yourself and upon others in your life in a different way. You will have developed the feeling that you deserve to be treated fairly and properly. You will probably, as many of our clients, find yourself chuckling at some of the excuses you used to find for behaving nonassertively. Not just your behavior will have changed. The "real you," the way you think and feel about things, will also have changed. As people respond to you more favorably, your self-esteem will increase. Your insight into your preassertive relationships will have grown. You will understand who expected to "get away with using you" and why. You will have found out who your "real friends" are—the people who like to see you happier and more content, not the people who had some stake in keeping you docile, quiet, and nonassertive. You will probably have some new friends and wonder why you remained so long in counterproductive relationships.

### BODILY SENSATIONS

The more assertive you are, the less likely you will be to experience the bodily sensations of fear and anxiety in social encounters. You will be less given to shakiness. Your heart will be less likely to "run away with you." You will find your stomach less tied up in knots. Your words will not get so "caught" in your throat.

### MEASURING GAINS

For a more formal assessment of your gains, retake the RAS on pages 137–39. See how many points you have gained. Consider a gain of twenty points or so to be highly significant for you. Go out and buy yourself something! This is a special occasion. You owe it to yourself.

Also, review your initial checking-off of problem areas on the assertiveness grid. Note the areas in which you feel you have made improvement. No assertiveness-training client makes improvement in all areas, so do not expect this. There simply is not sufficient opportunity in eight weeks, and it is not necessary that you become perfectly assertive under all possible circumstances. But pat yourself on the back when you note the number of areas in which you have improved. Focus on your successes and not your failures! But use grid areas in which you have not made gains in a decision-making process. Determine whether you wish to attack these areas or people, or whether these are rare and unimportant matters. Watch out for phony excuses, but also avoid perfectionism.

# THE GROUP APPROACH TO ASSERTIVENESS TRAINING

## Forming an Assertiveness-training Group

Many of you have friends, neighbors, coworkers, and other acquaintances who would also profit from behaving more assertively. You may wish to consider the advantages of running an eight-week-long assertiveness-training group that would meet once weekly. You could do this after you have undertaken your private eight-week program, or could run the group simultaneously. One of the great initial advantages for you is the assertive behavior you will employ in getting the group under way, something about which we learned indirectly when we discovered that our time-limited assertiveness-training groups were being continued by our clients—quite competently. Talking to people about the purposes of the group, showing them how assertiveness training can be personally advantageous, and taking the initiative to see that things run relatively smoothly—all these are highly assertive behaviors.

# Advantages to the Assertiveness-training-group Approach

## INTERSTIMULATION

In the group setting, each group member stimulates other group members to become more assertive. It is also highly effective for group members to be rewarded by other group members for their assertive behaviors.

## GROUP PROBLEM SOLVING

In the group there are many resources for formulating what types of assertive behaviors are likely to be effective for group members. Often we do not know exactly what to do about a problem though we recognize a problem exists. We may be too "close" to the situation. Each group member can offer suggestions for appropriate assertive behavior based on his own experiences. The give and take that occurs in the group during such problem solving is assertive in itself. When a suggested behavior sounds right to several people, there is reason to believe that it may work out.

## MODELING

In the group setting, members can demonstrate or model assertive behaviors that are suggested for other group members. Observing models is a quicker method for learning to adopt and adapt new behaviors than is the individual process of trial and error.

## BEHAVIOR REHEARSAL

The group is a marvelous setting for behavior rehearsal. When group members practice possible assertive behaviors in the company of warm, accepting group members, they do not feel so "alone" with their practice efforts. The group also provides constructive feedback to the rehearser to help the behavior become more suitable. Attention is paid to the content of the assertive behavior, tone of voice, and body posture. Assertive behavior practiced in front of others provides better preparation for "real life" situations than will assertive behavior practiced alone.

## ROLE PLAYING

In role playing, one group member rehearses a behavior while another group member acts as the recipient of the behavior. The recipient says things that are likely to occur in the real-life situation, and the rehearser gains experience in "fielding" these responses. Other group members can also *prompt* the behavior rehearser to make appropriate assertive comments as the situation evolves. We have found it effective for one group member to stand behind the rehearser and whisper the prompts as the conversation develops. The rehearser may incorporate the suggestion or not use it.

## DISINHIBITION

Observing other group members behaving assertively in the group and listening to their report of assertive behavior between group sessions have a disinhibiting effect on more anxious group members. They are likely to speak up and act assertively when they see others doing so and being rewarded for their behaviors.

# Format of the Assertiveness-training Group

Session 1

1. Each group member fills out the RAS and the assertiveness grid.

2. Through discussion with other group members, each member selects areas he feels it is important to work on. A major task for a woman in the group may involve becoming more assertive with her children, while avoiding aggressive behavior. Another woman may wish to become assertive with coworkers whom she finds to be "catty" and distant. A man may wish to become more assertive with his supervisor or his supervisees. Another man may wish to develop date-seeking skills.

3. Each group member is given the homework assignment of reading this chapter on asserting yourself.

4. Each group member agrees to three specific behavioral homework assignments. Begin with less-threatening assertive behaviors, such as complimenting someone, smiling and saying "Hi," or asking someone for a small favor. In progressive weeks, the homework assignments will gradually become more demanding.

## Session 2

5. During the second session, the chapter on asserting yourself is discussed in detail. Each group member is provided an opportunity to react to it. Areas that seem relevant or irrelevant to the lives of specific members are highlighted. Attention is paid to the all-important distinction between assertive behavior and aggressive behavior.

6. Each member discusses the three assertive behaviors used during the week prior to the session. He reports the situation he was in, what he did or said, the response to the recipient of the assertive behavior, and how he felt about behaving assertively in that situation. Successful assertive behaviors are greeted with group praise. In cases in which assertive behaviors have been counterproductive, the group troubleshoots the problem. Did a smile appear phony? Was the behavior employed at the wrong time? With the wrong recipient? Was the behavior aggressive rather than assertive?

7. Significant time is spent planning assertive behaviors relevant for specific group members and practicing them in the group through behavior rehearsal and role playing. Behavior rehearsers receive constructive social feedback. They are prompted as needed.

8. Each group member is given the homework assignment of engaging in twenty assertive behaviors prior to the next group meeting. For each behavior, the group member will write down (a) the situation he was in, (b) what he said or did, (c) the response of the recipient of the behavior, and (d) how the group member felt afterward.

## Sessions 3 through 7

9. During sessions three through seven, steps six through eight are repeated.

Each group member reports some of his homework assignments. He is praised for carrying out preplanned assignments satisfactorily. Reasons for behavioral failures are explored.

As group members gain increasing knowledge of the problems that other group members face, they pinpoint more specific responses from which they feel other members will profit. Any group member *must* have a veto over any specific assertive behavior that is recommended for him. But he should also be willing to engage in open and frank discussion of his reluctances. Sometimes he may find that his excuses do not hold water. At other times they will be accepted as valid.

It has been our experience in assertiveness-training groups that group members may come to expect too much from one another too soon. They may not be capable of accurately putting themselves in the other person's place. A woman may assume that another group member's husband is no more difficult to deal with than her own, that he would simply "have to see reason," but he may actually be much more threatening than her own husband, more fixed in his ways, and potentially physically abusive.

Agreed-upon new behaviors are practiced in the group setting through behavior rehearsal, with other group members role-playing the antagonists in the rehearser's life.

The homework assignment of twenty assertive behaviors between sessions remains constant, but intermittently includes specific new behaviors that have been recommended by, and, if possible, practiced in, the group. There should be some variety to these assignments. Group members should not be choosing only nonthreatening areas and endlessly repeating entry-level assertive behaviors; there is also great value in the repetition of useful and productive assertive behaviors.

## Session 8

10. The last session begins with any event that occurred during the past week that a member would like to discuss. But during the last session, all members need not report. Only those assigned behaviors that promised to be problematical or behaviors that occasioned unforeseen difficulties should be pursued.

11. Each group member retakes the RAS, scores it, and determines what gains he has made. As a rule of thumb, a gain in the neighborhood of twenty points may be considered significant. It is also useful, if possible, to compare those items in which change occurred and those in which change did not.

12. Each group member compares his first assertiveness grid with a new blank one. Areas in which improvements have been made are checked off. It is not unusual for the assertiveness-training experience to have underscored initially neglected areas in which assertive behavior would be of use. This will help point to directions for future growth.

13. The group "expresses feelings" about the progress of each group member and about the experience of having been a group member. Some groups contract to continue meeting

for another four to eight weeks. It has been our experience that such contracting is sometimes more the product of a sense of "loss" of the group than the need for continued group assertiveness training. Therefore, we recommend a respite of at least a month before the group reconvenes to discuss the possibility of continuing assertiveness training.

# General Group Considerations

## NUMBER OF PEOPLE IN THE GROUP

We have found that the successful assertiveness-training group has six to ten members. This assures a sufficient pool of knowledge about what type of behavior would be assertive and appropriate in a given situation. Such a group is large enough to provide interstimulation and support for becoming more assertive, but small enough not to be unwieldy. It is also a fact of life that not every group member will be able to attend every session despite the best of intentions. But with six to ten, a strong core will remain if one or two members have the "flu" or cannot attend for other reasons.

## WHO SHOULD BE IN THE GROUP?

Unless the group develops a focus in addition to assertiveness training, as in the case of the currently popular "women's consciousness-raising group," we recommend that members of both sexes attend and that an age span of twenty years or so be sought. This will be beneficial for group problem-solving for heterosexual interactions and parent-child relationships. It is valuable in behavioral rehearsal and role playing. A male group member whose major problems include beginning conversations and knowing what to say to members of the opposite sex will profit from behavior rehearsal with a woman group member role-playing the recipient of his attentions. A woman having difficulty standing up to her husband will profit from behavior rehearsal with a man role-playing her husband. A young man having difficulty denying requests from his mother will profit from role playing, with a somewhat older woman role-playing his mother.

## SHOULD THE GROUP HAVE A LEADER?

Research in group dynamics has suggested that leadership develops within groups, whether preplanned or not. Usually, group members manifesting qualities like general intelligence, likability, and knowledge relevant to the tasks at hand tend to assume or be placed in leadership roles.

But the assertiveness-training group is a specialized, time-limited group whose sense of direction is already dictated by the group format. What is essentially required is an agreement as to how long the group should run and then, perhaps, the rotating appointment of clock watchers to mention that it is time to proceed to another agenda item. (In general, group meetings running longer than two and a half to three hours become burdensome. Taking breaks from the agenda items is also desirable.)

The "leaders" will lead in other, subtler ways, and need not be appointed or elected. They may tend to offer a bit more than their share in providing information, playing roles, prompting behavior rehearsers, and emotionally supporting group members who are attempting to behave more assertively.

# GETTING OUT FROM UNDER: THE WOMEN'S ASSERTIVENESS-TRAINING GROUP

A powerful variation of the assertiveness-training group is the women's assertiveness-training (WAT) group, which limits its membership to women, and focuses on problems that are specific to women who desire equality with men in the expression of sexuality, the right to advancement in the business world, and the sharing of household chores, including the responsibility for handling money.

## Women's Assertiveness Training vs. "Consciousness Raising"

Dr. Janet Wolfe of the Institute for Advanced Study in Rational Psychotherapy in New York City has found WAT groups to be more effective than the widely used "women's consciousness-raising group."[26] In consciousness-raising groups, the group focus is usually on *discussion* of issues common to women. Dr. Wolfe found that although women who participate in such groups felt that they had come to understand better the reasons for their hesitation to seek equality with men and assert themselves in social interactions with men, they did not necessarily learn to *behave* more assertively or acquire improved social skills.

The format of the WAT group may be identical to that of other assertiveness-training groups, including group problem solving, modeling, behavior rehearsal with social feedback, between-meeting homework assignments in behaving more assertively, and the offering of group support. Over an eight-week period you will not only gain knowledge of the reasons for which you had refrained from acting assertively in the past, you will also learn to act more assertively. You will build new social skills week by week, tackle progressively more involved homework assignments, and have the opportunity to discuss your successes and your failures with your peers.

## Confronting Sex-role Stereotypes

As Dr. Wolfe and Dr. Iris G. Fodor of New York University suggest,[27] WAT groups provide an ideal milieu in which you and your peers can help each other challenge some irrational beliefs and sex-role stereotypes you may have acquired during your childhood.

As you practice your homework assignments, you will find that you often meet with opposition from your husband or boyfriends, male family members, male supervisers or coworkers, and others who have some stake in keeping you "in your place"—in your passive, submissive role. Some of your most aroused adversaries will ironically be other women who feel that you are invalidating their back-seat life styles. The WAT group will permit you and your colleagues to provide each other with emotional support as you attempt to change the expectations of those you live, work, and play with.

Although the format of the WAT group may be identical to that of assertiveness-training groups including women and men, the topics for discussion and the homework assignments will take on different and additional flavors.

# Increasing Sexual Assertiveness

Researchers Noel R. Carlson and Diane A. Johnson of the University of Minnesota have run workshops in which women become more sexually assertive.[28] Their group agendas have helped women to challenge traditional, irrational beliefs that the woman should learn how to behave sexually from men only, that the man should be the partner to initiate courtship or sexual activities, that a sexually assertive woman is sluttish or "castrating," and that it is incumbent upon women to use whatever artificial means are available—such as makeup and "hygiene sprays"—to make themselves more appealing in their competition for men.[29]

Women, in short, are often reluctant to take the initiative or the responsibility in their sexual interactions. They often permit themselves to sit home bored if they are not asked out for the evening. They tend to view their only power as a filtering one: the ability to say "Yes" or "No" to men who choose them out. If they desire a particular man, they are commonly reluctant to express their feelings and intentions directly. They often resort to indirect techniques for gaining the man's attention, getting "in his way," subtle flirting, and other behaviors that they feel will give them a way out if they are discovered "at their game."

If women are married or involved in other more or less stable relationships with men, they are often hesitant to initiate sex. Many of our clients have told us that their husbands or other partners would view them as "oversexed" or "crazy" if they ever followed through on their sexual urges and from time to time fondled or patted their partners. Some clients have even wondered aloud if they were abnormal for having such desires. Yet their partners look upon it as perfectly normal to pat or pinch them, often in ways that are decidedly demeaning and nonsensual. The WAT group provides a setting in which you can learn to take more responsibility for your sexual behavior, in which you can discuss and rehearse specific social skills that will make you more effective sexually. You will also find out that you are not alone in your urges and in the sometimes demoralizing expectations of your sex partners.

## Women on the Way Up

The WAT group also provides a forum in which you can explore nonassertive behavior in the business world and obtain group feedback concerning between-meeting homework assignments in which you strive more actively to get ahead and to be treated as equals with men at work. For some women in the business world, nonassertiveness is an expression of shyness or social withdrawal. But for other women it has been suggested that success may be *feared*.

### FEAR OF SUCCESS: THE HORNER STUDY

Dr. Matine Horner of Harvard University ran an experiment in which she asked male and female college students to write brief stories about a student who, at the conclusion of the first term at medical school, is at the top of the class.[30] College women were informed that the medical student was female, and college men that the medical student was male. The stories about the two medical students were strikingly different, based on the sex difference alone.

The majority of college women wrote stories in which they either attributed the female medical student's success to an anomaly or predicted a future of isolation. Some attributed her high grades to an illicit relationship with a powerful professor who acted as her benefactor. Some suggested that mistakes had been made in the grading system or, perhaps, that a computer had confused her grades with those of another student. Even college women who acknowledged that the grades might have been earned tended to predict that the female medical student would lose friends, remain single, and become progressively isolated. With few exceptions, college men elaborated upon the male medical student's success as a natural event, predicting future wealth, interpersonal happiness, and prestige within the peer group.

It was assumed that the college women were projecting their *own* qualms about academic and professional success experiences into the stories they wrote. Thus there is reason to believe that many women are nonassertive at work because of fear of social sanctions they might incur if they were to become more successful vocationally.

In the WAT group, time may be profitably spent having group members explore their fantasies about what might happen to them if they were to "succeed"—to get promoted, to be placed in a position of responsibility over men as well as other women, or to be given responsibility for the management of large sums of money. Once such fears have been laid out and examined, and irrational beliefs are seen to be just that—irrational—specific behavioral assertive homework assignments are given to help group members counteract their fears and provide them with the opportunities for self-expression that they had been denying themselves.

In assertiveness training with working women, we have often found the client to be her "own worst enemy," with her fears about getting ahead far exceeding the realities of her situation. Once previously nonassertive women do attain greater "success" and live with it for a while, they become gradually more comfortable in their roles and tend to wonder how they could ever have allowed themselves to take a back seat to less-well-qualified men.

## Revolution Begins at Home

Each client's home situation is different, but it is common to hear women who are married or living with a man express the desire to:

- write checks and handle money
- have more input concerning large purchases, such as a home or an automobile
- get a job despite possible jealousies over who will be making more money, or the possibility that the woman will be "exposing herself" to flirtatious men
- negotiate the carrying-out of household chores, ending the idea that certain types of housework are to be done by women
- negotiate child-rearing chores, bringing to a crashing end the mystique of the mother-child relationship (which usually means that the woman is the one to change diapers at four in the morning) and focusing, instead, on parent-child relationships

Our clients complain that if their men do perform household chores, they tend to be limited to traditionally "masculine" jobs such as taking out the trash or mowing the lawn. These chores can be and often are performed by the woman, yet it is relatively rare that the man will take it upon himself to vacuum, wash dishes, or hang up soggy towels after showering.

In the WAT group, ask each group member to discuss how the household chores might be distributed if she were living with a female roommate, and not a man. A reasonable contract taking into account the special skills, the desires of each roommate, *and* the total requirements of keeping the household in good order would probably emerge. Such a contract need not have riders just because the roommate also happens to be the woman's husband or boyfriend.

Our clients complain that they are expected to know how to raise children and that their male partners find it "natural" that the woman should be getting up in the middle of the night, washing diapers, feeding and burping infants, and providing the types of stimuli that will entertain the infant and help the infant get a "head start" with its cognitive development. There is no denying that everything else being equal, a woman is more likely to know how to care for an infant. But this is not because "a mother knows." This is not magic or vibrations or even genetics. It is simply a result of the cultural expectation that female children begin to help take care of younger children in their families when they are old enough, and that girls, once they reach their teens, are to engage in chores like baby-sitting if they want to earn spending money. Women learn *through experience* how to rear children. Some of our clients are shocked to hear that men have equivalent learning ability, especially our male clients seen in marital counseling—who would typically rather *not* have learning ability in this sphere.

The WAT group is also the ideal setting to explore irrational beliefs about child rearing, develop strategies for eliciting the cooperation of male companions, rehearse the behaviors that stand some chance of gaining male co-operation, and soothe the feelings of the woman who chooses to assert herself in the home—sometimes winning, sometimes losing, sometimes compromising, and never again falling for the nonsense that certain social behaviors are masculine and others are feminine and must always remain so.

# THE RATHUS ASSERTIVENESS SCHEDULE (RAS)

The RAS is a thirty-item self-report test of assertiveness that has been shown to be valid with both normal[31] and psychiatric[32] populations. You may use the RAS to establish whether or not your self-directed assertiveness-training program is leading to gains in assertiveness. Follow the directions given below in taking the RAS.

## RAS[33]

DIRECTIONS: Indicate how descriptive of you each item is by using the code given below. Mark your answers lightly in pencil if you wish to reuse the RAS.

*Assert Yourself*

3   very much like me
2   rather like me
1   slightly like me
—1   slightly unlike me
—2   rather unlike me
—3   very unlike me

———— 1. Most people seem to be more aggressive and assertive than I am.*

———— 2. I have hesitated to make or accept dates because of "shyness."*

———— 3. When the food served at a restaurant is not done to my satisfaction, I complain about it to the waiter or waitress.

———— 4. I am careful to avoid hurting other people's feelings, even when I feel that I have been injured.*

———— 5. If a salesman has gone to considerable trouble to show me merchandise that is not quite suitable, I have a difficult time saying "No."*

———— 6. When I am asked to do something, I insist upon knowing why.

——— 7. There are times when I look for a good, vigorous argument.

——— 8. I strive to get ahead as well as most people in my position.

——— 9. To be honest, people often take advantage of me.*

——— 10. I enjoy starting conversations with new acquaintances and strangers.

——— 11. I often don't know what to say to attractive persons of the opposite sex.*

——— 12. I will hesitate to make phone calls to business establishments and institutions.*

——— 13. I would rather apply for a job or for admission to a college by writing letters than by going through with personal interviews.*

——— 14. I find it embarrassing to return merchandise.*

——— 15. If a close and respected relative were annoying me, I would smother my feelings rather than express my annoyance.*

——— 16. I have avoided asking questions for fear of sounding stupid.*

——— 17. During an argument I am sometimes afraid that I will get so upset that I will shake all over.*

——— 18. If a famed and respected lecturer makes a statement that I think is incorrect, I will have the audience hear my point of view as well.

——— 19. I avoid arguing over prices with clerks and salesmen.*

——— 20. When I have done something important or worthwhile, I manage to let others know about it.

——— 21. I am open and frank about my feelings.

——— 22. If someone has been spreading false and bad stories about me, I see him (her) as soon as possible and "have a talk" about it.

——— 23. I often have a hard time saying "No."*

——— 24. I tend to bottle up my emotions rather than make a scene.*

——— 25. I complain about poor service in a restaurant and elsewhere.

——— 26. When I am given a compliment, I sometimes just don't know what to say.*

——— 27. If a couple near me in a theater or at a lecture were conversing rather loudly, I would ask them

     to be quiet or to take their conversation else-
where.

———— 28. Anyone attempting to push ahead of me in a
line is in for a good battle.

———— 29. I am quick to express an opinion.

———— 30. There are times when I just can't say anything.*

The total RAS score is tabulated by first changing the *sign* of all items followed by an asterisk (*) and then adding the item scores. For example, if the response to an asterisked item is 2, place a minus sign (—) before the 2. If the response to an asterisked item is —3, change the minus sign (—) to a plus sign (+) by adding a vertical stroke.

The average RAS score is somewhere between 0 and +10, with scores potentially ranging all the way from —90 to +90. About two thirds of the college and university population[34] score between —15 and +34. As you progress through your assertiveness-training program, look upon a gain of twenty points or so as significant.

# 6

# BT PROGRAMS FOR GREATER SEXUAL FULFILLMENT

## THE MISERY OF SEX

Although Dr. William H. Masters and Virginia E. Johnson of the Reproductive Biology Research Foundation in St. Louis[1] and other researchers have demonstrated convincingly that the size of the penis is unimportant in bringing a woman satisfaction, men still tend to belabor the physical adequacy of their sex organs. Since our society still promotes a sexual double standard, most teen-aged girls worry about how far they should "go" in sexual activity prior to marriage. Some worry that no man will want to marry them if they are not virgins. Others are literally concerned about the prospects of hell and eternal perdition. Other women are raised with the notion that sex is essentially painful, a duty that must be performed for the sake of procreation and their husbands' carnal satisfaction. Men raised in similar homes learn to pay little attention to pleasing their wives sexually. Many believe that all sex is basically sinful, but that some sexual behaviors are less sinful than others.

Some clients approach us literally afraid that they are losing their minds. They have been fantasizing about sex, against their wills, and "decent" people don't do that. It is frustrating for the therapist to learn that a simple reassurance in this matter sometimes does little more than convince the client that the therapist is "in league with the devil." We have lost track of the suspicious looks we have received when we have tried to free our clients of some of their more prohibitive beliefs.

Other people, in active rebellion against "the standards of the past," demonstrate their liberation by having intercourse with whomever they can, wherever they can. College women have complained to us of the widespread expectation that the freshman year is the year in which they must "overcome" their virginity. Women's liberation becomes women's obligation. Somehow "liberation" does not include the right to say "No." College men also complain of severe peer pressures to become involved in group or other sexual activities that they find distasteful, for the sake of being "with it."

## Performers or Spectators?

These conflicts place many of us into positions in which we become our own "spectators" during sexual activity, as noted by Masters and Johnson.[2] Rather than fully enjoying the occasion for sex and allowing ourselves to lose ourselves in pleasure, we tend to watch every move we make, wondering if we will measure up, hoping we won't make a mistake. These harsh self-evaluations lead to what is probably the single greatest inhibitor of adequate sexual functioning: *performance anxiety*. We question our ability to perform sexually. The man tries to "will" an erection. The woman tries to "force" an orgasm. Sexual problems are equated with personal failure and loss of self-esteem. Thus we watch ourselves carefully. Perpetual self-observation increases our level of anxiety, and, as the vicious cycle completes itself, anxiety makes it less likely that the man will achieve erection and delay ejaculation. Anxiety makes it less likely that the woman will experience orgasm.

## Overview

The self-directed BT programs presented in this chapter will teach you how to reduce the anxiety that interferes with your ability to achieve sexual gratification in the privacy of your own home. Step-by-step procedures are presented for the man to help him overcome problems of impotence and premature ejaculation. Step-by-step methods are presented for the woman to help her deal with the pressures or misunderstandings that may prevent her from achieving and enjoying orgasm.

Finally, a section on myths that interfere with sexual enjoyment will help you understand whether your perception of certain sexual issues interferes with your capacity to find sex pleasurable and perform adequately and fulfillingly.

Our techniques derive largely from Masters and Johnson,[3] Dr. Helen Singer Kaplan of Cornell University,[4] Dr. Lonnie Garfield Barbach of the University of California at San Francisco,[5] and our own clinical experiences.

*A Word of Caution*

Before you attempt any of the BT self-help procedures outlined in this chapter, you should have a checkup by your family physician or a medical specialist to ascertain that your sexual equipment is in good physical working order.

# MALE SEXUAL PROBLEMS
## Impotence

## Defining the Problem

Impotence is defined as the inability of a man to achieve or sustain an erection. A few men, suffering from "primary" impotence, have never achieved erections. For most men with impotence, the problem is "secondary" to certain situations or their own self-defeating expectations. They may not achieve erection as frequently as they would desire, or they may lose their erection during intercourse. Perhaps they can only achieve erection through masturbation, viewing erotic photographs or films, or with occasional partners, such as prostitutes.

### AN ERECTION CANNOT BE WILLED

An erection is an involuntary response to a sexually arousing situation. The greatest single inhibitor to achieving and maintaining an erection is performance anxiety, the fear that the man will not be able to satisfy his partner sexually.

## PERFORMANCE ANXIETY AND THE SELF-FULFILLING PROPHECY

Many men experience problems with impotence following one or two "failure experiences." Greg, a twenty-seven-year-old office worker, complained of periodic impotence. "I can get it up every now and then, but not regularly. . . . If I do get it up, I'm afraid I'm going to lose it." His impotence began with his first effort to initiate intercourse with a new sex partner following his divorce. It was late at night and he had been drinking heavily. Fatigue and alcohol[6] are known to inhibit the erectile response, but Greg interpreted his impotence as a mysterious mortal blow to his masculinity. When the occasion for a repeat performance arose, Greg became immediately overwhelmed by anxiety, though he was fully alert and had not been drinking. Nonetheless, his performance anxiety prevented him from achieving erection, further compounding Greg's self-condemnations and increasing his expectations of future failure. A vicious cycle ensued.

## BREAKING THE VICIOUS CYCLE

The BT program for treating impotence breaks down the vicious cycle of initial failure→anxiety→continued failure→greater anxiety. The BT approach teaches you to relax in the presence of your partner. As you become more relaxed, spontaneous sexual responses will follow naturally.

## SETTING THE STAGE

Once the physician has ruled out the likelihood of any medical disorder, treatment of impotence involves setting the stage for achievement and maintenance of an erection through the reduction of performance anxiety. Provided that you find your wife or other sex partner sexually desirable, treatment focuses on establishing *nondemand* but stimulating sexual contacts. Intercourse is temporarily set aside as the goal of sexual interaction. Intercourse is approached gradually, only as you become progressively more comfortable with your sexual contacts and regain confidence.

## PLEASURE VS. ANXIETY

During each step in the BT program, focus on the sexual pleasure you are receiving. The program is designed so that pleasure will be "stronger" than anxiety during each step. If the program is carried out to the letter, you will probably experience no performance anxiety at all. Our clients report difficulties when they try to "jump ahead" a step or two in the program.

## ACHIEVING THE CO-OPERATION OF YOUR PARTNER

The BT program for treating impotence assumes the total, understanding co-operation of your sex partner. She must temporarily forgo expectations of achieving orgasm through intercourse, and join you in a series of sexual exercises that will decrease your performance anxiety. She must enter into an open contract with you that she will not expect penetration and orgasm during these sessions. You and she should also discuss unintentional noises or gestures that may have signaled impatience in the past so that she will be less likely to emit them during treatment. By reading this section, she will become more aware of ways to solve the sexual problem you share.

## REWARDING YOUR PARTNER

But the exercises can also be extremely pleasurable for your partner, so long as her expectations are modified. The treatment sessions are pleasurable since they include body contact, kissing, and petting according to a graduated schedule. She can be brought to orgasm during these sessions through means other than intercourse, perhaps by manual or oral stimulation. She will thus have the opportunity to explore avenues for sexual pleasure that you might not have previously taken. In the long run, of course, she may expect you to maintain erection through orgasm. But some women who help their partners through this program discover means to sexual fulfillment that are as pleasurable as or more pleasurable than intercourse and choose to repeat them as often as possible.

# Six BT Steps for Treatment of Impotence

## STEP 1: RELAXING IN THE NUDE WITH YOUR PARTNER

Lie in bed with your partner in the nude. Subdue the lighting. Watch television, make small talk about the events of the day, or make love talk. Visually explore your partner's body. Similarly, permit her to satisfy any curiosities about the details of your body.

Stay with Step 1 for at least an hour a day for three days. Do not push forward prematurely. It is necessary for you to learn on a "gut level" that you can experience and enjoy your partner's nudity without having to "perform."

If by lying nude in bed with your partner you achieve erection, fine. But do not attempt intercourse. If you do not achieve erection, this is also fine. The purpose is to avoid experiencing anxiety in the presence of your nude partner, to avoid equating nudity with performance anxiety.

*If anxiety is too strong* . . . If you do experience strong anxiety during Step 1, employ a preliminary substep in which you desensitize yourself to being in the nude with your partner. "Fear" of female sex organs is discussed in the chapter on fear. Many of the techniques in that chapter can be employed. With the threshold method, you and your partner might gradually undress and gradually approach the bedroom. Through gradually prolonging exposure, you would spend progressively greater amounts of time in the nude with your partner. If necessary, you could employ systematic self-desensitization (SSD), constructing a hierarchy of imagined scenes involving gradually approaching the "target" behavior of lying in the nude by your partner.

## STEP 2: NONGENITAL MASSAGE

Take turns with your partner massaging one another, as in the methods prescribed by Masters and Johnson and Helen Singer Kaplan.

*Learn to receive pleasure.* Do not massage each other simultaneously, as a couple might engage in mutual petting prior to intercourse. Take ten to fifteen minutes massaging each other. Lie on your stomach or on your back. Alternate. Do what feels good. Allow yourself to receive pleasure without worrying about reciprocating. Note that:

- You need not be an expert at massaging. Systematically and gently massaging another brings pleasure.
- When you are receiving massage, you should be concentrating only on the pleasure you are receiving. You should not be planning what you will do when your turn to deliver massage comes. Do not heighten performance anxiety by worrying about whether the massage you give will be as good as the one you receive. Be selfish! Enjoy the pleasure for its own sake, not as a prelude to intercourse.
- You should not hesitate to inform your partner as to what feels good, either by saying so straightforwardly or by using appreciative sounds or gestures.
- The massage should be principally in nongenital areas so that you learn to associate pleasure, not anxiety, with being touched. During nongenital massage the hands may brush against the genitals or the woman's breasts. If so, let it happen naturally, but without obligation. There should be no intentional massage of genital areas until all anxiety that may have been associated with Step 2 dissipates.
- Some couples enjoy using body lotions during nongenital massage. Masters and Johnson recommend usage of lotions and oils. We have found that some couples enjoy them, but others find them "messy." This is entirely your choice. Experiment at will. Do what gives you pleasure.
- Nongenital massage will obviously be more pleasurable if both parties have recently showered or bathed.
- It is wise to pick a time of day when you and your partner are alert. You should not be fatigued. You should not be experiencing time pressure, as in the case where you have to keep an engagement. There should be no question of maintaining privacy.
- If erection is achieved, fine. But do not have intercourse. If not, also fine.

Nongenital massage should also be carried out for three days, for at least an hour a day. If you have any hesitancy about moving on to Step 3, remain with Step 2 until all concern diminishes.

## STEP 3: GENITAL MASSAGE

After three days of nongenital massage, the focus of massage may become genitally oriented. But intercourse is not to occur, even when erection is achieved. For men without medical impediments to achieving erection, erection is usually initially achieved during any of the first three steps. In Steps 1 and 2, the erection is ignored in the sense that the penis does not become the focus of the stimulation being applied to you. Your erection is not a "signal" for intercourse. You maintain the erection without feeling that you must "do" anything about it.

*When erection occurs.* In Step 3, when erection occurs, have your partner continue to stimulate your penis. You may wish to become more specific and vocal about the type of stimulation you are enjoying. Focus on enjoying the sensations in your penis and in your testicles. Do not think about intercourse. Merely enjoy your partner's stimulation while you achieve erection.

*If you lose your erection.* Loss of erection during Step 3 may indicate that you have become anxious about the situation. Check your thoughts to determine whether you were thinking ahead to the next steps in treatment. Or you may have begun to worry about your past "failures." Allow yourself to relax. If you have developed progressive self-relaxation (PSR) skills, as outlined in the chapter on anxiety, you may take a deep breath, tell yourself to relax, and exhale. Remain in the situation. Allow your partner to continue genitally massaging you while you relax and you will again achieve erection. *Do not interpret loss of erection as a signal to leave the situation.*

*If you ejaculate.* It is common for men to ejaculate during Steps 2 and 3 of training and, rarely, during Step 1. Ejaculation is usually the result of pleasurable stimulation to the point of orgasm and is not to be avoided, just as permitting your partner to achieve orgasm through massage during Steps 2 and 3 is desirable. We have found that the period following ejaculation is ideal for you to caress and massage your partner, attending to her sexual needs and her pleasure. Ejaculation will also serve to relieve any residual stresses or tensions you may be experiencing during treatment. It will help to strengthen the association between massage of your partner's and your own genitalia and *lack* of performance anxiety. After ten to thirty minutes have passed, you will probably reachieve erection. You may again desire to receive genital massage.

There may be times when something about your ejaculation is displeasing. Perhaps you feel you have ejaculated "prematurely," following only a few moments of caressing. Or perhaps you ejaculated while in the process of losing your erection because of some intrusive thoughts. In such cases it is better to remain with the situation than to "call it a day." Spend some time massaging your partner and focusing on her pleasure. Take a brief nap. Or simply lie together in the nude and discuss the issues of the day. When you feel the desire, ask your partner again to massage you genitally. If you ejaculate again, fine. If not, also fine. Focus on the pleasurable sensations in your penis and testicles. Allow yourself to live in the moment, not in your sexual past or future.

*Oral stimulation.* During Step 3 many couples employ oral stimulation, cunnilingus and fellatio, as well as massage and manual genital stimulation. Whether your partner uses fellatio largely depends on whether she finds this mode of stimulation palatable. Some women love to perform fellatio, others tolerate it, and still others greet it with great discomfort and disdain. Do not urge your partner into performing fellatio if she finds it discomforting. This will damage the growing sense of mutual trust based on bringing nondemand pleasure to each other. But if your partner does enjoy it, fellatio offers some advantages in treatment to overcome impotence:

1. It provides still another type of stimulation during which you can achieve or continue to experience erection.
2. The mouth feels similar to the vagina, and you can expect some "transfer of training" to occur when you do have intercourse.
3. Although the mouth is similar to the vagina, you will not be so likely to experience performance anxiety during fellatio as during intercourse because you will not

have the feeling that it is desirable to "hold on" to your erection until your partner achieves orgasm.

## STEP 4: EJACULATION WITHOUT INTERCOURSE

You are ready for Step 4 when you have reliably achieved and maintained an erection through Step 3. We recommend that you move on to Step 4 when you have reliably maintained an erection for at least three sessions.

Step 4 is the achieving of ejaculation through means other than intercourse. This may mean through manual or oral stimulation, or through a combination. The purpose of achieving ejaculation through means other than intercourse is to increase further the strength of the association between pleasure and sexual contact with your partner. This will help you *unlearn* further the "gut level" association between performance anxiety and sexual contact with your partner.

As you are being sexually stimulated during Step 4, allow yourself simultaneously to stroke or massage or stimulate orally your partner's body. But if you find that simultaneous sexual stimulation produces anxiety, spend at least three sessions first during which you and your partner take turns arousing one another, as you had done in Step 3.

Many men will already have achieved ejaculation during Steps 2 and 3. Nevertheless, devote at least three additional sessions, in Step 4, to achieving ejaculation through means other than intercourse.

*The fallacy of the importance of simultaneous orgasm.* In Step 4, do not be concerned that you bring your partner to orgasm manually or orally as she is bringing you to ejaculation. This concern will only create another sort of performance anxiety: You will try to get your "timing right." Do reward your partner by bringing her to orgasm manually, orally, or through whatever means she desires, but do not attempt to have your orgasms coincide.

The "myth" of the importance of simultaneous orgasm has diminished the sexual pleasure of couples and led them to wonder if they were failures because their timing was not perfect. During Step 4, your attitude should be, "I shall do what I *enjoy* doing to my partner while she is bringing me to orgasm. I shall allow myself to focus on my pleasure. I shall not get upset over silly ideas about what I *ought* to be doing." If you wish to stroke your partner's breasts while she brings you to ejaculation, do so. If you wish to kiss her or to caress her buttocks, do so. If she does achieve orgasm shortly before or after you do, and you both find this pleasurable, fine. But do not aim for this. It represents counterproductive sexual idealism and has created more problems than it has solved.

## STEP 5: NONDEMAND INTERCOURSE

Once you have learned to associate pleasure and not performance anxiety with being brought to orgasm by your partner in Step 4, you are ready to experiment with intercourse. But intercourse must be nondemand at first. This means that you are to focus expressly on your own pleasure during intercourse. Your partner is *not* to expect you to maintain your erection until she achieves orgasm. This *must be accepted by your partner and by you.* A twenty-nine-year-old college professor found it devastating when his wife "clutched desperately at me and begged me to keep it up just a few moments longer" as she continued to thrust in an attempt to attain orgasm during Step 5. The professor's performance anxiety became immediately elevated, and his erection was consequently lost. It was necessary for this couple to return to Step 2 for several sessions before progress to Steps 3, 4, and 5 could be reinstigated.

*Experiment.* In Step 5, experiment with intercourse in various positions and concentrate on enjoying the sensations of intercourse. Allow yourself to ejaculate inside your partner when you wish. If the thought of ejaculating inside your partner arouses any anxiety, you may choose to ejaculate extravaginally for three preliminary sessions. But most clients are capable of initially ejaculating inside their partners in Step 5 so long as they do not feel the need to bring their partners to orgasm through intercourse, or "get the feeling" that their partners resent their achieving ejaculation through intercourse when they are making no similar demands.

We have not found that any particular position is reliably more helpful than another in Step 5. Take positions that you enjoy. Vary them at will. Focus on the sensations of intercourse, not as preparation for orgasm for your partner, not as preparation for ejaculation—enjoy the sensations for their own value.

*Allow youself to be selfish.* Use assertive thoughts. You *are* worthy of the pleasure you are allowing yourself to experience! Focus on intercourse as a method of experiencing ·pleasure for its own sake for at least seven sessions. This does not mean that your partner will be thoroughly forgoing orgasms through this period. She should not seek to achieve orgasms through *intercourse*. But if your thrusting brings her pleasure, she should let you know by saying so or making appreciative sounds or gestures. If she cannot "help herself" and experiences orgasm through intercourse, fine. But she should not be "working at" achieving orgasm through intercourse. Bring your partner to orgasm through other means, as during earlier steps.·

*A word to the female partner.* What you expect from intercourse in Step 5 is crucial. If you expect and attempt to achieve orgasm, this will re-create your partner's destructive performance anxiety. The optimal way to help your partner achieve and maintain erections is to go into intercourse sufficiently aroused and lubricated so that the sensations are enjoyable for you, but not to seek an orgasm actively. This is a temporary measure. The long-term payoff is obvious.

## STEP 6: HELPING YOUR PARTNER ATTAIN ORGASM THROUGH INTERCOURSE

Once you have developed confidence that you will achieve an erection when stimulated by your partner, and have had at least seven sessions in which you ejaculated intravaginally, it is time for you and your partner to ease into intercourse through which you may both achieve orgasm—if this is indeed your preference as a couple.

Step 6 begins to occur "naturally." As you lose fear that you will not be able to maintain an erection, you will engage in further experimenting and probably would, without our cue, have begun to urge your partner to have an orgasm through intercourse. Our only injunction is to practice Step 5 for at least seven sessions.

. An occasional "relapse" is normal. Do not be surprised if on one or two occasions you have difficulty achieving or maintaining erection. It is normal for any man to intermittently experience "erectile incompetence." This does not mean that you must return to Step 1 of the treatment procedure. The next time you have sex, the problem may not recur. Nip self-defeating ruminations like "Oh, my God, it's back again!" or "What's the use?" in the bud. Adopt a wait-

and-see attitude. If the problem does persist, return to Step 5 for another few sessions. When you feel ready, simply suggest to your partner that she may feel free to achieve orgasm through intercourse, if she desires.

Most clients who undertake the BT treatment plan for secondary impotence find that they and their partners, more often than in the past, commonly choose to have orgasms through manual or oral stimulation, either in addition to or instead of intercourse. A twenty-two-year-old student reported that he would typically prefer to bring his partner to orgasm through intercourse but then achieve ejaculation through fellatio. The spouse of a forty-nine-year-old physician reported that while her husband generally preferred to ejaculate through intercourse following the program, she would sometimes choose intercourse and at other times prefer manual stimulation. She confessed that she thought she might prefer manual stimulation to intercourse on an ongoing basis, but felt that this was "gauche."

In the event that you and your partner both choose to achieve orgasms through intercourse, we have found that it is usually more successful for the couple to bring the woman to orgasm first than to strive for simultaneous orgasm. Certainly it is counterproductive to aim for the man to ejaculate first, since the penis then goes into the "refractory phase" and may become flaccid rather promptly. But a few women report that the man's ejaculation provides the ultimate stimulus for orgasm. To each his own.

# Premature Ejaculation

Premature ejaculation is a relative phenomenon. Some men ejaculate upon first nude contact with their sex partner or upon brief petting. Others ejaculate after a few minutes of intercourse when their partners would prefer a half hour or forty-five minutes of intercourse. Some men with generally excellent ejaculatory control intermittently ejaculate prematurely. We define premature ejaculation as ejaculation occurring before you *choose* to ejaculate.

There is much speculation as to why some men have difficulty maintaining control of ejaculation prior to or during intercourse. Masters and Johnson[7] pointed out that in our culture some men first learned about intercourse in situations where they might be discovered, such as in back seats of cars at drive-in movies, and it was necessary to be quick about sex. Prostitutes will also typically rush the young man toward completion of the sex act. Others have speculated that traumatic experiences incurred during certain periods of the male child's growth process might have caused anxieties that led to premature ejaculation.

Regardless of how or why a male comes to ejaculate prematurely, it is known that anxiety increases the changes for loss of ejaculatory control. An extremely high anxiety level, in fact, can promote involuntary ejaculation without erection. Thus any man who worries that he will lose control of ejaculation during a sex act increases the probability that he will. This is another example of the self-fulfilling prophecy. Men who ejaculate prematurely also have low "tolerance" for the pleasurable sensations of intercourse. "Folk knowledge" encourages such men to divert their attention from intercourse, to recall stock quotations, baseball averages, or to work out office problems. Such diversion of attention interferes with sexual enjoyment and may also lead to loss of erection entirely, especially if the cognitive tasks chosen for diversion of attention are complex.[8]

Attainment of ejaculatory control focuses on (1) decreasing performance anxiety during intercourse and (2) increasing tolerance from the pleasurable sensations of intercourse.

## Treatment for Men with Wives or Other Reliable Partners

The following techniques assume total co-operation from your sex partner, who should also read this section. They may place some burden on her because she will both act to help you learn to attain ejaculatory control and temporarily forgo expectation of achieving orgasm through intercourse. However, you may bring her to orgasm in the early stages of training through manual or oral stimulation. Her expectations regarding the manner in which she will achieve orgasm through the training period must change so that neither of you will experience performance anxiety or a sense of failure associated with her achieving orgasm through means other than intercourse.

We have found that some women, for a variety of reasons, prefer to forgo achieving orgasm at all during training. Often women believe that orgasm attained through means other than intercourse will not satisfy them. Such women should read the section on sexual "myths" before becoming hardened in their position. In short, women who are open to experimentation, to achieving sexual fulfillment through differing avenues, serve, in our experience, as better partners in helping their men learn ejaculatory control.

## LOCATING THE PROBLEM

Once you have achieved the co-operation of your partner, identify just where *your* problem with premature ejaculation lies. Below is the hierarchy of sexual stages with which we shall be working. Place a check mark next to those stages that you can accomplish *without* fear of ejaculating.

___Stage 1: being nude with your partner

___Stage 2: engaging in foreplay with your partner

___Stage 3: entering your partner in the female-superior position (Figure 6.1) and remaining motionless

___Stage 4: engaging in active, thrusting intercourse with your partner in the female-superior position

___Stage 5: engaging in intercourse in the lateral position (Figure 6.2)

___Stage 6: engaging briefly in intercourse in the male-superior position (Figure 6.3)

___Stage 7: engaging in intercourse in the male-superior position for prolonged periods of time

Once you have identified those stages of sexual activity that you know you can accomplish without ejaculating, begin your BT training program at the next higher stage.

## EXPERIMENTING TO PINPOINT THE PROBLEM

Given our check list, some clients report that they know they can "handle" Stages 1 and 2, have "failed" in Stages 5 through 7, but have never tried Stages 3 and 4. If you are in a situation like this, your initial step includes experimenting with your partner to determine what happens during vaginal containment or active thrusting with her in the superior position. Some clients have found that experimentation with the female-superior position has, in effect, solved their problem. The sensations of intercourse are less impelling for the male in this position, and many men who had been able to "hang on" for only a minute or two in the male-superior position

**FIGURE 6.1**
**INTERCOURSE IN THE FEMALE-SUPERIOR POSITION**

Intercourse in the female-superior position is less likely than other positions to stimulate the prematurely ejaculating male to orgasm. The position also helps the woman with situational orgasmic dysfunction experiment to find sexually-arousing stimulation. Psychologically, it may also help her feel more "in command" and give her "permission" to express sexual strivings. (Modified from Masters and Johnson: *Human Sexual Inadequacy*, 1970, Little, Brown and Company, Boston.)

have been able to enjoy intercourse indefinitely in the female-superior position.

But some clients and their partners have been resistant to employing the female-superior position. One man remarked that the "one on top" is the aggressor, and he did not think that this was a "proper role" for his wife. We have also found that some women brought up with strict notions of what is "prim" and "proper" are reluctant to take the superior position. They would rather not be "responsible" for thrusting. One prostitute in therapy seen for other than sexual reasons reported that she would do almost anything a male client wanted her to do, for enough money, but she would *not* take the female-superior position. It appeared that other positions permitted her to conceptualize herself as an innocent victim of circumstances. Women helping their sex partners attain ejaculatory control should be willing to take active, supporting roles throughout training. If they cannot do so initially, perhaps talking through their feelings with their partners will help. If not, professional counsel may be indicated.

## STARTING GUIDELINES

Once you have located the problem and your partner's co-operation has been secured, begin the BT program at the stage above the last one checked off. Throughout the program, specifically focus your attention on pleasurable sexual sensations.[9] Do not merely permit yourself to enjoy them. Allow your enjoyment to be enthusiastic. Establish an open communication system with your partner, using words, sounds, or gestures so that you will learn what each of you finds pleasurable.

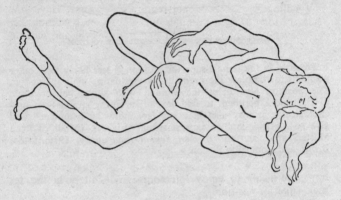

FIGURE 6.2
INTERCOURSE IN THE LATERAL POSITION

Intercourse in the lateral position provides both partners with maximum freedom of bodily movement. While more stimulating than the female-superior position for prematurely ejaculating male, it is less stimulating than the male-superior position and serves as an intermediary step between female-superior and male-superior intercourse. (Modified from Helen Singer Kaplan: *The New Sex Therapy,* 1974, Brunner/Mazel, New York.)

# Seven Stages of Training for Ejaculatory Control

## STAGE 1 TRAINING: EJACULATION AND . . .

If you experience ejaculation in the presence of your nude partner, without foreplay or touching, simply permit yourself to do so and try to enjoy the experience. Do not condemn yourself. Do not think of yourself as a failure! Initial ejaculating is *part* of the training process for men in Stage 1.

However, change what happens *after* you ejaculate. Rather than embarrassedly bringing your partner to orgasm through manual or oral stimulation and then quitting, or rather than immediately turning away and ending the sexual interaction, remain in the situation.

Presumably your penis will have become flaccid. Whether or not you maintain a partial erection, use the situation to explore your partner's body, to engage in bodily contact, petting or fondling—acts that do not require intercourse. Have your partner fondle your genitals or apply oral stimulation, whichever you both prefer and find nonstressful and pleasurable. After ejaculation you may prefer to wait two or three minutes before your partner directly caresses your genitals, since some men report immediate stimulation to be physically discomforting. Nevertheless, use this time to explore your partner's body visually, manually, and orally. If your partner happens to achieve orgasm, fine. But there should be no felt obligation to provide your partner with orgasm in Stage 1 training. Stage 1 is to be undertaken leisurely. Orgasm for your partner is possible and not to be purposefully avoided, but conceptualizing orgasm for your partner as a requirement will only heighten the performance anxiety of both partners and delay progress.

*Focus on pleasurable sensations.* No two men are alike, but it is reasonably safe to assume that ten to thirty minutes following ejaculating, through mutual caressing and kissing, you will again have achieved erection. Focus on the pleasurable sensations in your penis, especially the sensations that occur as you again begin to build toward orgasm. Simply stop whatever you and your partner are doing when you feel that continued stimulation will again prompt ejaculation. Learn what your "point of no return" is—that is, the point of sexual arousal beyond which there is no preventing ejaculation. Stop just short of this point in your mutual or unilateral caressing. Do *not* attempt to take your mind off the penile sensations. Enjoy them to the fullest. If you find that enjoying these sensations promotes ejaculation, stop a bit earlier in receiving caresses next time. This is a trial-and-error procedure. It is normal to make several "mistakes" as you and your partner learn how to stop just short of your point of no return.

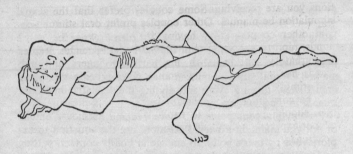

FIGURE 6.3
INTERCOURSE IN THE MALE-SUPERIOR POSITION

Intercourse in the male-superior position is highly arousing for the male and constitutes the last step in treatment for premature ejaculation when combined with the "stop and go" method.

Therefore, your "mistakes" are not mistakes at all—they are essential elements in a learning process.

Most couples find that it takes fewer than ten sessions to bring the male to the point at which he is capable of experiencing his partner's nudity, and enjoying it, without ejaculating.

## STAGE 2 TRAINING: STOP-AND-GO
## METHOD WITH PETTING

In Stage 2 training, we again focus on learning what your "point of no return" is. If merely being touched by your partner in the genital area causes you to ejaculate, begin with your partner caressing you in safer regions. Employ the nongenital massage technique (Step 2 in treatment of impotence) for three sessions before you reinstigate caressing of your genitals.

*The "stop and go" method.* We now introduce the "stop and go" method first written of by Dr. James H. Semans[10] on which you will rely heavily during further stages of training. The stop-and-go method will teach you to tolerate and enjoy the sensations that precede ejaculation *without* producing ejaculation. Develop a system of open communication with your partner, using words or gestures, whereby she repeatedly brings you close to the point of no return and then discontinues her caressing, while you focus on the pleasurable sensations you are receiving. Some couples prefer that the sexual stimulation be manual. Other couples prefer oral stimulation. Still other couples enjoy having the man guide the wife's hands, reporting that the man thus directly associates favored masturbatory motions with his partner's fingers and also "lends her strength." Many women dislike being guided in oral stimulation, however, and it is imperative that her comfort be considered as significant as the man's pleasure. The man should not hesitate to explain what he enjoys, but he cannot expect to secure his partner's co-operation by causing her to gag.

*Find your own positions.* Masters and Johnson[11] suggested that the position for this type of training should be with the female leaning against a headboard, cushioned comfortably against a pillow, with the male lying on his back, his legs spread open before her (Figure 6.4). Dr. Helen Singer Kaplan[12] shows the woman sitting alongside the man, while he lies on his back. We have found an effective position in which the man lies on his back with his head supported by a pillow. His partner may lie alongside him with her upper torso propped up by pillows. The man thus has the opportunity to take his partner's nipples into his mouth if desired. His hand may readily stroke her breasts or buttocks. We have found that there is no single best position for ejaculatory training. We inform our clients of some positions and suggest they find positions that work best for them.

*Gradually approaching the "point of no return."* In Stage 2 training, your partner gradually approximates the foreplay that has, in the past, rapidly brought you to orgasm. If stroking the penis has caused orgasm, your partner at first merely rests her hand on your penis. You permit yourself to enjoy thoroughly the sensations of her attentions, and signal her when you feel you will be able to tolerate gentle stroking without ejaculating. If continued caressing by your partner has brought about orgasm, have her discontinue her caresses when you feel you are approaching the "point of no return." *Enjoy the pleasure. Wait for the sense of nearing ejaculatory inevitability to pass. Then have your partner caress you again.* Gradually you will tolerate pleasurable pre-ejaculatory sensations longer and longer without loss of control.

*If you ejaculate "prematurely" in Stage 2 training . . . If*

FIGURE 6.4.

THE MASTERS AND JOHNSON POSITION FOR PENILE STIMULATION

This position is recommended by Masters and Johnson as a position for teaching the male ejaculatory control. After the male is brought to the point of ejaculation by his partner's manual stimulation, Masters and Johnson recommend the "penile squeeze" technique to prevent ejaculation. We recommend the "stop and go" method for those not under the direct care of a sex therapist, but the "stop and go" method may be used successfully in the position recommended by Masters and Johnson. (Modified from Masters and Johnson: *Human Sexual Inadequacy*, 1970, Little, Brown and Company, Boston.).

you do have an orgasm during training, do not condemn yourself. Enjoy the orgasm fully. Then, as in Stage 1 training, remain in the situation and continue with mutual stimulation. Do not be concerned that on a few occasions you passed the point of no return. After ejaculating, you will be physiologically incapable of immediately ejaculating again. Take this opportunity to have your partner caress your genitals. If there is some discomfort having your genitals caressed immediately following ejaculation, have your partner wait a couple of minutes first. After ten to thirty minutes, when you have recovered your erection, return to the stop-and-go method.

We recommend using the stop-and-go method for at least one half hour for ten sessions. Culminate each session by achieving a purposeful orgasm through manual or oral stimulation. At the culmination of a session of Stage 2 training, also bring your partner to orgasm through means other than intercourse.

*Prolonged masturbation.* When you have completed ten sessions of such foreplay and experience little fear of ejaculating, begin to have your partner bring you as close as possible to the point of no return—without ejaculating—through manual or oral stimulation. Then, upon your signal, have her discontinue stimulation. Follow the system originated by Dr. Helen Singer Kaplan: Approach orgasm three times without ejaculating, and ejaculate without hesitation during the fourth period of stimulation.[13]

If on occasion you ejaculate during the first or second period of stimulation, do not think of this as a failure. Remain in the situation. Engage in whatever postejaculatory activity you and your partner find pleasurable. When you reachieve erection, continue with this stop-and-go method. Approach orgasm another two times without ejaculating. Then on the second or third buildup, purposefully ejaculate.

We recommend ten sessions of prolonged masturbation. During this period of training your partner should also receive sexual pleasure, but through means other than intercourse. The timing is up to you as a couple. Some of our clients' partners have preferred to attain orgasm prior to the session. Others prefer orgasm following the session. Some prefer multiple orgasms during the interludes between stimulating their partners. Variety appears to be the rule. Some women prefer oral to manual stimulation. Others enjoy using vibrators. The major impediment to your partner's using a vibrator during sessions, assuming experience with vibrators, is her fear of *your* jealousy. If your partner generally prefers self-stimulation to achieve orgasm, it is often desirable for you to participate in ways your partner suggests. She may wish you to gently kiss her nipples, to grip her buttocks, or to do other things. In this manner you share giving pleasure. There is less likelihood that you will think of yourself as the one doing all the "taking."

## STAGE 3 TRAINING: NONDEMAND VAGINAL CONTAINMENT

In nondemand vaginal containment, intercourse begins in the female-superior position (Figure 6.1). Do not engage in thrusting after entry has been accomplished. Take time to focus on and enjoy the sensations of intravaginal containment without feeling the necessity to "perform." Engage in enough movement to provide the stimulation necessary to maintain erection. If you feel that you are about to ejaculate, there are several options:

- Press your penis inside your partner as hard as you can—without hurting your partner or yourself—until the feeling of being too close to the point of no return passes.
- Have your partner "lift off" your penis. In this option, the arranging of a signal and timing are important. You may wish to have your partner lift off somewhat farther away from the point of no return because the act of withdrawing from the penis may be in itself highly stimulating.
- Allow yourself to ejaculate, fully focusing on and enjoying the sensations. Then remain in the situation, enjoying a brief rest or little acts of love. Perhaps bring your partner to orgasm manually or orally. Re-enter when erection has been reachieved.

During each session, once you have experienced nondemand vaginal containment for several minutes, ejaculate purposefully, through active thrusting or in any manner you desire. Focus on the sensations and enjoy them fully.

*The stop-and-go method vs. the penile-squeeze technique.* Masters and Johnson[14] have used the "penile-squeeze technique" with excellent success as a method of preventing ejaculation. Although this method is usually painless, some clients have complained of discomfort using it. Furthermore, it is a difficult method to learn from a book. We believe that it should be learned from personal contact with qualified therapists who can provide exact instruction in its use through demonstration with models, indicating the exact amount of pressure to apply, exactly where, and exactly when. The stop-and-go method is more readily learned. Errors in timing are possible with both methods, but with the stop-and-go method, there is no chance of physical discomfort.

### STAGE 4 TRAINING: INTERCOURSE WITH THRUSTING

You will find that it does not take many sessions to experience the pleasures of intravaginal containment without threat of ejaculation. At this point begin mild thrusting. Have your partner thrust in opposition to you at the pace you set. Try to approach your point of no return and then stop. Use the stop-and-go method in this manner to prolong intercourse.

You may use various strategies in the stop-and-go method to show your partner when to stop. Our clients have successfully used the following:

- Place your hands on your partner's hips to indicate that she should discontinue all movement while you press firmly into her to prevent ejaculation.
- Lift your partner's upper thighs or buttocks with your hands or fingers as a signal that she should rapidly "lift off" you and withdraw containment of your penis.
- Make some type of appreciative sound that is an agreed-upon signal that your partner should cease doing the last thing she began to do, such as caressing your testicles, because it is so pleasurable that ejaculation may be precipitated.

*Spice.* A good deal of variety is possible in the female-superior position. During a particular session you and your partner may take turns thrusting mildly. You may generally thrust mildly, but occasionally engage in a few more rapid thrusts—with the understanding that your partner is not to take this as a signal for total self-abandonment. You may stroke or kiss your partner's breasts. Upon your suggestion, your partner may reach down behind her and lightly caress your testicles to provide additional stimulation. Many clients who initially undertake intercourse in the female-superior position as a "training device" become so enthralled with its variations and possibilities that it becomes a staple in their sexual diets.

*Orgasm.* As Stage 4, training proceeds, you will find yourself progressively more capable of enjoying and tolerating high levels of sexual stimulation. When you feel that you have reached a desired level, indicate to your partner that she may take more of a role in varying the rate of thrust, the angle of thrust, and guide you in providing her with additional sources of stimulation, perhaps to her breasts, her clitoral region, or her buttocks or anus. *But for a few sessions have your partner prepared to "stop" upon your signal, since the new combinations of activity may occasionally tend to precipitate orgasm.*

Once you feel that most of your partner's sexual behaviors in the female-superior position will not precipitate ejaculation, suggest to her that she feel free to achieve orgasm through intercourse. In fact, having been given the opportunity to experiment herself, she may have already begun to experience orgasms. Have each sex act culminate with an orgasm for yourself. Your orgasms may be achieved through intercourse or other means. This is a matter of preference, as it is for your partner. But you will now have the *option* of providing your partner with orgasm through intercourse.

*"Relapses."* Once you have achieved ejaculatory control in the female-superior position, do not construe occasional premature ejaculation as a sign of failure. It happens to everyone. Sometimes your partner was particularly alluring. Sometimes the setting was unusually romantic. Be assertive with yourself! Tell yourself that this was *not* a setback. When you feel yourself passing the point of no return, allow yourself to enjoy ejaculation completely. Have a standing agreement with your partner that this will intermittently, and possibly unpredictably, occur. None of us is perfect. After you have ejaculated, remain in the situation. Depending on circumstances and your mutual mood, bring your partner to orgasm through means other than intercourse or wait until you reachieve erection and bring her to orgasm through intercourse. Whatever you do, don't go on a guilt trip. Guilt trips are punishing to your partner as well as to yourself. Worst of all, after a while guilt trips are boring.

## STAGES 5 THROUGH 7

Stages 5 through 7 are a matter of altering position and increasing the amount of time that can be spent in intercourse without ejaculating. The male-superior position is mentioned last not because it is the most desirable position, the "ultimate" position, or the goal that every couple should be striving for; it is simply the position in which most clients report difficulty maintaining ejaculatory control.

Once you have achieved satisfactory intercourse in the female-superior position, you will find intercourse in the lateral position (Figure 6.2) to be slightly more arousing. Many couples are especially pleased with the possibilities for simultaneous petting and thrusting provided by lateral intercourse. The position provides free movement for both partners.

The same considerations apply to the male-superior position (Figure 6.3). Use the stop-and-go method. The same considerations apply to any new position you undertake. Initial novelty may be quite arousing, and the stop-and-go method may be employed to prolong intercourse.

Thus, in self-training for ejaculatory control, the initial methodology is time-consuming and, occasionally, tedious. Your partner must be willing to follow your signals or the process is doomed to failure. During early stages of training your partner forgoes any attempt to reach orgasm through intercourse. This is frustrating for many women. Others ironically learn acceptable substitutes or preferable methods for achieving orgasm. During later stages of training, your partner may begin to experience orgasms, but they remain secondary to the goal of teaching you ejaculatory control. Thus you are relieved of performance anxiety and permitted to focus on maintaining your pleasurable pre-ejaculatory sensations over prolonged periods of time. Once self-control is learned, many variations are possible. Self-control will transfer into a variety of positions and techniques. When transfer is not automatic, assertive use of the stop-and-go method remains always at your disposal. You can train yourself to extend pleasurable sexual intercourse markedly. Your partner will find that her efforts have paid off in full for both of you.

## Treatment for Men Without Regular Partners

Discussion until now has assumed that you had a partner who was willing to make the effort to help you gain ejaculatory control. But many men without reliable partners also suffer from inability to control ejaculation. You may date regularly but look forward to dates with a mixture of anticipation and dread because you cannot predict whether you will be able to control ejaculation if the occasion for intercourse arises. Anxieties may be compounded by having two things to worry about: whether you will be having intercourse *and* how capably you will perform.

Treatment in this situation involves three steps: (1) controlling your self-defeatist attitudes about your possible forthcoming sexual performance, (2) prolonged exposure to pre-ejaculatory sensations through a controlled masturbation procedure, and (3) use of other then penile stimulation when engaging in sex.

## STEP 1: CHANGING
## SELF-DEFEATING ATTITUDES

When you examine your thoughts prior to or on a date, you may repeatedly ask yourself questions such as, "What if I have to prove myself tonight?" "What if I ejaculate too soon and leave her high and dry?" "What will she think of me if I can't control myself?"

The facts are that many men who usually demonstrate excellent ejaculatory control will ejaculate prematurely with a new sex partner. Novel sexual stimulation may be highly arousing, but may also produce severe anxiety. Failure the first time with a new partner, or even the second or third time, need not be considered failure at all. It can happen to the most controlled of men. Many women find it extremely satisfying to think that *they* were so arousing that the man could not readily contain himself. One twenty-two-year-old female graduate student in anthropology, being seen in therapy for other than sexual reasons, commented ironically about a new boyfriend, "No matter what I do, he can keep control. One of these days I'm going to turn him on so much that he'll just lose his control and 'come' whether he wants to or not!" This woman's sexual encounters were decidedly counterproductive—power plays rather than affectionate relations. But her remark illustrates that many women construe a man's prematurely ejaculating in terms of their own capacity as "turn-ons"; they are complimented and not necessarily disappointed.

So cut off self-defeatist thoughts! Repeat assertive statements to yourself like, "I'll be all right after things settle down," "Well, she's really turning on to me," "It'll be exciting to see what she's like with her clothing off," "This is going to feel good," and "If the relationship is going to come to a quick end because I ejaculate too early, it wasn't going to be worth a hell of a lot anyhow." Look forward to the occasion. Pat yourself on the back that this attractive young woman is going out with you, that she is attracted to you. If you don't feel this way, why go out at all? Your first performance does not have to win the lady's heart. You are not Errol Flynn—the film script does not give you just one opportunity to win the lady's hand with the perfect kiss.

## STEP 2: PROLONGED SELF-MASTURBATION

Engage in a specific program of learning how to prolong pre-ejaculatory sensations through self-masturbation.

Masturbation is usually done specifically to relieve sexual tensions. It is carried out as rapidly as possible. In the BT program to learn ejaculatory control, bring yourself near the point of ejaculation and then discontinue self-manipulation, focusing on the pleasurable sensations while the penis remains erect. Allow these sensations to subside, but reinstitute the procedure before the penis becomes totally flaccid or soft. Several clients have reported successful training experiences when they have followed instructions analogous to Dr. Helen Singer Kaplan's procedure for learning ejaculatory control with a female partner. They caress themselves to the point of ejaculation three times without ejaculating, and then ejaculate following the fourth buildup. This provides for systematic release of sexual tension.

*As arousing as possible.* Pay attention to details of the masturbation situation. It should be sexually arousing. You may place photographs of arousing, provocative women in convenient places. The sensations of vaginal containment are better approximated if you use a lubricant such as Vaseline or K-Y Jelly. Lying in bed is preferable to using the bathroom because the former more closely approximates the actual sexual situation. Propitious placement of a towel will help maintain neatness. Allow fantasizing to bring you closer to the sensations of actual intercourse. Recall stimulating women with whom you have been. Recall tactile and olfactory sensations as well as visual memories.

Pick a time of day when you feel alert and are not likely to be interrupted by predictable visits or phone calls.

*The point of no return.* Each man quickly learns what his point of no return is—the point beyond which he can no longer stimulate himself and prevent ejaculation. In undertaking this BT program, it is normal to make some errors and go beyond the point of no return. We learn by trial and error. Many undertaking this program are overly cautious and stop self-stimulation well below the point of no return. This slows progress. Be risky. Find that point and stop just short of it. With practice this becomes an easy task.

Focus on the pleasures of the pre-ejaculatory sensations.

By using this BT procedure two or three times a week (more often if desired), you will learn to maintain yourself at a pleasurable plane just below the point of no return for protracted periods of time. This will transfer increased control of pre-ejaculatory sensations into heterosexual encounters. You will also find that masturbation itself becomes more pleasurable.

After two or three weeks, you will be able to maintain pre-ejaculatory sensations over prolonged periods. At this time you will wish to decrease the frequency of buildups during a training session since you will consume the same amount of time with one or two buildups that you had previously consumed with four.

## STEP 3: PLEASING YOUR PARTNER

When the occasion for intercourse arises, use the techniques you have practiced alone with your partner. Do not be afraid to suspend thrusting when you feel that you are about to reach the point of no return, and then reinstigate thrusting when ejaculatory inevitability has passed. If your partner asks what you are doing, or looks at you quizzically, make an assertive statement: Compliment her by telling her forthrightly that she is so arousing that you were about to ejaculate, and that you wanted to rest a moment so that you could extend the mutual pleasure. This is perfectly accurate.

Use techniques discussed for treating premature ejaculation in men with reliable partners. Suggest that your partner get into the female-superior position. Take moments off in which only she thrusts and you enjoy the sensations without thrusting yourself. If this, too, become overly arousing, place your hands on her hips to suggest that she pause for a moment. Or press your penis into her as deeply as possible while you pause. Maintain this pressure without thrusting and your partner will probably experience pleasurable clitoral sensations. Meanwhile your sense of approaching ejaculatory inevitability will pass. Rather than thrust actively, you may also maintain the deep penetration and move your hips about. This is stimulating to your partner but not so highly arousing for you.

Remember that rapidity of thrust is not the optimal technique for helping your partner enjoy intercourse. She will enjoy variety in the rate of thrusting. At times do not move at all—just press hard when fully contained. At other times move slowly and deliberately. Try a few rapid thrusts when you feel least likely to ejaculate. Then slow down when you feel that the sensation may stimulate you to the point of no return.

If you ejaculate before you might have liked, remember that sexual activity between two people is a mutually acquired skill. Few sex acts near perfection the first time, or the first ten times. Tell the woman that she was highly arousing. This is true and you are expressing a feeling. Assertive talk can decrease anxiety. Wait fifteen or twenty minutes and repeat intercourse. The second time your physiological arousal will be less powerful and some of the novelty of the situation will have diminished. Both conditions will help you control ejaculation. Lower physiological arousal, a decrease in novelty, and your self-training will permit you to remain longer at a pleasurable pre-ejaculatory level.

Also remember that intercourse is not the only means by which your partner can achieve orgasm. If you ejaculate you need not discontinue caressing her breasts and genitals, perhaps bringing her to orgasm through manual or oral stimulation. Be assertive: Ask your partner what she likes. Or continue a variety of stimulation with her, paying attention to the kisses and caresses that cause her to breathe more heavily and emit appreciative sounds. Repeat these caresses.

Your partner will respond more fully to you if you are the type of person who is sincerely interested in bringing her pleasure. If the two of you have a sexual future together, it is more likely to be based upon the type of person you display yourself to be during sexual activity *and* at other times, than on whether you controlled ejaculation during the first few episodes of intercourse, allowing your partner to climax through penile stimulation.

# Retarded Ejaculation

## Three Steps for Self-treatment

Retarded ejaculation, as premature ejaculation, is a relative concept. Some men can ejaculate almost at will during intercourse with their sex partners. As men age, it typically takes somewhat longer to achieve ejaculation. Some men can ejaculate readily through masturbation, or with prostitutes or mistresses, but not with their wives, suggesting that their "retardation" is a psychological problem that has something to do with the relationship rather than with the sexual apparatus itself.

Because of these psychological implications, treatment of retarded ejaculation is not always straightforward. Great amounts of guilt or anxiety may accompany the sexual efforts of men with this dysfunction. With a forty-seven-year-old engineer who had difficulty ejaculating, it appeared that he was using his problem as an indirect method of expressing anger toward his wife. He was depriving her of the privilege of providing him with pleasure. For these reasons men with retarded ejaculation may choose to seek professional counsel.

Self-treatment of retarded ejaculation involves (1) increasing the level of comfort that you experience during sexual activity with your partner, (2) bringing about ejaculation through the stimulation of your partner by means other than intercourse, and (3) gradually associating ejaculation with intercourse.

## STEP 1: INCREASING YOUR COMFORT LEVEL

In order to increase your comfort level with your partner, follow the first three steps in the BT program for treatment of impotence: relaxing in the nude with your partner, nongenital massage, and genital massage. Obviously the goal of these activities is not to help you attain erection; it is to help you learn to enjoy the sexual stimulation of your partner in gradually more arousing situations. The pleasure of the non-demand sexual contacts will help reduce feelings of guilt or anger you may be harboring toward your partner. They will also relieve you of performance anxiety. If you achieve ejaculation during these activities, excellent.

## STEP 2: EJACULATING AS A RESULT OF YOUR PARTNER'S STIMULATION

If you do not achieve ejaculation through nongenital or genital massage, try ejaculating in any way that you can after having been sexually aroused by your partner. Self-masturbation is a common technique. If masturbation in your partner's presence would prove too embarrassing for you, you may at first become as aroused by her as possible and then leave the room to masturbate, as suggested by Dr. Kaplan.[15] After a while you will feel less concerned about self-masturbation in your partner's presence. A social worker in his thirties reported that masturbating in his wife's presence was facilitated by *mutual* self-masturbation. Observing others, including your sex partner, engage in activities that are usually guilt- or anxiety-inducing has a disinhibiting effect.[16] It will also be of help to know that Georgia Kline-Graber and Dr. Benjamin Graber[17] have found "masturbation together" to be a useful step in helping *women* learn to achieve orgasm through intercourse.

## STEP 3: LEARNING TO EJACULATE THROUGH INTERCOURSE

Masters and Johnson and Helen Singer Kaplan both consider the ability to ejaculate somehow in the presence of your partner to be a breakthrough point. The social worker we treated remarked that he no longer felt that he was "withholding" ejaculation from his wife. The engineer reported that ejaculating in his wife's presence seemed to dissipate anger he felt toward her.

At this point the task becomes to ejaculate inside your partner by having her stimulate you to the point of no return and then quickly entering her. We have also found that it is possible to accomplish this by self-stimulation to ejaculatory inevitability followed by entry into your partner. Ejaculation is then facilitated if your partner is well lubricated and thrusts rapidly once you have entered her. Masters and Johnson suggest that your partner stimulate you in the female-superior position (Figure 6.1) and place your penis inside her and thrust rapidly once you have reached the point of no return.[18] Dr. Kaplan suggests a male-superior position in which your partner, by reaching underneath, can continue to stimulate you manually once you enter her, thus "easing" the transition from manual to intravaginal stimulation to achieve ejaculation.[19] Dr. Kaplan notes further that the use of vaginal lubrication in manually stimulating your penis will help strengthen the association between ejaculation and vaginal containment.

If you find that you have reached the point of no return before entering your partner, but ejaculatory inevitability disappears upon entry, begin by entering your partner while you are already in the process of ejaculating. Repeat this procedure several times before you again attempt entry just as you are about to ejaculate.

As in the treatment of impotence, we have not found any one position to be superior to another in the treatment of retarded ejaculation. Nor do we have research evidence that demonstrates the superiority of having your partner stimulate you to the point of no return over self-stimulation to this point, prior to entry. Logic would suggest that having your partner stimulate you to the point of ejaculatory inevitability indicates that she is arousing to you and that you have sufficient trust in her to permit her to caress you in an arousing manner. But this does not imply that your partner's inability to stimulate you manually or orally to ejaculatory inevitability suggests lack of sexual appeal or lack of sexual trust—it may as readily imply lack of sexual skills, or in the case of manual stimulation, lack of strength. Use what works for you.

## Painful Intercourse

### A Case for the Specialist

If you experience ongoing painful intercourse or painful ejaculation, consult your family physician. Any number of medical problems may be responsible for this discomfort. If your physician finds no medical reason for the pain, and it is further determined that your partner has no physical impediments—such as physical obstructions or failure to lubricate—seek further professional counseling.

Similarly, if you require further clarification or help with any of these behavioral programs for overcoming sexual problems, consult a behavior therapist or other professional sex therapist.

# FEMALE SEXUAL PROBLEMS

## Achieving Orgasm

Whereas anxiety in male sexual performance may lead to premature ejaculation, anxiety accompanying female sexual activity may impede orgasm entirely. Achieving orgasm for the woman is essentially setting the stage on which an orgasm can occur, then *letting go* of any anxieties that may interfere with achieving orgasm.

## Setting the Stage

Setting the stage for orgasm involves the creation of a situation in which all stimuli are conducive to achieving orgasm. The circumstances under which lovemaking occurs should be secure—that is, the bedroom door should be locked if there are children afoot in the house so there is no fear of discovery. You should be alert and interested in lovemaking rather than having to be "talked into it." This might mean that lovemaking ought to occur at a time more desirable than just prior to sleep, when the metabolism is slowing down and the body is expecting rest. You should desire the partner you have chosen. He should co-operate with you in such a way that you become aroused and lubricated. You must be open and honest enough so that you can let him know, through words or gestures when you are ready to receive his penis.

Setting the stage has its mental or cognitive counterparts. You should be "ready" for sex in terms of attitudes and beliefs. Are you looking forward to sex as an opportunity to have fun and engage in a mutually satisfying activity with a partner with whom you are comfortable, or do you fear sex as a situation in which you must "do your duty" for your mate? Have you been brought up with beliefs that sex is sinful and permissible only for procreation, or do you feel that you have a right to enjoy yourself during sex? Do you believe that it is all right to focus on your own pleasure and your own bodily sensations, or do you feel that you must do everything solely for your partner's benefit? Do you believe that there is something "dirty" about sex?

These factors are more important for women than for men because achieving orgasm for the woman largely involves letting go of mental and bodily vigilances and allowing herself to experience a variety of pleasurable sensations. If she views herself as a vulnerable victim, ruminating about what a wrong she is doing or what she is doing wrong, she will not find it easy to "let go."

## Achieving Orgasm Is an Acquired Skill

Knowing what it feels like to achieve an orgasm is extremely important. We have seen some women in the clinic who do not honestly know whether they have ever achieved orgasm, either through masturbation or through intercourse. Research has shown that women who masturbate during their teens appear to experience more orgasms through intercourse than women who do not have a history of masturbating.[20] This is consistent with the concept that *achieving orgasm can be a learned skill*. Many children have been severely punished for "playing with themselves," although it would appear that all children left to their own devices will start to "play with themselves" during the first couple of years of life—as soon as they learn that touching certain bodily parts brings pleasure. Parents punish their children for masturbation because of religious beliefs or because of misguided notions concerning the possible physical and mental consequences of masturbation. A girl strongly punished for masturbation at a very early age is likely to develop some fear of manipulation of her genitalia, and is likely to be deprived of the self-experimenting that would make it easier for her to achieve orgasm later. She may not be able to examine her own genitalia visually without experiencing severe bodily sensations of fear. She may go so far as to avoid certain birth-control devices, like a diaphragm, because she doesn't want to touch herself "down there." Her "private parts" remain private—even to her. She develops little concept of female genital anatomy and is at a loss to understand how manipulation of specific areas is likely to bring her pleasure.

## The Nature of the Female Orgasm

Masters and Johnson and other sex researchers[21] report four definable phases to both the male and the female orgasm. These are, for both sexes, the excitement phase, the plateau phase, the orgasmic phase, and the resolution phase.

### EXCITEMENT PHASE

In the female, the excitement phase is marked by lubrication and lengthening and distending of the vagina, responses that are involuntary and that prepare the vagina to receive the penis. Various tissues become engorged with blood, causing the labia minora (Figure 6.5) to swell and the labia majora to flatten and recede, allowing smoother entry of the penile shaft. The nipples become erect, and the breasts of women who have not suckled children swell in size. Muscles

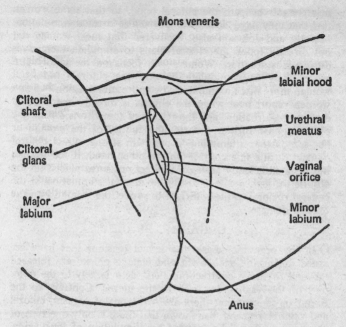

**FIGURE 6.5**
FEMALE GENITAL ANATOMY

(Modified from Masters and Johnson: *Human Sexual Inadequacy,*
1970, Little, Brown and Company, Boston.)

tense, both voluntarily and involuntarily, and many women
who contract their rectal sphincters report increased sexual
stimulation. Some women desire to have the man stroke the
anus, which is an erogenous zone, during intercourse, or to
place a finger inside the anus, which appears to produce sensations similar to contracting of the sphincter muscle and
provides the rectum with a resistance against which to contract the sphincter.

## PLATEAU PHASE

The plateau phase is marked psychologically by increased
sexual tension and physiologically by increased engorgement
of the vaginal region with blood, so that the outer part of the
vaginal opening actually decreases in circumference. The clit-

oris retracts beneath the clitoral hood, so that some women feel that they have "lost" it if they utilize manual stimulation. Masters and Johnson also discovered that most women did not directly touch the clitoral glans to stimulate themselves during masturbation. Women who focus on the clitoris are more likely to manipulate directly the clitoral shaft, but women more often manipulate the entire mons region.[22] Some women report pain when the clitoris is directly encountered during masturbation, and the retreat of the clitoris during the plateau phase further suggests the futility of the woman or her sex partner attempting to maintain strong, direct clitoral contact during intercourse. On the other hand, if the woman has been sufficiently aroused, indirect pressures placed on the clitoris through penile thrusting or manual stimulation in the general region is quite sufficient to propel the woman into the orgasmic phase.

## ORGASMIC PHASE

In the orgasmic phase, the sexual tensions that have accrued during the excitement and plateau phases are released through rhythmic contractions that occur largely in the outer part of the vagina, but also in the uterus. Contrary to the Freudian concept that there are two types of orgasm, clitoral and vaginal, research has shown that there is only one type of orgasm, whether it be induced by stimulation of the vagina, the clitoris, or both regions. The rectal sphincter may also rhythmically contract during orgasm. Psychologically, orgasm is experienced as intense physical pleasure combined with a sense of release of tension. Physiologically, the heart rate and the respiration rate are markedly increased over their usual levels during orgasm, and muscles in various bodily groups are tensed. The buildup of blood in various vessels that had led to engorgement and enlargement of the genitals and the breasts is released.

## RESOLUTION PHASE

During the resolution phase, the woman's body returns to the pre-excitement quiescent phase. The clitoris descends rather rapidly after orgasmic contractions have ceased. At this time, postorgasmic clitoral massage may prove extremely pleasurable. The innermost part of the vagina contracts while the outer part, which had decreased because of engorgement, again dilates. The labia minora and the labia majora return to their usual appearance. Breathing and heart rate slow to their normal rhythms. In contrast to the man, the woman may go on to experience multiple orgasms if she is again sexually stimulated in the resolution phase.

## SPICE

Women vary in the types and amounts of stimulation they appear to require in order to achieve orgasm. For some women, stimulation of the breasts is important. Other women report no erotic sensations from fondling of the breasts (although they can often experience pleasurable sensations from manipulation of the breasts if stimulation of other erogenous regions is consistently paired with fondling of the breasts). Some women thrive on stimulation that is as direct to the clitoris as possible, whereas other women find direct clitoral stimulation painful or insignificant in comparison to indirect stimulation resulting from manual, oral, or penile stimulation of the genital region or vagina. Some women desire anal stimulation prior to or during orgasm. Others are repulsed at the thought. Some women desire oral stimulation of the breasts, genitals, or anus. Some women feel more comfortable with the male atop them in "missionary position." Others desire to sit astride their partners in the female-superior position, which provides them with greater latitude of movement and control of erotic stimulation.

Of particular interest is the Masters and Johnson discovery that women tend to achieve the most intense orgasms through masturbation, with their next most intense orgasms achieved through mutual masturbation or petting with a partner. Intercourse yields the third most intense orgasm.[23] Here, too, psychology is paramount. The woman who hesitates to masturbate for religious or ethical reasons is less likely to enjoy masturbation than the woman who does not share her concerns.

## BT Programs for Achieving Orgasm

If you have difficulty achieving orgasm, first determine whether your problem is "primary" or "secondary." *Primary orgasmic dysfunction*, as the term is used by Masters and Johnson,[24] refers to women who have the feeling they have never experienced an orgasm. *Secondary*, or "situational" *orgasmic dysfunction*, refers to women who have achieved orgasms, but not as frequently or with as much pleasure as they would like.

## Seven BT Steps for Treatment of Primary Orgasmic Dyfunction

Our treatment of choice for primary orgasmic dysfunction is masturbation, initially suggested by Dr. Joseph LoPiccolo of the Division of Human Sexuality of the Psychiatry Department of the State University of New York at Stony Brook.[25] This approach is also recommended by Dr. Helen Singer Kaplan of the Cornell University College of Medicine[26] and Dr. Lonnie Garfield Barbach of the Human Sexuality Program of the University of California at San Francisco.[27] While no two practitioners emphasize the exact same sequence of "steps," the essentials of the technique are similar from researcher to researcher.

### STEP 1: ACCEPTING MASTURBATION

Learning how to experience orgasm by yourself is a logical prerequisite to experiencing orgasms with someone else,[28] and is enjoyable for its own sake.

If you have never achieved orgasm through masturbation, it may be that you were taught that sex is "dirty." Your parents may have punished you for manipulating your genitals during infancy. You may be literally afraid to touch yourself. You may be uncomfortable or experience a confusing jumble of sensations whenever your partner touches you "down there." You may be afraid to "let yourself go." At times you may have felt that you were on the verge of having an orgasm, but then the sensations faded. The seven BT steps for treatment of primary orgasmic dysfunction will help you "unlearn" feelings and fears that interfere with your ability to experience highly pleasurable bodily sensations through self-masturbation, and ultimately, if desired, through the attentions of your partner.

*Use of systematic self-desensitization.* If you have difficulty accepting the idea of self-masturbation, you may refer to Chapter 3, on fears, and undertake a program of SSD with masturbation as the "target behavior" prior to actually masturbating. One twenty-eight-year-old client who could not bear the thought of touching herself in her genital region was taught progressive self-relaxation (PSR) and then learned to imagine herself masturbating without experiencing the bodily sensations of fear. Relaxation readily transferred to actual masturbation.

*Use of assertive statements.* Several clients have found it helpful to use spoken or thought-assertive statements that granted them permission to "let go" and masturbate, and, as other assertive behaviors, tended to reduce anxieties and fears associated with the concept of masturbating. Each client constructs statements that sound right for her. Statements that are used frequently include:

- My body belongs to me. I am free to do with it as I please.
- I am entitled to experience pleasure.
- The Shakespearean quote: "There is nothing either good or bad, but thinking makes it so."
- I am an adult and capable of making my own decisions.
- I am *not* a child. My mother is *not* going to run into my room and slap my hand.
- I may do as I please in the privacy of my own home.

One twenty-two-year-old graduate student in psychology wrote several such statements down on small index cards and placed them by her toothbrush in her bathroom. Each time she went to brush her teeth she read the cards to herself in random order. She was instructed to be certain that she read them emphatically to herself. Several times she dropped a statement or two and added others as new, relevant ideas occurred to her. She reported that they began to "sink in" after a week had passed. This technique is similar to the Graber[29] method of tape-recording "suggestions" to the effect that you are enjoying masturbation. If you repeat such self-assertions and believe in them, they will help you overcome many of your qualms. Once the program is further underway, pleasurable sensations derived from self-stimulation will help to counter remaining fears and misgivings.

Some clients, of course, have no difficulty accepting the concept of masturbation. Being told by their therapist that masturbation is permissible seems sufficient. Other women, especially those with strong, orthodox religious convictions that masturbation is sinful, may find it impossible to entertain the idea of self-masturbation. Such early learning may take a good deal of verbal therapy to overcome, even when the client is motivated to do so.

## STEP 2: DESENSITIZATION TO YOUR OWN GENITALS

Explore your genital area, both visually and manually. You may find it most comfortable to sit on your bed with your legs spread, holding a mirror between them. Locate the various anatomical parts shown in Figure 6.5. No two women look precisely alike. Do not be concerned with the differences between your anatomy and the figure. Variation is the rule. Do not worry about whether your genitals are attractive or unattractive. This is truly a case in which, as Shakespeare wrote, "Beauty is in the eye of the beholder." If you learn to allow your genitals to bring you pleasure, they will become beautiful to you.

Many women are convinced that their genitals are ugly. They sometimes wonder in the therapeutic session, "How can my husband stand to look at me down there?" or plaintively say something like, "If we ever made love with the light on, I think he would learn to hate me." On the contrary, for the large number of men a woman's genitals are an alluring object of great mystery. For other men, the sight of that which brings them pleasure is pleasurable itself.

*Use of relaxation and assertive statements.* Clients who are anxious about exploring their genitals have been helped to overcome their qualms about self-examination through the use of progressive self-relaxation (PSR) and assertive thoughts, both of which dispel anxieties and fears.

You may read Chapter 2 to develop PSR skills. Then, prior to and during self-examination, take deep breaths, tell yourself to relax, and exhale. Focus on sensations of warmth and bodily comfort. Momentarily close your eyes and focus on a pleasant scene that is unrelated to self-exploration. Then continue with your self-examination. If you again begin to feel anxious, discontinue for the day. But repeat the procedure over the next several days. You will find that you can examine yourself for progressively longer periods of time without incurring the bodily sensations of anxiety, so long as you never allow your anxiety to build to the point where it counters the feelings of relaxation you have summoned. In several days you will be able to explore yourself indefinitely, without anxiety.

One woman reported that she found it helpful to continue to use assertive statements to dispel anxiety, as she had done in initially coming to accept the idea of masturbation. She repeated the following statements to herself emphatically as she explored her genitals:

- I have a right to get to know my body.
- This is *me*, not a foreign object.
- My vagina is as much a part of me as my eyes, nose, or hair.
- I look as I look. "Beauty is in the eyes of the beholder."
- I have a right to be proud of my body. If a man can be proud of his penis, I can be proud of my vagina.

If you decide to use this technique, construct statements in a similar vein that sound right for you. Make your spoken or covert tone of voice sincere and emphatic. This is the truth you are speaking to yourself! If it takes a while for your "guts" to catch up with your thoughts, this is perfectly predictable. It does not mean that the thoughts are untrue. It only means that you are still experiencing some of the visceral learnings you underwent as a child though your thoughts have achieved adulthood.

## STEP 3: A RELAXED SETTING

Create a relaxed setting for masturbation. It is one of the most important activities of your life. Treat it as such. Select a time of day when you are interested, alert, and not pressed for time. If you share a home or apartment, select a time when you are not likely to be discovered or distracted.

Choose warm, comfortable surroundings for this experience: mats and pillows, your bed, your bath. Subdue the lighting. Use mirrors, candles, scents, oils—anything you find sensual.

## STEP 4: SELF-MASSAGE

When you are settled and relaxed, massage yourself all over, perhaps with body oils. At first do not concentrate on your breasts or your genitals, but do not feel that you should avoid these areas. As suggested by Dr. Barbach,[30] discover what caresses are pleasurable for you and repeat them. If you enjoy encompassing your breasts, stroking a nipple, or circling your belly, do so. If you enjoy massaging the mons veneris above the clitoris, do so.

If you find some of these activities anxiety-inducing, you may approach the "troublesome" areas intermittently and casually, after having first massaged other bodily areas so that you are feeling generally warm, comfortable, and sensual. When your anxiety becomes noxious, move elsewhere. Then, when you have once more established pleasurable sensations, return. You will find that you can gradually spend longer periods of time massaging anxiety-inducing bodily areas. This is a method for directly counterconditioning anxiety induced by self-manipulation with pleasurable sensations. The rule of thumb is always to keep the anxiety at a tolerable level. At first, stroke the problem areas only occasionally. Make each total self-massage session as pleasurable as possible. Soon you will find that the direct bodily pleasure you receive from caressing previous problem areas counterconditions any remnants of anxiety.

*PSR*. You may also use PSR skills developed from Chapter 2 during Step 4. Once PSR skills have been firmly developed, take intermittent deep breaths as you massage yourself, tell yourself to relax, and exhale. At first you may wish to focus specifically on relaxing muscle groups in the abdominal and leg regions. Permit these areas to become warm, comfortable, and heavy. Breathe easily and regularly. But if at some point you feel that continuing self-massage may elevate anxiety to the point where it is not readily quelled by PSR, discontinue self-massage for the day. Briefly focus on something pleasant and nonsex-related, perhaps a forest or a beach scene. Continue your self-massage and PSR on the next day and you will be able to go farther.

Some women find it extremely pleasurable to take a hot, relaxing bath prior to self-massage. Some women prefer to massage themselves with soap while they are in their tubs. Soap acts as a lubricant, and warm bath water is an erotic stimulus for many women.

## STEP 5: USE OF FANTASY

As you may read in the section on sexual mythology, erotic fantasies are not for men only! After you have begun to find the self-massaging caresses that make you feel good, fantasize an erotic adventure with a sexually appealing partner, and associate these fantasies with self-massage and stimulation of your genital region.

Your sexual fantasies may include your boyfriend, your

husband, a former boyfriend, a movie or television actor—whatever turns you on. Some clients have reported guilt at fantasizing about anyone but their husbands. We usually point out that there is a difference, for the faithful-minded, between fantasizing an erotic experience with someone you find sexually attractive and actually "cheating" on your husband. It is important for you to learn to associate arousing thoughts with pleasurable bodily sensations. Later, if you desire, the pleasure you derive from erotic fantasies can be paired with having sexual activity with your husband. This will help you to view him as a more erotic figure.

*Visual aides.* Some clients choose to view photography of partially clad or nude men or women while they massage their bodies. Such photos are readily available in magazines such as *Playgirl*. Some clients have preferred photographs of persons engaged in intercourse or other sexual activity. This is entirely a matter of personal preference. Select the images, mental or photographic, that you find appealing, and then use them in differing combinations around you to provide pleasurable stimuli. Many men use photographs of nude and provocative women when they masturbate. What is sauce for the gander may as well be sauce for the goose.

## STEP 6: GENITAL MASSAGE

As you employ your erotic fantasies or photographs, begin to focus on massaging your breasts and your genitals. It is natural for you to find it pleasurable to stroke your clitoris, but be aware that as you become more aroused, your clitoris will "retreat" under the fold of your clitoral hood and you may "lose" it.[31] Thus you may wish to massage your entire genital region. Continue to stimulate your clitoris indirectly by stroking your labia and inserting one or more fingers an inch or so into your vagina. Movements in this region will "tug" on the clitoris in much the same way that a thrusting penis provides indirect, yet potent stimulation when you are highly aroused without actually touching the clitoris. You may wish to use a small amount of Vaseline or K-Y Jelly as you massage your genital region. This will assure sufficient lubrication.

Many women report that they use their dominant hand to massage their genitals and the other hand to stroke their breasts or nipples. Others use both hands to massage their genitals. No two women masturbate exactly alike.[32] Use these exercises to determine what types of self-caresses bring you a maximum of pleasure, and repeat these caresses while you concentrate on your erotic fantasies or photographs.

Allow your legs, your pelvic region, your entire body to move in any way that increases your pleasure. Some women prefer to lie on their backs, others recline partially, and some support themselves on their knees and heads, well buttressed by pillows, as they reach below and behind with both hands to provide clitoral, vaginal, and anal stimulation. Enter one or more fingers into your vagina and thrust against them if this is pleasurable. Focus on the sensations in both the clitoral and vaginal areas, and on your erotic fantasies. You may breathe through your mouth to take in more air. Permit whatever sounds develop deep within you to be expelled with your breath. You are alone and expressing your own right to experience pleasure. Whereas during nongenital massage you may have focused on keeping your abdominal and leg muscles relaxed, do not hesitate, now, to press rhythmically against your hands.

## STEP 7: PERMITTING ORGASM

*Allow* orgasms to occur spontaneously by continuing to stroke yourself pleasurably, maintaining erotic rhythmic body movements and pursuing your erotic fantasies. Don't concern yourself with thoughts like, "When is it going to happen?" "How long will it take?" or "What do I have to do in order to have an orgasm?" You then assume the spectator role rather than the performer role.

*An orgasm cannot be forced.* An orgasm is a reflex that occurs spontaneously in the presence of erotic, sensual stimulation and in the absence of anxieties and self-defeating ruminations. But an orgasm cannot be willed or forced.

Some women using the prescribed technique achieve orgasm within an hour. They did not have particular anxieties concerning their bodies or masturbation, only misinformation, or, incredibly, total lack of information. All they needed was "permission" and some guidance.

Other clients have required up to eight weeks of desensitization to fears or ill-based mores in addition to self-massage. If you require several weeks to reach orgasm, do not be discouraged. Using these BT steps, we have had over a 90 per cent success rate in helping preorgasmic women become orgasmic. It is always a thrill when we are told, "Well, you've given me my first orgasm, doctor." But we are *quick* to point out that the client has accomplished orgasm by herself with some guidance and encouragement.

Your first orgasm may be relatively weak or strong. You will experience vaginal contractions occurring slightly more frequently than one per second, a release of much or all of the sexual tension that had been building, and a sense of psychological pleasure that no one has ever painted well enough with words. It is typical for clients to report that their orgasms become increasingly "stronger" and more pleasurable as they masturbate. This is perfectly consistent with the view that attaining orgasm is an acquired skill.

Do not be disheartened by "setbacks." It is not uncommon to experience one orgasm and then to look forward with such anticipation to the second that performance anxiety inhibits the orgasmic reflex. Allow yourself to relax. Focus on your step-by-step accomplishments. Reflect on the fact that you know it is possible for you to have orgasms and permit yourself to lose yourself in the pleasurable sensations you bring about by self-caresses and erotic fantasy.

Trying to have an orgasm every time you masturbate may create performance anxiety. Worrying about whether you will masturbate well enough turns masturbation into a task rather than a pleasurable experience you can give yourself. Remember this rule and you will find your sexual learning experiences more productive: *Self-masturbation may be undertaken because it feels good, and not only as a means for achieving orgasm.* Masturbation allows you to pay attention to your own body, to please yourself, not others. *Be assertive with yourself and insist that you are entitled to give yourself pleasure.*

## A NOTE ON VIBRATORS

Some women choose to use vibrators in masturbation. This is a fully acceptable and desirable practice. The vibrator commonly accelerates the process of learning to have orgasms. The vibrator also tends to approximate the penis, suggesting that orgasms achieved through use of the vibrator may transfer more readily to sexual intercourse than orgasms achieved manually. On the other hand, as Dr. Kaplan notes,[33] some women seem to become "hooked" on their vibrators, finding it difficult to surrender them or to achieve orgasm in other manners, including intercourse. One twenty-year-old nursing student reported that she had named her vibrator "Elvis." We were afraid to inquire why. She became capable of achieving orgasm regularly with her vibrator, but not with male sexual partners, though she did enjoy penile stimulation. Her orgasmic problem became "situational" rather than primary—resulting from the nature of fleeting relationships in which she did not sufficiently assert her own sexual needs or develop trust in her partners, enabling her to "let go."

But there is no reason to surrender the vibrator. If you enjoy the sensations it provides, that is all the justification you require for using it. Our clients have also reported that when their sex partners work to make themselves as attractive and reliable as their vibrators—and men can still do some things, especially orally, that vibrators cannot—their learning how it feels to have orgasms with the aid of the vibrator gives them sensations of building toward orgasm that they can recall and attempt to reproduce through intercourse. It then becomes up to them to show their partners what types of erotic stimulation they should continue. Be assertive! Your partner will not read your mind.

## A SUMMARY WORD

The woman who knows what an orgasm feels like and how to bring one about is more likely to experience orgasm through manual or oral stimulation, intercourse, or the use of an instrument such as the vibrator. Many women who learn to achieve orgasm through masturbation also begin to experience orgasm through intercourse. But if this is not the case for you, you are not alone. Read the program for secondary orgasmic dysfunction for women who can achieve orgasm through masturbation.

*Masturbation: Why stop?* We do not feel that once you learn how to achieve orgasm with a partner you should surrender masturbation as a secondary or somewhat illicit avenue toward orgasm. There will be many times when you are in the mood to achieve orgasm and your partner is unavailable. Orgasms achieved through masturbation and through intercourse, moreover, appear to have somewhat different sensations, although the vaginal contractions that occur in both instances have been shown by Masters and Johnson[34] to be identical. It may occur that you will desire to achieve orgasms through masturbation as well as through intercourse. There is room for both.

# Treatment of Secondary Orgasmic Dysfunction

Secondary orgasmic dysfunction refers to those problems in which the woman has achieved orgasms in the past but no longer achieves them, achieves them less frequently than she would like, or experiences less pleasure than she would like through orgasms. Secondary orgasmic dysfunction has also been labeled "situational" orgasmic dysfunction by Masters and Johnson,[35] since the woman is capable of having an orgasm, and it is thus assumed that the current causes of the orgasmic dysfunction deal with the circumstances under which she tries to achieve orgasm.

Many of the reasons for secondary or situational orgasmic dysfunction are similar to those for primary orgasmic dysfunction and have to do with the woman's beliefs. Some women have been raised to believe that sex is essentially dirty and sinful, albeit sometimes necessary for purposes of procreation. Some women were punished for "playing with themselves" as little girls, and now associate a great deal of learned or conditioned fear or anxiety with sexual activity. Very often the punishments occurred at such a young age that the woman has no conscious recollection of them. It is a fact of learning that words are easier to remember than picture images, and many of these acts of punishment occurred prior to the age of language acquisition, before the girl was capable of labeling what was happening to her. Nevertheless, on a "gut level," the thought of allowing her genitals to be manipulated causes fear and anxiety.

We have heard many young women say that they feel there is nothing wrong with sex. In some cases they say that they are currently at odds with the teachings instilled by their parents or their religious backgrounds. Why, then, when they can understand that there is nothing evil or sordid about sex, do they still have difficulty "letting go" and enjoying the experience? Much of our functioning is on a conscious level, and women whose attitudes are "prosex" will ultimately have fewer sexual problems than women who are philosophically opposed to sexual activity—but we have also been learning on an automatic "gut" level since entering this world. What has been learned on a gut level must sometimes be unlearned on a gut level. We shall discuss this further.

Some women have little or no difficulty achieving orgasm through masturbation, but cannot achieve orgasm with their husbands or other sex partners. In these cases there is usually something lacking in the relationship with the partner—sympathy, empathy, patience, or, possibly, sexual skills. A woman in this situation poses yet a different problem.

## Program A: For Women Who Rarely Experience Orgasms or Experience Nonsatisfying Orgasms

Rarely achieving orgasm or achieving nonpleasurable orgasms is closely related to never having achieved orgasm. Assuming that a gynecologist has given you a clean bill of health, it has been our experience that women who rarely achieve orgasm, even through masturbation, experience a great deal of *performance anxiety*, and tend to feel uncomfortable in manipulating their own bodies due to moral restrictions. For these women we recommend the same program that was recommended for women with primary orgasmic dysfunction: self-masturbation. The steps in this program were already outlined, and the program should run more smoothly and rapidly for the woman who has some idea of what an orgasm is like and of the type of self-stimulation that is pleasurable.

If you rarely achieve orgasm, following the seven BT steps on pages 178 through 185 will

- get you used to the idea that you are allowed to seek your own sexual pleasure
- make you less dependent on sex partners and their whims and fancies when it comes to achieving satisfaction for yourself
- desensitize you, if need be, to your own genital organs
- teach you to associate feelings of relaxation with sexual activity, thus counteracting performance anxiety (Learning to relax during masturbation is also a "gut level" type of learning that may help counteract some negative early learning experiences you may have had about sex and, especially, about self-manipulation.)
- put you more in touch with specific types of sexual stimulation that lead to your having orgasms (This will be information that you can later teach sex partners so that

they will become more proficient in meeting your needs.)

- give you practice in "letting go," that all-important prerequisite to experiencing orgasm
- heighten the pleasure you experience during orgasm

All of these goals will be beneficial for you in achieving orgasms with your chosen sex partner. They will tend to "liberate" you of restrictive beliefs that you may have grown up with.

## Program B: Four BT Steps for Women Who Successfully Masturbate to Orgasm

If you can achieve orgasm through masturbation, but not through intercourse, you need to learn to associate the two. This requires the full co-operation of your male partner.

### ATTAINING YOUR PARTNER'S CO-OPERATION

Men sometimes feel threatened if women make suggestions about the way that sex ought to be handled, or show any signs that they are failing to enjoy fully men's efforts to provide them with pleasure. There are some men who believe—as, unfortunately, also do some women—that sexual pleasure is proper for men only. Thus you may have to tread carefully in gaining your partner's co-operation. But if your marriage is one in which you are deathly afraid to discuss this matter with your husband, you may be in need of marriage counseling or of a new sex partner.

Most couples presenting themselves for sex therapy make great gains in relatively brief amounts of time. But the sexual growth activities that are prescribed in the clinic presume the full co-operation of both sex partners. However, most couples who would profit from sex therapy are not necessarily in agreement concerning the need. You may see a problem where your partner does not. If your partner agrees that a problem exists, he may feel that visiting the professional sex therapist is an invitation to invasion of privacy. Or you may both agree that a problem exists and both be willing to seek professional counsel, but not be able to afford the sometimes expensive counsel offered through many sex therapy programs, especially the programs requiring approximately two weeks' residence at the clinic.

Ask your partner to read the entire section on women's sexual problems to alert him to your needs and to help him understand more fully the attitudes and behaviors that he should adopt to help you attain sexual fulfillment with him.

The man, of course, has a great deal to gain from helping his partner achieve orgasms during foreplay or intercourse. She will be more willing to have intercourse. She will appear less moody and irritable. She will be more highly aroused and better lubricated. Thus entry of the penis will be smoother and the sensations more pleasurable for both partners. There will be greater honesty and openness in the marriage. Some women who dread or merely tolerate sex but refrain from telling their mates will be able to open up in bed and elsewhere. The bedroom is not one isolated part of a marriage. A woman achieving greater pleasure in the bedroom will look more favorably on her marriage in general.

Assuming the total co-operation of your sex partner, learning to have more frequent orgasms through intercourse is a straight-forward matter.

## STEP 1: TAKING TURNS PETTING

Take turns petting to learn what turns each other on.

In taking turns petting, you devote several sessions of an hour or so to receiving pleasure from and giving pleasure to your partner through manual and, perhaps, oral stimulation. The purpose of taking turns petting is to provide both of you with a learning opportunity to become more stimulating to one another, and to assure that there is reciprocity or an immediate "payoff" for your partner. The purpose of this exercise is not to achieve orgasm, but to learn the technique of mutual pleasuring. It is possible for you to have sessions in which you alone are the recipient of sexual attention. But taking turns will make you a more effective stimulator for your partner and relieve feelings of selfishness or guilt that you are allowing yourself to take too much pleasure. Guilt over receiving pleasure is another common reason why some women have difficulty achieving orgasm through intercourse.

Taking turns in petting will also give you experience in giving your partner pleasure when you are feeling no psychological demand to experience an orgasm. This will help you to get over the feeling that orgasm is something that you or your partner are demanding of you.

*Giving feedback.* Concerning the actual techniques employed in these petting sessions, the main rule to keep in mind is that you are to stop hoping and praying that your partner will read your mind to find out what stimulates you sexually. It will be up to you to show him or tell him.

Masters and Johnson[36] suggest use of a position for this type of instruction that is intended to allow your partner and you freedom of movement so that you can guide his fingers and hands through the types of strokes and caresses that will arouse you (Figure 6.6). The man sits behind you while you place yourself between his legs with your back to him. This positioning may be carried out in the bed or elsewhere. We have a word of warning, however, that comes from clients whose beds have been on wheels or coasters or otherwise not very firmly set in place. As the male has leaned back for support, the bed has moved forward. Happily, we have no injuries to report, but do be sure that your bed is firmly set against a wall or headboard if you choose this position. We agree with Helen Singer Kaplan that the position chosen for this exercise is not very important, so long as both partners are quite comfortable and there is ample freedom for you to guide your partner's hands. A front-to-front position will also allow your partner to apply oral stimulation.

The essential factor in Step 1 is teaching your partner what you like, what "turns you on." Several sessions of about an hour or so each should be devoted to this type of physical guiding of your partner. You should have no hesitation to tell him or show him how to stroke you in a different area, to stroke you more lightly or with more force. When it comes to stimulation of your clitoral region, as Masters and Johnson note, you will probably wish to have your partner momentarily enter his finger in your vagina to obtain some lubricating fluid, since no lubrication emanates from the clitoris. Or else Vaseline or K-Y Jelly may be used.

*Receiving pleasure.* When it is your turn to receive pleasure, you must allow yourself to be selfish, to concentrate on your pleasure alone and to use your partner's hands, fingers, and mouth as though they were your personal toys. Similarly, when it is your partner's turn to receive pleasure, he should be permitted to guide you as freely. Perhaps the one exception applies to oral stimulation, which is not possible for some persons to apply without great arousal and

FIGURE 6.6
A FAVORED POSITION FOR TEACHING THE MALE HOW TO
STIMULATE HIS PARTNER'S GENITALS

This position is recommended by Masters and Johnson and Helen Singer Kaplan. The woman sits between her partner's legs, leaning comfortably back against him, and guides him verbally or with her hands through movements that she finds sexually arousing. This position permits the woman to concentrate on her own pleasure, and is especially useful with women who must learn to receive pleasure without immediately feeling the need to reciprocate. (Modified from Masters and Johnson: *Human Sexual Inadequacy*, 1970, Little, Brown and Company, Boston.)

anxiety. If this is the case, such stimulation must be forgone, since it is implausable to attempt to force anyone into enjoying the active role in cunnilingus or fellatio.

*Problem spots.* Some couples report that a session of mutual petting has not gone well. In these cases, we usually find that one or both partners did not stick to the "rules." Sometimes the man tried to bring his partner to orgasm by stronger petting than she desired. Sometimes the man has ejaculated during petting and the woman has been "shocked" that he has experienced orgasm while she has not. Or it may be that disputes have arisen over who was giving or receiving more.

A little common sense will answer some of the problems.

Your partner should make *no effort* to do anything other than what you show him to do. While he is pleasuring you, it is his job to learn what you find arousing and stimulating, and to remain fully open to learning new things from you. If your partner ejaculates during his "turn" in receiving pleasure, we do *not* feel that this is necessarily a negative event. In fact, if you were to bring your partner close to the point of orgasm but then "let him down," or make him feel he must discontinue receiving pleasure at that point, this would be highly frustrating. There is nothing to gain by your partner's suffering at this point. However, it is incumbent upon you not to feel "insulted" or vaguely hurt that your partner has ejaculated while you have not achieved orgasm. It would be wiser for you to share his pleasure, recognizing that your achieving orgasm was not necessary for him to receive pleasure. *This will in the future serve to reduce the pressure you may have felt to feign an orgasm when you did not achieve orgasm. Permitting your partner to ejaculate though you do not achieve orgasm will help liberate you from the psychological need to fake orgasms.*

If you or your partner feel that you have not been receiving as much as you or he ought to, clearly this calls for open discussion. Such complaints usually emanate from feeling that your partner is co-operating "just to make me happy," or from his feeling that he has been reduced to nothing more than a sex tool to give you pleasure. Feelings such as these ought to be brought into the open, and if they cannot be resolved through discussion sessions that remain warm and loving, marriage counseling may be in order.

## STEP 2: ACHIEVING ORGASM THROUGH MANUAL OR ORAL MEANS

Once the woman is feeling aroused and lubricated, Masters and Johnson[37] and Helen Singer Kaplan[38] suggest that the next step ought to be "nondemand coitus" or intercourse during which the woman does not feel the requirement of achieving orgasm. We believe that an intervening step, while optional, is often helpful, and thus delay "nondemand" intercourse to the third step.

Therefore, we recommend that once you feel that your partner has learned to arouse you to the point of reaching orgasm, you then allow yourself to have orgasms through your partner's manual or oral stimulation. Note that we have said *allow* yourself, not *force* yourself.

The purpose of Step 2 is to teach you, on a gut level, to experience orgasms through the manipulations and attentions of your partner. Repeating this technique through several sessions will reinforce the association between your partner and orgasm before you become reinvolved in intercourse. It will also help set the stage for achieving orgasms through intercourse by showing your partner, and yourself, certain things that you can do during intercourse to increase your pleasure.

The logical reciprocation during Step 2 is for you to bring your partner to ejaculation through manual or oral means. Thus you reacquire the expectation of achieving orgasm through each other's caresses. We have often been asked, "Who should achieve orgasm first?" Initially our response was that this was immaterial. But we have, over time, developed a rule of thumb: *Everything else being equal, the partner who is less likely to lose interest in sex upon achieving orgasm should achieve it first.* In this manner, reciprocation with greater motivation is likely to be achieved. We recommend engaging in Step 2 for about a week before going on to Step 3.

## STEP 3: NONDEMAND INTERCOURSE

Once you have been aroused and lubricated to the point where you desire orgasm, we recommend, as do Masters and Johnson,[39] that you lower yourself onto your partner and insert his penis into your vagina. This is the female-superior position (Figure 6.1). Your major goal at this point in therapy is to learn to associate sexual arousal, as learned through the pleasuring sessions, with vaginal containment of the penis. Whereas it was possible for your partner to experience orgasm during petting in Step 1, it is now important that neither of you attempt to achieve orgasm. This is the nature of nondemand intercourse. It is intercourse that is undertaken for the pleasures of the moment, not because it leads to orgasm, and certainly not because it leads to procreation.

*Positioning.* Helen Singer Kaplan notes that sex therapists other than Masters and Johnson suggest different positions for this first intercourse, and Dr. Kaplan herself believes that any position desired by the couple is the appropriate position. We would favor the female-superior position for three reasons. First, it allows you to be the literal prime mover—that is, you can control the depth and rate of thrusting, which should be at first carried out slowly, with you again focusing on the sensations in your vaginal and clitoral region and, in effect, developing the feeling that your partner's penis is yours, to do with as you desire. Second, the female-superior position, especially for women who have never used it, carries the psychological advantage of placing you "in the driver's seat." It is a position that gives you the prime responsibility for the motions of intercourse and allows you the most freedom of motion. Thus you will come to feel that intercourse belongs to you as a technique for obtaining pleasure just as much as it belongs to your partner. Again, this can be a "liberating" experience. Third, your partner is least likely to ejaculate in the female-superior position, thus prolonging intercourse.

*To err is human* . . . If your partner feels that he is going to ejaculate, he should tell you or signal you, and the two of you should stop thrusting, separate if necessary, or, in some cases, press together as hard as possible in order to prevent ejaculation. At this point your partner's ejaculating would interfere with your opportunity to continue experimentation with vaginal containment of his erect penis. However, no man can control himself *all* of the time. An intermittent "error" must be forgiven, and nondemand intercourse should ideally be continued after a half hour or so, when your partner has again achieved erection.

## STEP 4: ORGASM THROUGH INTERCOURSE

Helen Singer Kaplan has in our view made significant advances in helping the woman achieve orgasm through intercourse by associating other methods of vaginal-clitoral stimulation with penile stimulation in those cases where simply continuing thrusting to orgasm seems doubtful or insufficient.[40]

Step 4 ideally grows out of Steps 2 and 3. Having experienced orgasm through the stimulation of your partner, and having experienced pleasurable intercourse with your partner, a great many women can simply extend intercourse through harder thrusting to achieve orgasm.

*Use of manual or artificial stimulation.* Other women do not make this connection so easily. Dr. Kaplan's techniques are then called for. If you are having intercourse in the female-superior position, you may desire to guide your partner's hand to provide additional clitoral stimulation as the penis continues to provide intravaginal stimulation. You would thus be simulating the sensations that helped you achieve orgasm during Step 2, and your partner's task will be facilitated by the experience he achieved while you guided him in the exercises of Step 1.

If your partner's manual stimulation of your clitoral area is insufficient, you may, if you are both sufficiently "liberated," employ a vibrator while you are having intercourse. The vibrator may be held by either partner, although the man often prefers to manipulate the vibrator because it helps him feel that *he* is bringing you to orgasm. But do not hesitate to show him how to use the vibrator most effectively! It is also possible for you to self-manipulate your clitoral region while you are having intercourse. All these alternatives are workable.

Do not try to force the orgasm. Simply attend to the sensations in your clitoral and vaginal regions, give yourself permission to let go, and focus on erotic fantasies.

*Transition to penile stimulation to achieve orgasm.* If you have achieved orgasm through combining penile with manual or artificial (as in the case of the vibrator) stimulation, the next step is to make the transition to penile stimulation alone. Note, however, that there is no necessity to make this transition unless you and your partner feel the need. And, if you do choose to make the transition, you may still wish occasionally to employ other means of stimulation for the sake of variety.

Transition may be achieved in a straightforward manner. Simply remove the hand or vibrator from the clitoral area *just* prior to your experiencing orgasm. This may at first mean that you remove the hand or vibrator a fraction of a second prior to orgasm.[41] Let us call this the point of "orgasmic inevitability," when it might take an earthquake accompanied by lightning to prevent the orgasm. Then, as time goes on, you remove the additional source of stimulation earlier and earlier. This must be a gradual process. Removing the additional stimulation too early may prevent you from achieving orgasm and again re-create performance anxiety that will further tend to inhibit the "letting go" process that is fundamental to achieving orgasm. Thus choose a pace adapted to your needs so that you will feel at each step along the way that you are going to be reaching orgasm without difficulty. And it may be that for a while, you may wish to return to having orgasm as a result of combined penile and manual or artificial stimulation. This will tend to heighten the pleasure you will receive, provide variety, and also reinforce the association between penile stimulation and achieving orgasm.

In any event, once you have been achieving orgasm through the female-superior position, you will probably find that you can achieve orgasm through a variety of positions. If at first there is some difficulty in a new position, again guide your partner to provide additional stimulation or do so yourself.

*The importance of being selfish.* It is important to note that in achieving orgasm through intercourse, as in the mutual petting sessions of Step 1, you must allow yourself to be *selfish.* Certainly we would not wish to argue with the romantic notion that lovemaking ought to be both giving and receiving. But timing is important and it is unlikely that you can at the same time concentrate on your own bodily sensations, especially in the vaginal and clitoral regions, erotic fantasies, *and* all the sexual needs of your partner. Fortunately, this is not necessary. It is possible to take turns. We would recommend that in the normal course of events you and your partner first focus on your achieving orgasm and then on his achieving orgasm. However, we do not wish to stereotype sexual activity, and if you and your partner find workable and desirable alternatives as time goes on, do "whatever turns you on."

*Avoid self-defeating expectations.* Few women have orgasms every time they have sex. If you are prepared not to achieve orgasm sometimes, you will not feel like a failure when this occurs. Such knowledge will not help with the immediate sexual frustration you will feel, but it will be comforting to recall that intermittently not achieving orgasms is normal, and does not mean that you are "losing your touch." Remember, too, that practically all men at one time or another have difficulty achieving or maintaining an erection, or ejaculate prematurely. Men, especially when fatigued, may also not be able to achieve orgasm. You are a person and not a machine. You can set the stage for orgasms to occur, but you operate under so many complex stimuli from within and without that no two situations are going to be exactly alike, and nobody can perfectly predict that what worked on Monday will work the same way on Wednesday, or that what worked so well in February will also be as effective in April. Do not let periodic changes make you think that you are failing. Go "back to basics," perhaps to some more petting, to the vibrator, or to nondemand intercourse for a while. Relax your expectations and you will achieve greater sexual satisfaction.

# Painful Intercourse

Painful intercourse may result from any number of medical disorders, and a woman with this problem should discuss it with her gynecologist.

If you experience painful intercourse and have been assured that there are no physical impairments involved, you should assess your attitudes toward having intercourse with the man or men in your life. Do you *like* them? Are they clean? Do you think sex is dirty? Do you think that you are entitled to enjoy intercourse? Are there things that you would like to tell your partner to do but are afraid to mention? Are you expecting your partner to read your mind about your likes and dislikes? Are you being nonassertive in the bedroom? Are you feeling guilty about something? Are you worried about becoming pregnant? Do you engage in intercourse before you are sufficiently aroused? Do you feel the need to use an artificial lubricant, such as Vaseline or K-Y Jelly, but have the feeling that your sex partner will be "insulted" if you do so?

## THE CASE OF JACKIE

Jackie a twenty-five-year-old airline hostess, had enjoyed untroubled intercourse with her fiancé for two years, during which they had frequently discussed marriage, but Jackie had been reluctant to surrender her career. She then became pregnant and the couple married during her third month rather than abort the child, due to Jackie's ethical beliefs.

Following their quiet ceremony, and knowing that she would be forced to surrender her work, Jackie failed to lubricate, making intercourse painful. Assured by her gynecologist that there were no apparent medical problems, the couple sought therapy.

Jackie was in great anguish about both the child and the fact that the "one really good thing we had going for us," the couple's sex life, was painful. Following a few angry and tearful sessions during which Jackie ventilated her feelings, it became clear that she did not want to be in the marriage or keep the baby. She and her husband were able to annul the marriage. Jackie took a leave of absence when she began to "show." Four months later she delivered, surrendered the infant for adoption, and, following a rest period, returned "to the skies." A few months later, she reported no difficulty lubricating with a new sex partner.

Painful intercourse has thus always impressed us as a problem that is rarely subject to self-help behavioral solutions. We recommend that you contact the professional therapist if you cannot readily solve the problem by coming to grips with some of the questions we have posed.

# Vaginismus

## A Case for the Specialist

Vaginismus is the involuntary contraction of muscles surrounding the vaginal entrance, a condition that can make intercourse impossible and pelvic examination possible only under general anesthesia. Many factors, physical and psychological, may be involved in vaginismus, obviously including some aversion to be entered.

While behavioral techniques have been extremely helpful in dealing with vaginismus,[42] we feel that responsible behavioral treatment can only be carried out (1) after a certain differential diagnosis has been made by your gynecologist, and (2) under clinical supervision by a licensed psychologist, psychiatrist, or other professional who has had training in the techniques of sex therapy.

Furthermore, let us again suggest that you consult the professional with any persistent sexual difficulties.

# MYTHS THAT INTERFERE WITH SEXUAL FULFILLMENT

## Sex Should Culminate in Simultaneous Orgasm

Many couples adhere to this belief, find themselves falling short of it, and tend to feel that their sex lives are inadequate or lacking in romance. Examination of the origin of this belief may show that in the cases of some couples, one or both members are embarrassed to show strong emotional release unless the partner is doing the same. Most men, after ejaculating, find their penises becoming flaccid. The female partner is then often in a position in which she frantically tries to attain orgasm on what's left of the erection. Also, there is no reason that both partners should automatically choose to achieve orgasms through intercourse. For example, a man may occasionally desire to achieve ejaculation through manual or oral stimulation following his partner's orgasm.

From time to time we hear of an interesting occurrence. Some women report that they can feel the man ejaculating inside them, while other women report no sensation at all. Of the women who report that they can feel the man ejaculating inside them, a few maintain that this triggers their orgasms, or at least heightens them. This report is another example of the ways in which people differ, and helps point out why one strategy will work for one couple and be ineffective or counterproductive for another.

## Both Partners Should Be Totally Free and Liberated

This is a recently developed belief, apparently growing out of the "sexual revolution" of the 1960s. The point appears to be that nothing that any intelligent adult could crave sexually should be found to be disgusting, humiliating, or uncomfortable to his or her sex partner. Thus some men may expect their partners to swallow their semen, though their partners may gag, choke, and vomit. In other cases, practices such as anal intercourse are insisted upon with unwilling partners.

We have found that the most helpful stance to take is a neutral one in which it is allowed, in the liberal manner, that any sex act that is desired by consenting adults in private is acceptable. But we also find that one partner's insistence that the other engage in a sex act that is felt to be discomforting is a sign of lack of consideration and often results in the serious worsening of an already impaired sexual and marital relationship. We can assume that people are turned on or off by certain acts through a process that has occurred over a period of years. Processes that are learned also have the potential to be unlearned. But if one sex partner wishes to "desensitize" the other to the performance of a particular sex act, mature discussion on the issue should ensue. Both partners must come to joint decisions, without duress, and then it may be possible to apply the desensitization procedures described in Chapter 3. But it is inaccurate, cruel, and harmful to assume that a partner unwilling to engage in a specific sex act is being arbitrary or "behind the times." An "everybody's doing it" attitude heightens performance anxiety in the sex situation, and is also false.

## Sexual Activity Should Culminate in Intercourse

Couples very often are too tired or preoccupied to engage in intercourse, and when they are approached by their partners they tend to communicate nonverbal messages of disinterest through facial expressions and the tensing of bodily regions. A simple, honest remark about one's feelings is almost unheard of in these instances, yet it is highly desirable. Often, both partners may enjoy some petting, perhaps bringing one of them to orgasm. Intercourse is not always necessary.

## Sex Should Be Performed in the Dark or in Bright Light

The first part of the belief refers to ideas held by some who are "old-fashioned." The second refers to ideas held by some who are "liberated." Each couple must find for themselves the lighting arrangement that is most suitable and enjoyable. It has been our experience that some subdued lighting is a positive experience for most couples. It provides some visual sexual stimulation, but not so much that one is able readily to reflect on the flaws of the partner's body as well as the assets. Moderate lighting also avoids overstimulation of the visual sense to the detriment of the stimulation of other senses.

## The Male Partner Should be the Aggressor

There are at least two aspects to this belief that damage the ability of a couple to enjoy each other. First, the woman is denied the privilege of expressing her own sexual needs. Women who have difficulty expressing their needs in this area may also experience similar difficulty in other areas, and should pay strong attention to Chapter 5, on behaving assertively. Second, the male sometimes tires of being the aggressor, or at least finds a switch in roles to be stimulating. It may make him feel more desirable if the woman avoids behaving in an inhibited manner.

Sometimes a man is raised to believe that a woman who is sexually forward is behaving in a whorish or sluttish manner. Men who feel this way should recognize that they are not granting women the privilege of spontaneously feeling the sexual arousal that they, the men, commonly feel. Such attitudes run counter to the wealth of research evidence that women do experience strong sex drives when they have learned that they need not tightly control their bodily sensations.

The husband of a couple being seen in therapy complained that his wife was an inert "mount of Jell-O" in bed. However, she reported her fear that he would be turned off by her sexual advances, considering her "that kind of woman." In this case, ignorance of each other's attitudes was not bliss, and a successful resolution was achieved following a sharing of attitudes.

## Masturbation Is Bad, or at Least Second-rate

Dr. Albert Ellis has helped Americans deal with some of their fears that masturbation is basically unhealthy, could lead to insanity or, at the very least, adolescent dermatological disorders.[43] Research in the 1960s has actually shown that many women and men experience more intense orgasms through self-manipulation than they do through coitus.[44] This is not to suggest that coitus be abandoned in favor of masturbation. Petting, foreplay, and intercourse do more than relieve sexual desires; they reaffirm close relationships, and, very often, the trust one partner has in the other. But it is logical to suggest, especially for couples who are seeking variety in their sexual activities, that mutual masturbation, or masturbation in the presence of the partner, may provide additional modes for achieving sexual pleasure.

## Once I Get Married, Everything Will Work Itself Out

Since our society has long held double standards, being more prohibitive of premarital sexual experimentation and activities for females than for males, it has been more common for women than for men to believe that once they got married their sex lives would somehow automatically work out.

Sexual intercourse, or sexual activity between partners, involves a variety of discrete behaviors that may be conceptualized as skills. Intercourse between two people may be thought of as "putting a lot of things together." For example, if the man and woman already know what it feels like to have an orgasm, it is easier for them to experience orgasm through intercourse. This is in keeping with research that has shown that adolescents, male and female, who have masturbated prior to marriage tend to experience more sexual pleasure through their sexual relationship.[45]

## A Loyal Mate or Partner Does Not Masturbate

Through discussion with our clients, we have come to feel that it is something of an American ideal to "save" one's sexual desires for one's partner. A false assumption we often find associated with this belief is the idea that a person has only so much sexual energy, or so much sperm in the case of the male, and that if this "energy" is dissipated through masturbation it will detract from the quantity of energy that the couple may then apply to each other. Now, it would be nonsensical to state that if a man masturbates at 9:30 P.M., he will readily achieve an erection and be greatly inspired at 9:35 P.M. Human physiology does not work this way. But by 10:00 P.M. . . .

In the case of women, who are more capable of achieving multiple orgasms, we have found that many women are capable of masturbating in the presence of a partner, perhaps aided by a vibrator, and then are capable of being "driven to greater heights of enjoyment," to coin a phrase, through intercourse or petting with the partner.

## The Time to Have Sex Is After the Children Are Asleep and the Day's Work Is Done

This is probably the worst time to have sexual relations! Sex can acquire the sense of a duty prior to sleep. Spontaneity is destroyed. Both partners may be quite tired. The man may be incapable of achieving an erection, leading to great anxieties about the adequacy of his performance. Consider his plight. Not only has he "failed" to acquire an erection on one night, but he must wait until the next night, when he will again be fatigued, before he tries again.

We have found it worthwhile to encourage couples to become more spontaneous in their sexual interactions, so long, of course, as they observe the social proprieties demanded by law and custom. To illustrate: We know at least one popular sex-oriented magazine that publishes many letters from readers about public or semipublic intercourse. Our attitude is simply: Why are they trying so hard? On the other hand, we took it as a sign of growth when one man in his forties reached over to his wife while he was driving and fondled her breast. Why? Because he had felt like it. He grinned sheepishly as he reported the incident, and his wife was initially somewhat embarrassed, but this couple was clearly developing more gratifying sexual attitudes.

## The "Curse" of the Clitoral Orgasm

The psychoanalytic view of female sexuality that has had a strong influence on the thinking of many helping professionals and many laymen has held that a woman is meant to achieve orgasm only through the reception of the fully erect penis, and that the site of the orgasm must be inside the vagina.[46] Other orgasmic experiences become assigned the negative label, "pregenital." Such women are still functioning at a preadolescent level, according to followers of Freud. But many women find that they mainly experience orgasm in the clitoral region. Some view this as a failure. They feel that they are not having "the real thing," even though they experience intense pleasure. Clitoral sensations may recall thoughts of achieving orgasm through masturbation, and give them a sense that they are not functioning sexually as grown women.

Christie, a twenty-two-year-old woman, complained that her marriage was "on the rocks." She had masturbated prior to marriage and had experienced orgasms with strong clitoral sensations. She had assumed that once she got married, she would experience "the real thing," strong contractions in the vagina alone. She had had no difficulty achieving orgasm with her husband, for whom she had "waited," but she was shocked to find that the orgasmic sensations were markedly similar to those she had achieved through masturbation. Christie began to find that intercourse was making her feel increasingly that she was an adolescent, unworthy of an adult relationship. She withdrew from sexual relations, giving her husband a series of excuses, many of which were to the effect that "it" didn't feel right. This made her husband feel dirty, rejected, frustrated, angry, and, as he put it, "horny as hell." Christie only came to the clinic upon threat of separation or divorce. She was extremely reluctant to share what she viewed as a most sordid and revealing admission. However, therapy in this case amounted to one session of education. She was informed that the research done by Masters and Johnson demonstrated with hundreds of women from all walks of life that there really was only one type of orgasm, with both vaginal and clitoral sensations.[47] Other researchers, such as Dr. Seymour Fisher, found that some clitoral stimulation is essential for most women to achieve orgasm.[48] The vagina is sensitive to touch only near the entrance, and even women who report vaginal contractions during orgasm report them as occurring near the vaginal opening.

# I Can't Go to Bed with Someone I Don't Love

When we read the popular, "liberated" sexual literature, in magazines with photographs of nude women and men interspersed, we note that a certain point of view is being propounded to the American people in this and the last decade: Love and sex need not go together. It is possible to have some relationships in which deep feelings precede sexual acts, and others in which two mature, mutually attracted adults have sex soon after they meet, merely because they "want to." This attitude appears to have developed in order to combat the "old-fashioned" point of view that a woman (again, the standards have been different for men and women) should not go to bed with a man just for the fun of it.

What is missing in much of this popular philosophizing is the wide variety of individual differences. Some people can handle casual sexual relationships. Others cannot. We have noted that the difficulties arise when an individual raised consistently over long years according to a given set of standards suddenly decides that she or he is going to break loose of her or his bonds and become part of the swinging generation.

A twenty-three-year-old nurse, Connie, came to the clinic ostensibly because of a drinking problem and suicidal impulses. She would go out for the evening with a girlfriend, get drunk, be picked up by a man, bring him home, have sex with him, and wake up the next morning—sobered, looking at a sleeping stranger next to her whom she felt she hated, and contemplating placing a knife in his chest and then slitting her wrists. On several occasions Connie had toyed with wrist-cutting, and minor scratches were in evidence during several clinic visits. As her history and her behavior unfolded into a clear pattern, it became evident that she had been attempting to break away from her parents' standards and expectations, but that she could not accept the responsibility of breaking away. Thus, rather than focusing on the fact that her going out to drink with a friend led to predictable consequences, she chose to think that the alcohol was "doing it." This young woman's therapy is far from over. She must still attempt to make decisions concerning major conflicts. But she is no longer blaming her behavior on alcohol. She is capable of seeing how she had "set myself up" for sex to occur in a manner that for her was an expression of rebellion against her parents. She has also developed a meaningful relationship with a man with whom she can have sex without alcohol and with a minimum of guilt.

## It's Not My Marriage, It's Sex

Many people erroneously place the greater part of the responsibility for a nonworking marriage on bedroom activities. In the bedroom men and women have an excellent opportunity to punish one another in indirect ways. A woman may be too tired for sex, or she may be highly demanding. A man may insist on activities that his wife dislikes. They can communicate a world of hostility through subtle facial expressions of disappointment. Often they do not realize that they have chosen the bedroom as their battle arena, and come for therapy claiming that their marriages are fine, but they are having sexual difficulties.

You can test whether you are using your bedroom to express marital unhappiness through assertive discussions with your partner in which you take turns expressing what your partner's sexual behavior conveys to you. A woman may say, "When you come so fast, I think that you don't care at all about my feelings." Either partner may say, "When you don't show any pleasure, it makes me think that you are bored with me," or "When we only keep doing it one way, it makes me think that we're in a rut and you just don't care about trying to make our lives more interesting," or "When you try to get me to do something you know I don't like to do, I wonder if you really care about me." Bedroom behavior often has meanings that run much more deeply. If mutual discussion and sharing of feelings are insufficient in resolving your problems, you may seek professional marital counseling.

## My Partner Is Oversexed/Undersexed

A male client in his late twenties was recently telling us about his depressive state. One of his complaints was, "I just don't have no interest in sex no more, Doc. I mean, we used to do it three, four times a night. Now Sheila, she's feelin' good, and she can go every hour on the hour, but I lose all interest after I've done it the first time."

People develop the thought that they or their partners are oversexed or undersexed according to some frame of reference. The concept does not develop in a vacuum. Problems occur when one partner desires sex more or less frequently than the other, or when a couple meeting each other's desires and needs reads an article in some popular magazine or journal to the effect that couples "their age" tend to have intercourse more or less frequently.

Our philosophy urges the freedom of the individual. A person is entitled to as much sexual activity as he desires, so long as he continues to live up to the voluntary commitments made to others. If a man desires to ejaculate five times weekly, and his wife is interested in having intercourse only twice, it would be ideal if they enjoyed each other and the man then brought himself to orgasm additionally through means acceptable to both husband and wife. In some marriages it is agreed that the "oversexed" partner obtains additional gratification with partners outside the marriage. We have only seen a couple of cases in which this type of arrangement did not cause great distress. It is more common for the "undersexed" partner to help bring the other to orgasm through manual or oral stimulation, to have the other masturbate while they are together, or simply to know that the "oversexed" partner will be engaging in masturbation privately when it is convenient.

This is not very different from the situation couples find themselves in when they are separated for some days or weeks. They will operate according to their own needs, their rules of conduct, and their hangups. Some persons, remaining "faithful" and disdainful of masturbation, will simply abstain. Others, perhaps more liberated, will freely admit to their partners that they will be masturbating with some frequency while they are left alone. Many young couples accept suggestions that they freely discuss their needs and intentions with one another without great difficulty. However, you know your own situation—or you think you do—and you will have to judge whether or not you will share knowledge of all of your sexual activities with your partner. Such sharing can decrease feelings of guilt and increase feelings of trust, but unless it is sincere, it can provide a temporary glow that later gives way to feelings of regret or shame.

## My Partner Will Read My Mind

People deny that they hold this belief, but they behave as if they do in the bedroom. Something is wrong with their sex lives, but rather than discuss the problem openly with their partner, they show vague signs of displeasure and disapproval during lovemaking, hoping that the partner will "get the message." What the partner very often gets is fed up.

Jennifer, a twenty-one-year-old woman married to Ken for three years, came to the clinic for therapy to help her decide whether she wished to terminate her marriage. She felt she was pushing Ken away, and although she never denied him sex, she was not achieving orgasm. Jennifer actually found sex painful, but would not tell Ken because she did not want to hurt his feelings and had been raised to be demure in such matters. To compound the problem, Ken wanted sex daily.

After a few sessions, Jennifer came to see that a more important reason she was not telling her husband that sex was painful was that she was purposefully accumulating the injuries she was suffering. Her goal appeared to be that once she had reached a certain saturation point, she would leave Ken as a result of his insensitivity and not have to share the blame for a failed marriage.

Sex was painful and joyless, it turned out, because Ken did not engage in foreplay. Thus Jennifer did not become aroused or lubricate. She had assumed that he was being a bully with her, that he had no consideration for her feelings. In a joint session, Ken admitted that for him too the bedroom had become more of a battleground than a retreat for the sharing of pleasure. He had known his wife was unhappy, but she had not told him why. He had continued doggedly with his sexual efforts, not wishing to be a quitter, and hoped that he would provide his wife with some enjoyment. Instead, bitterness was increasing and spreading to other areas of the marriage. He was jealous of his wife's closeness to her father and brother, and would often sabotage family visits by finding other things that must be done at the last minute.

In a second joint session, both partners recognized that they had been assuming the worst of each other, and had allowed the situation to develop to the point of separation or divorce because they had simply not been able or willing to tell each other what they felt. They had assumed that if they loved each other, they would be somehow "sensitive" to each other's needs. Soon, sharing of feelings, complaints, and frustrations began.

After Jennifer told Ken about her concern over the lack of foreplay, Ken self-consciously initiated foreplay, which was reasonably effective despite his self-observation. They arranged a signal system whereby the wife indicated when she

was sufficiently lubricated and would, at such times, often initiate penetration. As time passed, self-consciousness decreased. The couple are now doing well.

## Nice Women Do Not Use Sexual Fantasies

Contemporary therapists do not view sexual fantasies, for
either sex, as signs of sexual maladjustment. Just the opposite.
Dr. E. Barbara Hariton of City College of New York found
that erotic fantasies are common among women, and that far
from being "escapist," they actually enhanced the woman's
sexual pleasure.[49] Dr. Hariton's work revealed that 65 per
cent of women sampled fantasized during intercourse. These
were women sampled at PTA meetings, church clubs, charity
groups—women identified as part of the mainstream of
middle-class America.

The two most popular fantasies entailed making love to another man—an old flame, a famous actor—and being overpowered by a faceless and nameless man. Women who
fantasized a great deal were found to be more impulsive, independent, nonconformist, and creative. These women reported that their erotic fantasies were sexually arousing and had
become part of their lovemaking routine.

## Erotica Is for Men Only

Are women turned on by erotic material? To find out, Dr.
Julia Heiman of State University of New York at Stony
Brook used a newly developed intravaginal device to measure
a woman's sexual response to erotic stimuli. Dr. Heiman had
predicted that women would be more turned on physiologically by tape-recorded stories with romantic content and no
explicit sex than by recorded stories with explicit sex. But the
results revealed that explicit sex, with or without romantic
trappings, were more arousing for women, as for men, than
stories with romantic content only.[50]

Is a woman who is turned on by erotica deviant? Dr.
Heiman's work suggests that she is quite normal.

# 7

# BEHAVE YOURSELF:
## BT Strategies for Making and Breaking Habits

Mark Twain remarked that it was easy to quit smoking—he had done it a dozen times. Many of us also stop from time to time, but then return to smoking. Why is it so difficult to abstain permanently? Or to remain on a diet? To improve studying or reading habits? To stop nail biting? Or to follow through on New Year's resolutions? If "willpower" alone has failed you, or if you have failed it, this chapter will help you use BT to begin living more effectively by breaking bad habits and strengthening desirable habits. Make no mistake; Behavioral self-control requires willpower and commitment. But it allows you to deal systematically with your problem behavior and to apply the principles of learning theory to help you develop strategies for behaving yourself.

Behavioral self-control refers to a series of integrated techniques designed to help people who feel that they are behaving in counter-productive ways, or not behaving often enough in productive, life-enhancing ways. In this chapter, the general techniques of behavioral self-control will be discussed. In the following two chapters, specific guidelines will be presented for two keynote problems: overeating and smoking.

# The Environmental Context: The *ABC*'s of Behavior

One major reason for failure in self-control is that people often don't take into account the environmental context in which behavior occurs. Psychologists have long studied the environmental events that pattern our behavior. Behavior (*B*) is related to what happens in the environment before (*A*) and after (*C*) it occurs. The behavioral psychologist attempts to discover the enviromental *A*ntecedents or stimulus cues for behavior, the *A*'s, and the resultant *C*onsequences, or *C*'s, of the behavior. To simplify the discussion of how to design BT self-control strategies, we will use the following *ABC* shorthand[1]:

1. Environmental stimuli or cues that are antecedent to our behavior=the *A*'s
2. The behaviors in question=the *B*'s
3. The environmental consequences or effects of our behavior=the *C*'s

# Antecedent Environmental Stimuli: The *A*'s of Behavior

The events or stimuli that occur in our environment partially determine how we behave. We learn to behave differently in different environments: at school, work, home, or in singles bars. Behavior (*B*) does not occur in a vacuum. One of the first tasks in the BT self-help strategy is to document the *A*ntecedent stimuli or cues that pattern our behavior.

The degree to which behavior reflexively follows the environmental *A*ntecedents varies with the type and complexity of the behavior. When we stop for a red light (*A*), our response (*B*) to this stimulus is more or less automatic. This is quite different from our response to guilt-laden cues like a mother's saying, "So why haven't you called lately?" In this book, we are concerned both with behavior that automatically follows antecedent cues (like fears) and behaviors in which a person's awareness plays a larger role, such as becoming more assertive, dealing with sex problems, and problems in self-control.

# Environmental Consequences: The C's of Behavior

In building effective self-control, it is important to discover and manipulate the environmental Consequences of effects (the C's) of our behavior.

Behavior that leads to positive reinforcements or payoffs tends to be repeated when the right stimulus conditions or A's repeat themselves. The term *positive reinforcement*, as used by psychologists, refers to any environmental event that increases the probability that a behavior that precedes it will recur. In terms of our code, positive reinforcements are C's that strengthen the B's they follow. Commonly, positive reinforcements are rewards, though we shall also describe how frequently occurring routine behaviors can be used effectively as positive reinforcers.

Behavior that leads to negative payoffs or punishments, or to no payoffs at all, may tend to fade rapidly. Thus, positive consequences or good C's strengthen the reinforced behavior, while punishment or ugly C's tend to weaken the punished behavior. But research shows that punishment is often undesirable, even if it can be effective. Most behavioral psychologists rely almost exclusively on positive reinforcement or reward strategies for shaping adaptive or desired behavior. But we shall present one method of self-punishment, called "response cost," which has been shown to be quite effective in changing bad habits.

# The ABC's of Behavior

Throughout this book, attempt to think of behavior in terms of this simple chain: Antecedent stimulus events→Behavior= reinforcement Consequences. Consider the following example: You finally land a date with that one person whom fate had intended for you. At that magical moment when your date looks fervently into your eyes (provides stimulus cues), you reach over for a tender embrace (emit behavior), but wind up with a "So what's for dinner?" (negative payoff). The next time these stimulus cues (A's) are evident, your response (B) will probably be different, and more cautious. The results of your behavior (the ugly $C$'s) encourage you to act differently when the situation again arises.

This example may seem trivial and oversimplified. However, the principle that behavior reflects its consequences is applicable in all spheres of our everyday life. Consider the $C$'s that shape problem $B$'s: the child whose temper tantrums generate attention, the wife whose chronic nagging produces an occasional night out, or the husband whose "can't make it" attitude leads to his wife's mothering him.

In addition, consider the $A$'s that initiate undesirable behaviors: the man who typically stuffs his face following a personal rejection, the teen-ager who smokes only at parties, the young man or woman who cries alone on Saturday night, but feels fine, although alone, on weeknights. Remember that Behavior reflects environmental Antecedents and Consequences.

# DESIGNING BT SELF-CONTROL STRATEGIES

The next two chapters will describe self-control strategies for problem eating and smoking. However, the basic BT self-help strategies can also be extended to problems like nail biting, difficulty in sticking to studying, excessive beer drinking, tardiness, and sloppiness. Devising a BT self-help strategy involves identifying the conditions (the $A$'s) under which the behavior (the $B$'s) takes place and what the usual results of the behavior (the $C$'s) are. Then the behavioral strategist attempts to change real-life $A$'s and $C$'s to shape more desirable behaviors.

The self-help program for making and breaking habits involves:

1. Behavioral definition of your problem Behaviors.
2. Counting the rate of occurrence of your problem $B$'s before and during the behavior change strategy.
3. Developing and implementing the behavior change strategy in terms of your knowledge of the existing stimulus and reinforcement conditions—the $A$'s and the $C$'s.

## Behavioral Definition of Problems

The identified problem and the self-control goal must be specified in terms of measurable or countable behaviors. If your problem is poor study habits, don't state the self-control goal as "becoming a better student." Be specific! You want to increase the number of hours spent studying every week. Here are some problems expressed in nonworkable terms and the corresponding workable behavioral equivalents:

"I want to be more popular."                =_"I want to increase my number of dates."

"I don't like being a shy person."          =_"I want to smile more often and engage in small talk more often."

"I want to be more up on current events."=_"I want to increase the number of newsmagazines I read."

Ronnie, an attractive nineteen-year-old secretary, complained early in therapy that she felt she was "immature," that she needed help "growing up." Her fiancé, Kevin, on whom she was very dependent, had insisted that she seek therapy to "straighten herself out." to change, as she put it, "my immature personality." Ronnie's expectation in therapy was that her personality was defective and that her relationship with her fiancé could only be improved if her personality were altered. It was explained that a BT strategy attempts first to define ambiguous unworkable terms, like "immature personality," in terms of measurable, behaviorally stated units. The behavioral questions to ask were: "Which behaviors or $B$'s was Kevin labeling as immature?" "Under what circumstances or $A$'s did Ronnie emit these behaviors?" "What were the consequences or $C$'s of these behaviors?"

In most cases, the problem can be defined behaviorally by identifying the $B$'s that indicate that a problem exists. After all, one doesn't observe a "problem personality," but rather makes such an interpretation following some observable behaviors. For example, you feel lonely because of few social contacts or activities. If you simply dwell on the inadequacies of your personality, you will make yourself feel worse and do nothing to help yourself. Define your problem in workable terms so that an effective change strategy can be developed. Change "loneliness" to infrequency of social contacts. Think behaviorally and proceed!

In Ronnie's case, it turned out that her use of childish sounds and facial gestures, and her frequent attempts to turn serious conversation into farce were the *B*'s labeled by Kevin as "immature." Thus the identified problem was the inappropriate emission of "baby talk." These *B*'s usually occurred when their conversation (the *A*'s) turned to "serious" topics like politics, religion, and future goals. The fact that Kevin criticized Ronnie for emitting these behaviors appeared contrary to the behavioral principle that negative payoffs (ugly *C*'s) usually weaken the behavior they follow. However, psychologists have found that behavior that is occassionally or intermittently reinforced may be highly resistant to weakening once the reinforcement is stopped. Upon considering the matter, Ronnie remembered that early in their relationship, Kevin would remark that her "childish" responses were "cute," thus positively reinforcing these behaviors (a good *C* for an unfortunate *B*). Ronnie also remarked that behaving "childishly" was the only way she knew how to act in interpersonal situations. As in the case of Ronnie, punishment alone is usually a poor strategy for changing undesirable behavior.

Now that Ronnie recognized the problem *B*'s, and the environmental context in which the behaviors occurred, a self-help strategy was developed. Ronnie recognized that she acted childishly whenever the conversation turned serious because she was afraid she "didn't know enough" to make significant contributions and was afraid of being ridiculed for offering her opinions. Rather than continuing this maladaptive behavior, Ronnie began to expand her knowledge by reading more widely about matters such as current events, history, and art. Once Kevin recognized that the "problem" was not in Ronnie's "personality" but was behavioral, he was more than willing to help directly in the treatment plan. Kevin was told to reinforce Ronnie positively for her attempts at serious talk, regardless of her level of sophistication, so that a receptive attitude for engaging in serious talk would be established. Kevin was told to ignore remnants of Ronnie's inappropriate "baby talk." Within several weeks "baby talk" was down to zero and Ronnie and Kevin were engaging easily in adult conversations.

# Counting the Problem Behavior: The Before, During, and After Figures

Counting the problem behavior provides an index by which to judge how significant and widespread the problem is, and to determine its *ABC*'s. Comparison of the frequency of occurrence of the problem before and after intervention will give you a good measure of the strategy's success or failure.

Other reasons for recording are not so obvious. People are very often resistant to keeping records of their undesirable behavior. The person who considers himself a light smoker may find, quite distressingly, that he is smoking 1½ packs a day. A person who bites his nails may find that he engages in this "minor" habit seventy-five times daily! The belief that ignoring something will cause it to go away is a common myth. An accurate self-record will also counter the self-rationalization, "It's no big thing anyway."

## SELF-RECORDING AS A BEHAVIOR CHANGE STRATEGY

In several research studies, the act of self-recording alone has led to changes in the rate of occurrence of the problem *B*. In one case, self-monitoring of study behavior led to higher grades.[2] In another study, people who merely kept records of their smoking frequency wound up decreasing their smoking rate.[3] Although simple self-recording alone may have strong benefits, we recommend integrating self-recording within a package of self-control strategies.

## BASELINE RECORDING

Records of the rate of the problem *B* prior to the start of the behavior change strategy are referred to as "baseline" data. Baseline data provide information about the usual frequency of the problem *B*ehavior. The important thing to remember when recording baseline data is that the record should reflect the usual rate of occurrence. Therefore, take one or two weeks to record baseline date *without* trying to alter the frequency of occurrence. To repeat for emphasis, the behavior change strategy *does not* go into effect until after the baseline data have been collected.

## WHAT TO COUNT

Most often the problem *B* is counted quite easily: number of cigarettes smoked per day, daily calorie intake, number of hours spent studying per night, number of dates per week, number of daily social conversations, etc. Be honest in baseline recording. Since you are your own judge, you only fool yourself if records are misleading. For example, time spent with a book open while daydreaming is not time spent studying.

## HOW TO RECORD

The record should be portable so that recording can continue wherever the behavior occurs. Woe to people who believe they will remember occurrences accurately when they get home. A three-by-five index card is usually sufficient for recording necessary information and is usually inconspicuous for recording purposes. However, if the frequency of the target behavior is particularly high, such as counting the number of times one says "you know" daily, or if a written record becomes cumbersome or conspicuous, use something like a miniature golf counter for recording daily frequencies.

Information about *A*'s and *C*'s of the problem behavior should be recorded wherever possible. This information will aid you in constructing your behavior change strategy. A typical record may be organized as follows:

DATE: March 10                PROBLEM BEHAVIOR: Nail biting

| OCCURRENCE | WHERE | WHEN | PRESENT ACTIVITY | FEELING STATE | OUTCOME |
|---|---|---|---|---|---|
| 1 | Living room | 10:00 | Reading | Bored | None |
| 2 | Dining room | 11:20 | Reading | Bored | None |
| 3 | Living room | 12:30 | TV | Bored | Yelled at by Mom |

Although indeed oversimplified for the sake of illustration, the utility of the running record should be clear. Were this hypothetical nail biter to examine the environmental context of his problem *B*, it would be clear to him that his problem *B* was related to his feeling bored (an *A*) and to the lack of consistent environmental sanctions placed on his behavior (harmless *C*'s). This analysis might lead to the following changes in the environmental context:

1. attempts to structure activities to reduce boredom (change the $A$'s)
2. if this is not possible, engaging in competing task (change the $B$'s) when bored, such as chewing sugarless gum
3. arranging bothersome environmental consequences (ugly $C$'s), such as enlisting the family's help for harsher reprimand, or a worse $C$: putting a nickel in a bowl each time—to be sent weekly to the most hated cause, such as a detested political party

## WHEN TO RECORD

Baseline data—daily frequencies and recording of $A$'s and $C$'s—are collected for one or two weeks prior to the start of your behavior change strategy. Continue recording daily frequencies of the target behavior *throughout* the duration of your active program in order to monitor your progress.

## HOW TO CHART BEHAVIOR FREQUENCIES

Your daily frequency counts should be transferred to a permanent chart at night. Charting changes in the frequency of the target behavior provides an immediate and clearly understood measure of treatment success. Returning to our nail biter, a typical outcome chart might be constructed as follows:

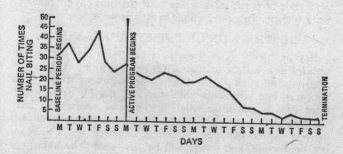

This type of chart is easily adaptable to most situations in which the problem $B$ is given in easily countable units. Hence our maxim: *Think behaviorally.*

## WHEN TO TERMINATE A BEHAVIOR CHANGE STRATEGY

Time of termination is usually an individual decision. You may wish to place a time limit on your intervention plan. You may leave it open-ended and terminate whenever the behavior is sufficiently changed, or when it is clear that the plan is not working. No intervention plan is sacred. You may try several plans until you find the strategy that works for you.

# Developing Behavior Change Strategies

Behavior therapists have developed a number of methods for using the environmental context to best advantage in changing problem behavior. Read through the following techniques and practice devising strategies for your particular problem $B$'s.

## STRATEGY 1: Manipulating the Stimulus Environment (The $A \rightarrow B$ Connection)

From your baseline data you should have a good idea of the $A$'s of the problem behavior. Under what circumstances does it occur? When? Where? With whom? While doing what? In what state of emotion? Manage your stimulus environment to work for you. This can be done in several ways.

### RESTRICTION OF THE STIMULUS FIELD

If your interest is in changing a bad habit that occurs frequently in a variety of places, restrict the problem $B$ to one environment, such as the kitchen or bathroom. If you feel you must bite your nails while watching the TV news, which these days is not so unusual, first remove yourself to your nail-biting area. In this way, the association between nail biting and various stimulus conditions, like watching TV, reading, conversing, and so on, will be weakened. The habit will become confined to a single stimulus-deprived area.

As the usual $A$'s weaken and lose their potency in initiating a problem behavior, the likelihood of that behavior occurring is reduced. The cost or $C$ of committing the act has been heightened as well: You remove yourself from a rich, rewarding milieu to a stimulus-deprived area. This increases the incentive to stop the habit. You are also forced to postpone the behavior, which may permanently interrupt your otherwise habitual *B*. If you use this procedure, you may select an unlikely and undesirable spot for your *B*, like your cellar or your attic. If you live in an apartment, try the bathroom. If your spouse yells at you for spending so much time in the bathroom, this will produce an additional and powerful ugly *C*. In Chapter 9, the extension of this stimulus-restriction method to the problem of smoking will be discussed.

## REMOVAL OF USUAL POTENT *A*'s

We have mentioned that when *B*'s are reinforced by good *C*'s, they tend to be repeated when the same stimulus cue (*A*) is presented. Thus we learn to stop (*B*) for a red light (*A*), since in doing so we *prevent* accidents and *avoid* traffic citations (good *C*'s). Just as constructive habits, like stopping at red lights, can be learned or conditioned, so indeed can maladaptive habits. Consider the following cases.

One serious handicap to most weight-control programs is the typical association or pairing of eating (*B*) and TV viewing (*A*). TV has become a most potent *A* for between-meal snacking, so that after many years of conditioning this behavior, many people routinely set themselves by the tube with boxes of crackers and potato chips. Most of us would agree that it is impossible to have only one. The pleasure of eating (good *C*) "stamps in" or reinforces this *A→B* connection, making it a difficult habit to break.

Often we hear the comments, "If it weren't for the damn TV, I'd have no problem losing weight," or "Whenever I watch TV, I instinctively start eating." Likewise for the association between partying (*A*) and smoking (*B*) or drinking (another *B*). Many people fail in attempting to quit smoking by exposing themselves prematurely to the "hazardous" *A*'s of the cocktail party.

Phil, a twenty-two-year-old law student, realized that engaging in social conversation with people who were smoking was a surefire stimulus (a potent *A*) for his own smoking. Thus, while he was on a smoking withdrawal program, Phil planned social activities with friends who were nonsmokers. Through restructuring his environment to include only nonsmokers, abstinence was achieved. After several abstinent weekends, he was able to say, for the first time, "I didn't think once of smoking tonight." As the habit of nonsmoking gained strength, he gradually introduced social activities with some of his smoking friends, but the $A \rightarrow B$ connection had been weakened to the point where he could continue his abstinence.

The curtailment of certain stimulus conditions ($A$'s), even temporarily, may bring about significant and positive behavior change. Review your baseline record to determine whether it is feasible to change your stimulus milieu ($A$'s) to alter the frequency of the problem behavior ($B$). If TV viewing is implicated as a potent $A$, watch less TV until you have developed a degree of mastery over the problem $B$.

## DEVELOPING ALTERNATIVE OR COMPETING BEHAVIORS: BRINGING IN NEW $B$'s

To break down the automatic features of habits, we have shown you how to restrict the stimulus field and avoid potent cues. A third method, use of competing behaviors, allows you to deal directly with these cues by interrupting the pairing of stimulus and response, of $A \rightarrow B$. Prevent the usual $B$ or response through using a new $B$—a competing response—in its place. First identify the existent connections between the usual $A$'s and the problem $B$'s. The following are typical examples:

| USUAL $A$ | MALADAPTIVE ASSOCIATED $B$ |
|---|---|
| Social conversation | Drinking |
| Feeling angry or lonely | Overeating |
| Sitting in class | Nail biting |
| Sitting in library lounge | Daydreaming |
| Work conference | Smoking |

Next, attempt to replace the conditioned maladaptive $B$ with a more adaptive, competing $B$. The new $B$ should be incompatible with the old maladaptive $B$. Drinking coffee is not an incompatible $B$ to smoking. Jogging is. If the new $B$ can be made to occur routinely in the presence of these usual $A$ cues, the old $A \rightarrow B$ connection should weaken. Reward yourself for emitting the competing $B$. Buy yourself a small something or pat yourself on the back. You deserve it!

The variety of competing $B$'s available is restricted only by your imagination. When feeling depressed ($A$) makes you think of burying your troubles in cheesecake ($B$), remove yourself from the kitchen and write down your thoughts instead (competing $B$). Reach for a pack of sugarless gum (competing $B$) when the potent signals ($A$) for a cigarette

(*B*) appear. Recognize these potent stimuli quickly and be prepared. Buy yourself worry beads to manipulate (competing *B*) while studying (*A*), rather than bite your nails (*B*). Reward yourself each time you engage in the competing *B* rather than the problem *B*. After several weeks, begin to "phase out" the reinforcers. Reward yourself every other time you use some competing *B*. Then every third time and so on, as the *A*→ problem *B* habit progressively weakens.

## STRENGTHEN *A*'s FOR DESIRED BEHAVIOR

Think in terms of using *A*'s to work for you. Plan to expose yourself to existing *A*'s that lead to desired behavior. If you're a poor studier (*B*) at home (bad *A*), but quite efficient in the library (good *A*), make use of the library more often. Reward yourself for spending more time in the library. In this case seek library time as the desired goal, not studying time. Succeed in the first, and the second is likely to follow. Also, study consistently in one or two places so that the stimuli or *A*'s present will acquire strength as potent new cues for studying.

## RESPONSE PREVENTION: MAKING THE *B* UNLIKELY OR IMPOSSIBLE

This technique refers to the practice of manipulating your stimulus environment (*A*) to prevent the occurrence of the problem behavior (*B*). The prodigal young man who attempts to improve his control over spending by opening a time-deposit account, and the dieter who goes to a "fat farm" in the mountains are both exercising self-control through response prevention strategies. How can you prevent problem behavior (*B*) by structuring your stimulus environment (*A*) to make the occurrence of the problem *B* impossible or highly improbable?

So far we have concentrated on changing problem behavior (*B*) through restructuring the stimulus milieu (*A*). The other key element in the environmental context—the reinforcement consequences (*C*'s) of our behavior—will enter next in our analysis of changing problem behaviors.

# STRATEGY 2: A Reward Is a Reward Is a Reward (The *B*→*C* Connection)

The use of rewards (good *C*'s) to shape our own behavior is omni-present. From rewarding ourselves with a nutritious snack later on for skipping a dessert at mealtime, to pasting gold stars on the good school reports of our children, the reward (good $C$) is certainly a potent behavior change tactic.

All rewards, however, aren't effective behavior shapers. The child who receives his allowance regardless of his behavior isn't motivated by the reward to behave properly. To use rewards as positive reinforcements in order to increase the rate of the rewarded behavior, adopt the following reward principles:

1. The reward (good $C$) must follow, rather than precede, the behavior ($B$).
2. The occurrence of the reward (good $C$) must be contingent on the occurrence of the behavior ($B$) (that is, no behavior, no reward).
3. The reward (good $C$) should follow the behavior ($B$) as quickly as possible.

## THE PRINCIPLE OF REWARD CONTINGENCY: YOU MUST HAVE GOOD $B$'s TO GET GOOD $C$'s!

The effectiveness of a reward in shaping behavior depends first and foremost on whether the reward is contingent on the occurrence of the target behavior. For example, if your employer paid your wages (good $C$'s) regardless of whether you worked ($B$), your salary would not be a contingent reinforcer for working. This principle, which works to maintain a steady labor force, is often misapplied in managing our own personal behavior. Effective self-control requires a reorientation of the way we reward ourselves. We must make our pleasures (good $C$'s) contingent on our achievements (good $B$'s). The person who spares himself nothing is using payoffs indiscriminately. The task in BT is to connect these payoffs to the occurrence of desired behavior, and desired behavior alone.

## THE PRINCIPLE OF IMMEDIATE REWARD: WHEN DO I GET MY $C$?

The effectiveness of any reinforcer or reward varies with the length of delay of the payoff. Achievement-minded parents who goad their ninth-grader on to study often fail to apply this principle. The parents stress the point that studying now will eventually enable the child to reap the benefits of being a doctor, a lawyer, or an engineer. When the child asks how long he must wait for these promised fruits of his labors, the parent replies, "Well, just three more years of high school, four years of college, three or four years more of professional school . . ." For a reward to become an effective incentive, it should follow more closely upon the completion of the desired behavior. Thus, to encourage Johnny to study more, a more effective tactic would be to make the amount of his weekly allowance contingent on the number of hours of studying time.

## THE PREMACK PRINCIPLE:
## A NO-COST WAY TO REINFORCE ONESELF
## OR WHEN A $C$ IS NOT A $C$

American life is often seen as increasingly materialistic. Our payoffs or rewards are often in the form of tangible goods, like cars, clothes, or stereos. However, tangible payoffs are very often ineffective behavior shapers. The "man who has everything" is not highly motivated by the lastest electronic wonder. To people inundated with material success, tangible rewards become devalued. To people whose daily life is a struggle to provide basic necessities, tangible payoffs may be too expensive to be practical behavior shapers.

Psychologist David Premack has studied the use of selected activities as contingent payoffs or reinforcers. Based on his studies, the Premack principle[4] states that if behavior $B_1$ naturally occurs more frequently than behavior $B_2$, $B_1$ can serve as a reinforcer for $B_2$. $B_1$ can become the $C$ for $B_2$.

Pick a behavior that occurs quite often during the day, like watching TV, combing your hair, showering, reading, walking, or leaving the house. Note that it's not necessary that the behavior be pleasurable. Routine behaviors that occur very frequently are appropriate, though frequently occurring aversive behaviors like taking out the garbage should be avoided. Next, select the behavior, $B_2$, you wish to increase, such as exercising, studying, brushing your teeth, or doing dishes. Now connect the two. Set up a schedule whereby you must do $B_2$ before you allow yourself to do $B_1$.

You might make watching TV (a $B_1$) contingent on doing the dishes (a $B_2$), or washing your face at night (a $B_1$) contingent on brushing your teeth (a $B_2$). Why take everyday reinforcers for granted? Use them to shape desirable behaviors. Carry through with the plan routinely and you should find desirable changes in the frequency of the target behavior.

You may actually wind up *enjoying* something you had avoided. Such is the nature of the $B \rightarrow C$ connection.

## REMOVING REINFORCERS THAT MAINTAIN PROBLEM BEHAVIORS

Investigate your baseline data to determine the reinforcers that maintain the problem $B$'s. If you are a poor studier and find that the usual consequence of leaving your books is that you switch on the TV (good $C$), TV viewing becomes an effective reinforcer (good $C$) for maintaining the very habit you desire to change, lack of "stick-to-it-iveness" in studying. To change the behavior ($B$), change the $B \rightarrow C$ connection. If TV viewing were made contingent on studying a certain amount of time, the tables would be turned, and you might be studying longer.

## USING A POINT-REWARD SYSTEM TO SELF-MOTIVATE

We've seen how the delay of reward is a critical factor in the BT self-control program. The dieter usually realizes that losing those twenty pounds is sufficient reward in itself. Yet this incentive is often too far off to offset the immediate gratification inherent in a piece of pie. To make the reward more immediate, behavior therapists use a point-reward system to bridge the temporal gap.

Jack, a college sophomore, found that his grades never matched his expectations. He felt that he simply lacked the motivation to study. Behavioral analysis of his problem studying redefined Jack's lack of motivation in terms of the lack of reinforcing consequences (good $C$'s) for studying behavior (good $B$). The long-term gratification of a fulfilling career was simply too remote to be effective. Other, immediate reinforcers needed to be found.

Jack was instructed to collect baseline data for one typical week to determine his usual frequency of studying behavior. Then he analyzed the stimulus conditions ($A$'s) during studying. While recording his hourly studying, he kept notes of where he studied, with whom, and when. He also noted the subjects studied. In reviewing his baseline data, Jack found that his studying usually occurred in a remote corner of the library, while he was alone, in the midafternoon, and most often in his two favorite subjects. Jack determined that there were several competing stimulus cues ($A$'s) that prevented studying behavior in other contexts. For one, when he attempted to study in a central library area, he was easily distracted by the constant parade of coeds. Studying at home was restricted by the blaring sounds of his neighbor's stereo system. Thus these other environments did not provide effective *A*'s for studying.

In his behavior change strategy, Jack decided to use his stimulus environment to best advantage. He began to make it a point to spend evening time in his "studying corner" in the library (studying *A*'s), and to reinforce this behavior he arranged a series of positive payoffs (contingent good *C*'s). For each evening hour spent studying in the library area, where the *A*'s favoring studying were dominant, Jack awarded himself five points. For studying in nonfavored subjects (extra good *B*), he received five points. For studying a straight hour and a half (target *B*), Jack rewarded himself with fifteen minutes of "people watching." In addition, each hour of studying was credited with ten points.

At week's end, points were exchangeable for desired activities (good *C*'s) of his choosing. If the week totaled one hundred points above his baseline record, Jack rewarded himself with a movie, a dance, or a concert. Two hundred points was worth dining out. Jack's studying rate increased rapidly, as he tied his pleasures to his achievements, and he was able to terminate his recordkeeping within several weeks. From Jack's report his studying behavior (*B*) became more routine, and he dealt with future lapses by reinstating the point-reward system (good *C* connection).

## SOCIAL REINFORCEMENT: SOME OF YOUR BEST FRIENDS MAY BE GOOD *C*'s

One of the most often overlooked sources of reinforcement is the social milieu—our friends, family, and coworkers. The pat on the back, or conversely, the scowling frown, shapes our behavior as well as our self-esteem.

Enlist your family and friends to begin to use social reinforcement ("good going" *C*'s) to help you in achieving your behavioral goals. Have them support you for progress with congratulations, smiles, encouragement, and attention. By the same token, have them disapprove of you or ignore you when you fail to meet targeted goals. Post your record sheet on the home refrigerator so that family members can get directly involved in shaping your day-to-day progress through contingent social reinforcement once you have undertaken your behavioral strategy—not while you are compiling your baseline record.

A word of caution: Too often people draw attention to themselves only for inappropriate behavior. Thus the child's temper tantrums are reinforced as they become the prime means for securing the busy mother's attention, however disapproving it is. By attending to the child principally when he is bad, mother is inadvertently reinforcing the very behavior she'd like to weaken! By the same token, friends or family who offer disapproving comments for your failures but are inattentive to your successes will undoubtedly handicap your efforts. Condemnation is not enough. They must also "accentuate the positive."

Also note that disapproval for your undesirable behavior is not disapproval of yourself. It is the behavior we wish to extinguish, not you!

## COVERT REINFORCEMENT: IMAGINING
## THE DESIRED $B \rightarrow$ GOOD $C$ CONNECTION

Imagine yourself acting assertively with an attractive member of the opposite sex. You become engaged easily in social conversation, and you express yourself directly, clearly, and without hesitation (the desired $B$). You have an air of certainty about your behavior, a self-assuredness. People begin to congregate about you. Everyone is interested in talking with you. Several ask if you're busy on the weekend. Friends congratulate you for your newly assertive behavior. "You've come a long way" echoes in your mind, and you feel great. You're overwhelmed with imagined or "covert" good $C$'s.

Or imagine yourself studying at home. Suddenly you get a phone call from your friends asking you if you'd like to go out. Before you know it, you're reaching for your coat. You're practically out the door filled with enthusiasm. Just then you say to yourself, "I can't go right now, I must study" (the desired $B$). Imagine yourself filling with pride, feeling good at having resisted temptation. You sit yourself down and study your targeted amount of time. Friends and family come by and remark how self-disciplined and what a fine student you are. Imagine your grade reports, with better grades than ever before. The world of possibility is opening up to you. You feel wonderful, and how proud others are of you. All these covert $C$'s!

Based principally on the work of Dr. Joseph Cautela of Boston College[5] behavior therapists have begun to have their clients use imagined scenes like these to promote, in real life, the types of desired behaviors dramatized in the scenes. Imagining or thinking about something is next door to doing it. Imagining positive reinforcement (covert good $C$'s) for emitting desired behaviors such as assertiveness and studying in spite of temptation may lead to an increased incentive to engage in these $B$'s in public life. Imagination serves as a testing ground, a protected inner environment in which behaviors can be rehearsed to "get the kinks out" before real-life testing.

The technique of imagining the desired behavior leading to reinforcement is called covert reinforcement.[6] In our usage the technique includes: (1) imagining yourself performing the desired behavior and (2) switching to an imagined reinforcing event like being warmly congratulated or achieving those dreamed-of goals. Use this technique several times daily until the sequence of covert $B \rightarrow$ covert $C$ becomes routine in imagination. Change the scene elements for variety, but retain the covert $B \rightarrow$ covert $C$ connection.

Then contract with yourself to actually engage in the desired $B$'s, such as date seeking, on a graduated schedule. Begin with the most basic behaviors, such as attending coeducational activities, then progress gradually to the target behavior of asking for a date, as in the graduated series of date-seeking skills in the chapter on becoming more assertive. Become comfortable at each step before progressing, but remember not to remain too long for fear of getting "stuck." Continue to rehearse the behaviors in imagination, use a tape recorder, or test out new behaviors with a good friend. We shall have more to say later on about shaping new behaviors through this method of gradual approximations.

## RESPONSE COST: USING
## SELF-PUNISHMENT TO MODIFY BEHAVIOR
### (THE UNDESIRED $B \rightarrow$ UGLY $C$ CONNECTION)

Psychologists would generally agree that in most situations self-change strategies based on positive payoffs are preferable to self-punishment strategies. It is easier for a person to reward himself for desirable behavior than to punish himself, even mildly, for undesirable behavior. Self-punishment can lead to failure, since the person would often rather "give up" than punish himself. Self-punishment is often socially discredited as "sick" behavior, and any form of punishment may engender an atmosphere of anxiety and possibly anger. These emotions can be frustrating and induce withdrawal from a behavioral program. Although punishment tends to suppress unwanted behavior, positive payoffs are more useful in shaping new, more desirable, and lasting behaviors. Still, self-punishment can have some place in the total self-control strategy.

The one self-punishment strategy we strongly recommend is the response-cost strategy. Response cost simply means that you must pay, in favored activities, goods or money, for engaging in the undesirable behavior. If you had several beers this afternoon rather than studying, you might decide to punish yourself by turning the TV off tonight and making up lost studying time. Or you might decide to surrender points— which had been exchangeable for money at a later time—for each cigarette smoked or cookie eaten (undesired B's).

Behavior therapists have found response cost to be an effective strategy for controlling undesired behavior. Drs. Leonard Epstein and Gerald Peterson[7] of Ohio University reported the case of an attractive female student who complained of being unable to stop pulling her eyelashes. She had been engaging in this behavior since she was five, and her eyelids were by this time almost completely bare. She had tried unsuccessfully to stop by "willpower alone." The one favored activity that could be sacrificed in a self-punishment strategy was listening to music. The student put herself on the following schedule: for each eyelash plucked (undesired B) she would not listen to music (ugly C) for the following six hours. The student was also urged to use eyedrops as a competing B to the hair plucking whenever she felt the "plucking urge." The results: A dramatic reduction in the habit was rapidly achieved.

Self-punishment (the ugly C) is usually most effective when combined with positive payoffs (good C's) for desirable behaviors. Say, for example, that you would sacrifice ten points for each hundred calories eaten between meals. In addition, you might award yourself ten points for each time you engaged in an incompatible response such as exercising or going for a walk whenever "cookie fever" grabbed you. You are eliminating an unwanted B→ugly C and replacing it with a desirable B→good C. The A, cookie fever, has remained constant, but will diminish with time, since the habit of following cookie fever (unfortunate A) with unwanted B will have been broken.

One interesting application of response cost was developed

by Drs. John Nurnberger and Joseph Zimmerman of the Indiana University School of Medicine.[8] They report treating a thirty-one-year-old assistant professor of modern languages for his inability to write his doctoral thesis. The client had been unable for more than two years to write a single page, although all of the preliminary research had been completed. The treatment plan for this problem emphasized increased self-control through response cost. Initially, the client was asked to postdate sizable checks to his favorite charities. If he failed to meet weekly writing goals, the checks would be mailed by the therapists. Although there was some initial progress in writing, the thesis was again stalled within a few weeks. To increase his motivation, checks were postdated to several organizations offensive to this client (the KKK, the American Nazi Party, and the John Birch Society). They were to be mailed if weekly goals were not met. With this contingency arrangement, writing speed improved rapidly, and within several months the 256-page first draft was completed. A follow-up interview ten months later revealed that the client had successfully completed the final draft and was to be awarded soon thereafter his Ph.D. degree.

# STRATEGY 3 : Behavior Shaping and Chaining

A behavioral strategy often fails because we attempt to master very complex or novel behaviors all at once, rather than in successive steps. In our divorced women's group, a frequent comment was that it is difficult to meet desirable men. As one of the group members stated, "They come up to you in the bar, dangling their car keys." The behavioral end goal—in this case meeting a man who was interested in more than a brief liaison—usually requires a series of steps to be mastered along the way. The BT approach attempts to shape these preliminary behaviors gradually, to provide success experiences at each step.

Group members were asked to identify the chain of behaviors considered necessary to master before reaching their end goal. The behavioral chain devised was: (1) first attend to one's own physical attractiveness through proper beauty care, attractive clothing, and weight reduction; (2) develop personal resources through reading current newsmagazines and attending extension courses in local universities; (3) learn to act more assertively in interpersonal situations, as in the chapter on becoming more assertive; (4) attend coeducational social activities such as church or temple groups, evening courses, Parents Without Partners, or do volunteer work; and (5) engage in previously rehearsed assertive responses in approaching and conversing with men.

To use behavioral chaining effectively:

1. Break down your end goal into the preliminary component steps.
2. Set weekly goals for yourself to master each of the targeted behaviors gradually.
3. Reward yourself for meeting weekly goals.
4. Attempt to accomplish the end goal following success at each previous step.

## SELF-CONTRACTING SUCCESSIVE APPROXIMATIONS TO THE GOAL

Behavioral end goals that require a significant change in behavior, such as smoking abstinence, may be approached through a series of successive approximations to the goal, to avoid trying and failing to master too much too soon. A self-contract denotes your timetable for completing each step toward the goal, and the reinforcers that will motivate you at each level. For example, if your goal is to increase your weekly reading time by ten hours, you may decide to use a self-control like the following:

1. Baseline week  Observed rate=4 hours average weekly
2. Week 1         Goal=6 hours weekly for 10-point payoff
3. Week 2         Goal=9 hours weekly for 20-point payoff
4. Week 3         Goal=14 hours weekly for 50-point payoff

Points could be exchangeable for equal money amounts or the equivalent in activities. Make sure that rewards are in tangible goods or activities. Money that just goes back in the bank is not usually a motivating incentive.

Keep four things in mind in using self-contracts:

1. The starting point may be very close to the baseline rate and the in-between steps quite small.
2. The initial steps are smaller than the later steps.
3. As you approach your target goal, the rewards are larger and more compelling.

4. The steps should progress toward the target goal; don't remain at any one step too long.[9]

Clients using self-reward and self-punishment procedures often comment: "Well, I really feel bad having to bribe myself to do things." Our reply is, "Is it really bribery to exercise enough self-control to tie your pleasures to your achievements?"

Once you've reached your goal, begin to phase out the reinforcer—that is, make the reward more difficult to obtain. In the example of increasing time spent studying, reward yourself biweekly for fourteen hours' weekly studying time, then triweekly, then monthly, until the behavior is well established.

## TO BREAK THE HABIT, BREAK THE CHAIN: MAKING A *B* INTO LOTS OF LITTLE *b*'s

The principle of chaining can be used to break undesired habits as well as to build constructive habits. Many beer drinkers, for health or weight reasons, need to restrict their daily intake. For many, beer drinking is a habit as intransigent as smoking. Beer is individually canned and stored conveniently in six-packs, making home beer consumption as easy as 1, 2, 3, 4, 5, 6, and so on. If controlling your home beer drinking has been a problem for you, you can help yourself exercise better self-control through *elongating* or *interrupting* the beer-drinking chain at each step.

The act of drinking beer at home can be broken down into the following chain of preliminary behaviors: (1) shopping for and storing the beer; (2) taking the beer from the refrigerator; (3) opening the can or bottle; and (4) drinking the beer. Learn to unhook the problem *B*eer drinking chain at each step. Develop the habit of buying a few cans or bottles at a time, rather than a few six-packs. That way you must go to the market to replenish your limited home supply every few days—a negative incentive for overindulgence. Set daily quotas for yourself. If you're tempted to drink *more* than your quota, stop yourself before taking the beer from the refrigerator (step 2 above). One thirty-four-year-old salesman made himself walk around the block to get to his refrigerator for an extra beer. While walking, he asked himself, "Is this beer really necessary?" He pictured his "beer belly" (or looked down) and considered how proud he would feel to thin down. The walk gave him time to summon the motivation he needed to exercise self-control. When he returned, he attempted to engage in a behavior that was incompatible with beer drinking, such as going for a drive, showering, or drinking water or fruit juice instead. In effect, he gave himself time to let the temptation pass.

If you can't interrupt the chain at step 2, elongate steps 3 and 4. Set a kitchen timer for five minutes and wait out the time before taking the beer from the refrigerator. Pause and reflect. "Must I *really* have *that* beer?" After taking the beer, hold it for one minute before opening. Then one minute further before drinking. Use your waiting time to build the motivation to break the chain right there. Engage in a competing response to help unhook the problem *B*eer-drinking chain. Remember that it's never too late to break the chain until the beer is completely consumed. If you succeed in interrupting the chain—and in rejecting that extra beer—reward yourself with self-congratulations or with a small gift. And feel good about yourself for exercising self-control.

Chain lengthening gives you time to summon your willpower to break the chain at its weakest link. Problem behaviors like excessive beer drinking, overeating, and smoking become so automatic and habitual that we are hardly aware of the steps in the behavioral chains that lead to the final behavior. Chain-breaking techniques make you attend to each step and thus help you to tackle problem behaviors step by step. These problem behaviors become laborious, even frustrating tasks, and lose some of their attractiveness.

# BT SELF CONTROL: A SUMMING UP

BT self-control involves applying a variety of behavioral techniques to help you master problem behaviors. All BT programs include: (1) behavioral definition of the problem; (2) self-recording; and (3) designing and implementing your behavior change strategy.

The various BT strategies for helping you reach your behavioral goals include:

1. Restriction of the stimulus field: Limit the *A*'s.
2. Removal of usual potent stimuli: Avoid potent *A*'s.
3. Use of competing or incompatible behaviors: Build *A*→competing *B* connections.
4. Strengthening *A*'s for desired *B*'s.

5. Response prevention: Make the occurrence of the problem *B* highly unlikely or impossible.

6. Premack principle: Use frequently occurring activities as *C*'s for good *B*'s.

7. Removing the usual reinforcers for problem behaviors: Disconnect problem *B*→good *C* connections.

8. Point-reward reinforcement: Build good *B*→good *C* connections.

9. Social reinforcement: Build good *B*→ "good going" *C* connections.

10. Covert reinforcement: Build imagined good *B*→imagined good *C* connections.

11. Response cost: Make the consequences for unwanted *B*'s to be costly *C*'s.

12. Use of behavior shaping and chaining to make and break habits.

# 8

## FAT:
## The BT Way to Take It Off
## and Keep It Off

The BT approach to weight control is neither a miraculous formula for instant reducing nor a fad diet. It is a scientifically developed program for lasting weight loss through changing maladaptive eating habits.

## The Fat Explosion!

With estimates of between forty million and eighty million obese Americans, the U. S. Public Health Service has stated that obesity "is one of the most prevalent health problems in the United States today."[1] Harvard University nutritionist Dr. Jean Mayer has suggested that obesity is marked regularly by improper food habits—an imbalance between calorie intake and energy expenditure.[2] Overweight people take in more energy in calories than they expend in bodily processes, work, exercise, and play. These excess calories are converted into body fat and molded into unsightly bulges.

## Pounds and Calories

One pound of fat is roughly equivalent to thirty-five hundred calories. Thus, if your weight is generally stable, the loss of one pound per week requires burning five hundred more calories a day than you take in. The goal of the BT weight-control program is to teach you adaptive behaviors to maintain a calorie-reduction plan, and then to help you keep that extra weight off.

## Dieting and Lasting Habit Change

Behavioral weight control applies the behavioral principles of self-control to help weight reducers control their problem eating behaviors. Overeating is a learned habit, which must be unlearned through attention to the behaviors of overeating. Few fad diets actually produce lasting weight change.[3] Weight recidivists may be successful in the short run in shedding pounds on a "quickie" diet, but fail to make a permanent change because their self-defeating eating habits remain unbroken. Although the weight often comes off, the fad dieter has not developed good eating habits to fall back on. The maxim of BT weight control is that lasting weight reduction comes only through habit change, through changing the behaviors of overeating.

## Dietary Promiscuity

Many Americans drift from diet to diet failing to recognize that it's not simply what one eats, but how, when, and where one eats that are significant in effective weight reduction. Do you routinely eat while watching TV? Do you shop before meals? Are you a social eater? Do you eat because others are eating? Do you eat quickly and finish everything on your plate? Do you know how many calories you consume daily? These questions describe the *ABC*'s of eating, from marketing to putting the food in your mouth, which become the focus of the BT weight-control program.

## Need for Commitment

State University of New York at Albany psychologist David Doty[4] explains to would-be weight reducers that they alone have the power to say, "I will do something about my weight." They must summon the motivation or willpower to put weight-control strategies into effect. However, the potential weight reducer also has the power to say, "I'd rather be fat," and, as Dr. Doty states, that individual probably will "stay fat, stay ugly, stay unpopular, stay self-conscious." Successful reducing will not result from simply "digesting" this chapter. Behavioral weight control aims at gradual and permanent weight loss through reorientation of eating habits. It requires a commitment to investigating your behavioral eating patterns, and changing maladaptive habits.

# BEHAVIORAL WEIGHT REDUCTION: THE THEORY AND EVIDENCE

The BT guide to lasting weight control recognizes that many people have difficulty achieving their desired goals by "willpower" alone. Willpower alone is often not enough because people fail to recognize the environmental context in which behavior occurs, the $ABC$'s of behavior, as explained in Chapter 7. Behavior ($B$) can be viewed in terms of two components: $A$ntecedent stimulus cues ($A$'s) and environmental $C$onsequences ($C$'s) or reinforcements. Behavioral weight control teaches you to manipulate both components to shape desired eating habits, and, consequently, trimmer waistlines.

## How Environmental Cues Relate to Obesity (The $A \rightarrow B$ Connection)

### WHAT TELLS YOU WHEN TO EAT?

Dr. Albert Stunkard[5] of the University of Pennsylvania asked obese and nonobese students to report to his lab at 9 A.M., following an overnight fast. The students were asked to swallow a stomach balloon, which, when partially inflated with water, provided measurements of stomach contractions. For the next four hours, the students were asked to indicate at fifteen-minute intervals whether or not they felt hungry. The results showed that nonobese students were more likely than obese students to report hunger at times of stomach contractions. The obese students more often reported hunger at times unrelated to their stomach movements. The study showed that nonobese people were more likely than obese people to use internal stimuli, such as stomach grumblings, as cues, or *A*'s, that they were hungry.

Columbia University psychologist Stanley Schachter and his colleagues attempted to determine what stimulus cues (*A*'s) obese people regularly use in determining when it is time to eat.[6] The results of these studies suggest that obese individuals are overly responsive to food-related cues in the environment in regulating their eating habits. Their eating is largely unrelated to their internal needs, but is rather controlled by external cues or stimuli (eating *A*'s), like watching others eat, TV food commercials, the sights and smells of food, or the time of day.

## BRINGING UP BABY

Dr. Schachter proposes that if we have been brought up in homes where family members predominantly ate when they felt hungry because their "stomachs were empty," and stopped eating when their stomachs were full, then we are more likely today to tie our eating habits to our internal needs. However, when our eating has been primarily conditioned by other, external-stimulus events, such as TV viewing, time of day, social conversation, or passing by a fast-food restaurant, we will "feel" hungry because of cues (eating *A*'s) unrelated to changes in our internal physiology. An external, cue-controlled eater may become obese, since his eating is "out of sync" with bodily needs, but is reactive to the omnipresent stimulus demands of our "try it, you'll like it" commercial milieu.

Dr. Schachter further suggests that termination of eating by the obese may be unrelated to internal cues of satiety. The "binge eating" observed in many overweight people, in which up to twenty thousand calories may be consumed at one time, suggests that internal need is not the determining factor for termination of eating. Rather, obese people usually stop eating simply when all of the food stimuli (eating *A*'s) are removed—through ingestion. In fact, some of us eat so rapidly—cheesecake, candy, whipped cream, peanuts—that we don't even give our bellies a chance to signal our brains that we've had enough.

## THE TYRANNY OF THE CLOCK!

The Schachter theory is based on a number of studies carried out over the past fifteen years. Schachter and Gross[7] used a doctored clock, running at either twice normal or half normal speed, to intentionally mislead student subjects as to the actual amount of time passed during an experimental session. The students were first individually occupied with irrelevant paper-and-pencil tasks for fifty minutes. They had not been advised of the actual purpose of the study, which was to determine how many crackers each of them would eat under one of two experimental conditions: (1) being told it was either thirty minutes later than it actually was, and hence closer to actual dinnertime, or (2) being told it was thirty minutes earlier than the actual time. Following the initial fifty minutes, the experimenters returned, asked the students to complete some additional irrelevant talks, and offered each of them a box of Wheat Thins.

The results were consistent with Schachter's theory. Obese students whose clock indicated that it was closer to mealtime ate twice as many crackers as obese students whose clock was earlier than actual time. This difference was not found for normal-weight students. The critical factor in determining how much to eat for the obese was the time on the clock, not the internal feelings or cues of hunger!

## OUT OF SIGHT, OUT OF MOUTH

In another experiment, Dr. Richard Nisbett[8] of the University of Michigan investigated how many roast beef sandwiches hungry normal-weight, underweight, and obese students would eat depending on the number of sandwiches available. While filling out some meaningless questionnaires in individual rooms, sandwiches and soda were made available to each student. They were told to eat as many as they'd like, since they would probably miss lunch in completing the study. They were informed that additional sandwiches, if desired, were available in a nearby refrigerator.

The experimenters found that normal and underweight students ate the same number of sandwiches, regardless of the number visible. However, obese individuals ate significantly fewer sandwiches than either normal or underweight individuals when one sandwich was immediately available, and significantly more when three were in view. Obese people used the sights and smells of food (food $A$'s), and not internal cues, in regulating their eating behavior more so than normal-weight or underweight people. Obese students did not, in general, help themselves to the sandwiches in the refrigerator. The food cues were not in plain sight!

## WHAT DOES WATCHING OTHERS EATING DO TO YOU?

Schachter and his colleagues[9] investigated the relative percentages of obese and normal-weight Jewish students at Columbia University who fasted on Yom Kippur, the Jewish Day of Atonement and a religious fasting day. Jewish students who had attended a synagogue at least once during the previous year were included in the study. The results showed that more obese students (83 per cent) than normal-weight students (69 per cent) fasted! The apparently greater ease in fasting for the obese students probably reflected the absence of food-related cues, in this case seeing other people eating, while the internal cues motivating normal-weight students to eat were present as usual.

## ENVIRONMENTAL DETERMINANTS OF OBESITY

These and other studies lend support to Professor Schachter's theory of external cue-determined obesity, and suggest that manipulation of stimulus cues (eating $A$'s) may be an effective remedy for helping overweight people regulate their eating behavior. Since these cues are omnipresent, we had better control them before they control us. Schachter's theory points to the need of the would-be reducer to become more aware of food-related cues in his environment and to restructure or eliminate them, as we shall see.

# BEHAVIORAL WEIGHT CONTROL: EMPIRICAL VALIDATION

Traditional treatments of obesity, ranging from medical advice to drugs, from dietary instruction to psychotherapy, have been notably unsuccessful.[10] Dr. Stunkard[11] has stated, "Most obese persons will not stay in treatment for obesity; of those who stay in treatment, most will not lose weight; and of those who do lose weight, most will regain it." In the traditional psychotherapeutic treatment of obesity, which focuses on the overeater's underlying personality and not on the behaviors of eating, it has been estimated that from 20 per cent to 80 per cent of clients beginning treatment abandoned their weight-reduction program before completion.[12]

## The BT Revolution

The BT or behavioral-control approach to obesity has brought about a growing revolution. Using a variety of behavioral-treatment approaches, significant gradual weight loss has been attained by subjects involved in controlled studies at Emory University[13] (.9 pound per week average over a 7-week program), USC[14] (5.1 pounds average after 4 weeks), Stanford University[15] (8 pounds average in 10 weeks), and twice at the University of Illinois (9.1 pounds average in 12 weeks,[16] and 13 pounds average in 11 weeks).[17] In most cases weight loss was either maintained or continued following the end of treatment, and relatively few subjects terminated treatment early.

### THE WOLLERSHEIM STUDY

Dr. Janet Wollersheim,[18] of the University of Illinois, compared various treatments of obesity in a study in which 79 overweight female students followed an 18-week-baseline, 12-week treatment, and an 8-week follow-up program. All of the students had reported prior unsuccessful attempts to lose weight, and most had been overweight since childhood or adolescence. The women averaged 157 pounds at the start of treatment.

The participating women were assigned randomly to one of the following treatment groups:

1. *Insight-oriented group.* This group was directed at elaborating the underlying reasons or unconscious motives for the participants' eating habits. The therapist led the discussion toward developing each student's understanding of her personality makeup in order to help them achieve their weight-reduction goals.

2. *Social pressure group.* Similar to many community-based weight-reduction programs, this group used peer pressure to help the participants lose weight. The group tasks involved a weigh-in and use of contingent comments ("This girl is really going places," or "What a shame, but you'll show us next week, won't you?") in order to highlight weight loss and gain. Weight gainers were asked to wear a pig-shaped red tag throughout the session, while losers wore yel-

low stars. Those whose weight remained the same wore a turtle sign. The woman who lost the most weight wore a star and a crown. The only instructions for weight loss given by the therapist was that each woman should reduce her caloric intake in her own way.

3. *No-treatment control group.* This group of women was put on a waiting list during the period of the study to determine what effect no treatment at all would have on weight control.

4. *Behavioral-treatment group.* BT group women were told that overeating was a learned habit that could be unlearned. They were taught relaxation procedures to use as competing responses in many situations in which they normally wound up eating. The women were asked to keep records of eating and to identify the *A*ntecedent stimulus conditions for eating. They were shown how to reward or punish themselves for controlled eating or overeating. The participants were instructed in techniques of chain breaking and manipulation of the stimuli tied to overeating, techniques explained in the chapter on making and breaking habits. Imagination was also used to make overeating a more unpleasant experience. Finally, the women were advised to obtain reinforcers (good *C*'s) from areas of life other than the kitchen. These techniques are elaborated in the self-help program outlined later.

The results: Twenty-five per cent of the women in the social pressure group, 40 per cent in the insight-oriented group, and 61 per cent in the behavioral-treatment group lost a significant amount of weight (9 pounds or more) during the 12-week treatment period. Students assigned to the waiting list gained an average of 2 pounds over the course of the treatment period. Statistical analysis showed that while all three active treatments were significantly more successful than no treatment at all, BT was the superior treatment.

## BUT CAN I DO IT BY MYSELF?

The available evidence suggests *Yes.* Dr. Richard Hagen[19] of the University of Illinois found that a BT weight-control program with a *written manual* was as effective as the same program applied by a therapist. Average weight loss for the manual-only group was thirteen pounds over an eleven-week treatment period.

## BEFORE THE PROGRAM, CONSULT YOUR PHYSICIAN

The BT program is designed for weight control through planned calorie reduction. Discuss your ideal calorie needs with your physician. A reduction diet of five hundred to one thousand calories daily makes sense for most people who are interested in losing weight (one to two pounds weekly) gradually while altering their eating behavior to make sure their weight reduction lasts. Ask your physician for a nutritious calorie-reduction diet that both limits calorie intake and provides sufficient nutrients for your particular health condition.

With the calorie approach to weight loss you don't have to fret about *never* being able to eat some favorite food again. You merely fit it within your total permitted calorie and nutritional plan. Gradual weight loss through reorientation of eating habits makes more sense than crash diets that change body weight but not the overeating behaviors that had caused the original weight problem. *Our guiding maxim is: gradually on, gradually off.*

# BT STRATEGIES FOR EFFECTIVE WEIGHT REDUCTION

You've seen your doctor. You know how many calories you need to skim from your present diet. You're now anxiously awaiting that new, thinner you. If you can now couple that enthusiasm with a commitment to changing maladaptive eating habits, you're ready to begin. To help you program permanent changes in your eating habits, begin to use routinely the following self-help strategies.

## STRATEGY 1 : Self-reward and Self-punishment (Changing the $B \rightarrow C$ Connection)

By now you should have begun to think of *B*ehavior in terms of the interplay of *A*ntecedent stimuli and *C*onsequent reinforcements. It is reasonable to suggest that since the long-term consequences of overindulging ourselves with chocolate cake are generally aversive—excess lard, unattractiveness, and health problems—overindulgent behavior should rapidly weaken and fade. If so, this chapter would be largely unnecessary. However, with many diet repeaters, this is hardly true. One reason may be that these ugly $C$'s are too delayed to be effective behavior modifiers. Although the rewards for eating are immediate—the taste and texture of food, and the feeling of fullness in the stomach—the rewards for refraining are not. In short, the immediate appeal of a calorie-laden dish simply "outweighs" the influence of the delayed averse $C$'s, and we find ourselves overindulging too readily.

Immediate rewards are more effective than delayed rewards of equal size. Our first task is to redress this imbalance, which pits the delayed rewards of a thinner, healthier you against the immediate delights of chocolate mousse, caramel custard, and on and on. To help you stick with your calorie plan through resisting inappropriate eating, use a self-reward, self-punishment system.

## STEP 1: BECOME A CALORIE COUNTER

Calorie counting, like any system of self-recording, allows you to quantify your successes and failures. Daily calorie records may belie the self-distortion, "I know I was good today." Obtain a food calorie list and record daily calorie intake by estimating the caloric value of everything that passes your lips. Everything!

## STEP 2: OBTAIN BASELINE DATA

With all self-control procedures you have to know where you are to know where you're going. Before beginning the program record your calorie intake for a two-week baseline period. For these baseline data to reflect accurately your usual intake, they should not be confounded by your attempts, however unwitting, to change your normal eating habits. Just eat as you would normally for the duration of the baseline period. The only difference is that you will be keeping records.

We have found that a small number of clients seem to go on a last-minute eating binge, or eating panic, while they collect baseline data. They view the data-collection period as their "last opportunity" to eat as they wish. Be forewarned of the possible temptation to gorge yourself before the "drought."

*How to chart.* Use a calorie chart like this one to record the caloric values of all foods eaten during the day:

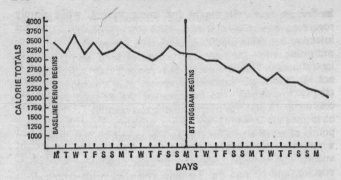

Continue to chart your calorie intake *throughout* the remainder of the BT program.

Much of the overeater's problem occurs because of between-meal snacks. To avoid the pitfalls of "junk food alley," the BT program calls for assessment of the *ABC*'s of this behavior. During the *baseline period only*, record the following information in a diary for each between-meal snack: *what was eaten, the number of calories, where you were, with whom, the time of day, what you were doing, your mood, and how you felt about your self-indulgence.* Become your own food detective to determine the *A*'s and the *C*'s of the snacking *B*'s.

If you're beginning to get edgy and you're wondering if this extra work is worth it, remind yourself how you look without clothes, and how good *you will feel* when that bathing suit follows the slim contours of your body, and not the bulges.

## STEP 3: PLAN YOUR DIET

If after consulting your doctor your goal is to lose one pound weekly, subtract thirty-five hundred calories from your average weekly baseline total and divide by seven. This will be your daily goal. Use your calorie book to plan meals and snacks within this calorie limit and to obtain proper nutrients. Don't use a "feast or famine" method in which binge eating is followed by crash dieting. Whatever your calorie goal, plan your diet for the coming week beforehand in order to stay within those limits.

*Don't use daily weights.* Researchers at Rutgers University[20] have found that daily records of weight loss are totally ineffective as a sole means for losing weight, while simply recording daily calorie intake *alone* does often lead to weight loss. Calorie recordkeeping helps you focus on calorie consumption. Your *behavioral* goal is not to lose pounds, but to lose calories. Daily body weight fluctuates naturally and is not an accurate day-to-day reflection of your progress. Just take care of the calories, and your weight loss will follow accordingly. In fact, we have had chronic pound watchers who have become demoralized by failing to lose a fraction of a pound *every* day, or by finding that they have actually gained a pound on a given day. *Temporary* failures to lose weight and temporary small gains are natural and to be expected. If you keep to the BT calorie approach, you *will* attain your long-term goals.

## STEP 4: USE MONEY TO REWARD AND TO PUNISH YOURSELF

Reward yourself at the end of each week with a preplanned amount if you've met your weekly *calorie*, not weight, goal. Pennsylvania State University psychologist Michael Mahoney[21] has found that self-reward for calorie reduction is more effective than self-reward for weight change. The amount of money involved should be sufficiently motivating to help you reach your goal. If you fail to meet your weekly calorie goal, punish yourself through sacrificing proportionate amounts.

*Can you trust yourself?* Emory University researcher D. Balfour Jeffrey[22] found that the amount of weight loss did not differ if weight reducers dispensed the rewards themselves or the experimenter dispensed them. In fact, weight reducers who managed their own rewards maintained their weight loss at a posttreatment follow-up evaluation better than those for whom the experimenter was the reward dispenser. Weight reducers using this self-reward system averaged a loss of one pound per week during the seven-week program, and maintained their initial weight loss at the six-month follow-up evaluation. So don't be afraid to be your own reward dispenser.

*How to proceed.* To implement the self-reward, self-punishment strategy, use the following system:

1. Reward yourself the full weekly amount for reaching

your calorie goal. This shouldn't be "paper money" that simply goes back into the bank. Treat yourself with the money to rewards that are tangible, such as small gifts or favored activities. You deserve it for taking care of your health and your looks!

2. Punish yourself in graduated amounts for increasing distance from your calorie goal. If your intake goal is 1,500 calories daily, and the week's award money is $20, the following schedule would be appropriate:

| AVERAGE DAILY CALORIE INTAKE (Goal=1,500 calories) | AMOUNT LOST |
| --- | --- |
| 1,501–1,600 calories | $ 5 |
| 1,601–1,700 calories | $10 |
| 1,701–1,800 calories | $15 |
| 1,801 + calories | $20 |

Be certain the penalty or response cost really hurts. The actual dollar amounts you select should be painful but not crippling to your weekly budget. An appropriate penalty might be to make out a blank check to a hated cause or atrocious political candidate at the beginning of the week. At week's end if you fail to meet your weekly goal, fill in the appropriate dollar amount and mail it at once.

*Shaping behavior toward the goal.* If your intended calorie goal seems too restrictive, too difficult to master all at once, set up a schedule of gradual approximations to the target goal. Set your first week's calorie goal at one third of the target, next week two thirds, and finally the total goal the third week. For example, if your target goal is to cut nine hundred calories daily from your diet, you might begin reducing your baseline daily rate by three hundred calories during the first week, six hundred calories during the second week, and nine hundred calories thereafter. Make the reward or punishment contingent on meeting your weekly goal, not your ultimate target goal. There is no such thing as too small a step. Smaller steps simply delay your calorie- and weight-reduction goals. But you're headed in the right direction.

*Use additional contingent rewards.* Congratulate yourself for your successes! If you pass up the usual doughnut and coffee at the office, buy yourself a little something. In fact, use the money you'd normally spend on excess snack foods on tangible goods or favored activities instead.

Dr. Stunkard[23] suggests a less self-serving reward: Donate money to a favorite charity. If you reach your calorie goal, send the preplanned amount. If not, mail the penalty amount to that hated cause, or give it to your brother-in-law.

Enlist your family's help. Post your calorie chart on the home refrigerator and have your family convey approval for your progress, and disapproval, though with implied encouragement, for not meeting your goals. That is, don't have them just say, "What a pig!" Have them say, "We're disappointed with what you did this week, and we hope you'll do better next week. We know you can."

Investigate weight-control programs in your community (for example, Weight Watchers, Overeaters Anonymous) that rely on mutual support, peer pressure, and nutritional guidance to help members maintain diet control. Remember that contingent social reinforcement (good social $C$'s) is a most potent behavior shaper. In addition, groups provide an opportunity for people with similar problems to lean on each other for mutual support, encouragement, and caring. If you can go it alone, fine. However, if you feel a group might help, don't be afraid to reach out to others. A note of caution: Don't use attendance at a group as an alternative to changing maladaptive eating habits.

One last word: Don't use food as a reward. Avoid rewarding yourself or your children with food. Why train your children to eat whenever they've accomplished something worthwhile? This pattern may last into adulthood. Food has enough appeal without taking on excess meaning.

## STRATEGY 2: Exercise—A Much-maligned Benefit

*Myth:* Exercise leads to increased appetite and eating, which cancels out its beneficial, weight-reducing effects. In point of fact, in our overmechanized and sedentary style of life, moderate exercise may actually reduce overall food intake. Research has shown that sedentary people actually eat more than moderately active people.[24] Witness the housewife or househusband whose major daily activity is snacking. Vigorous exercise before eating has actually been found to reduce appetite.[25] Exercise relieves boredom, a prime antecedent for eating, and is a competing response to eating. It also burns up calories.

Dr. Richard Stuart and Ms. Barbara Davis, in their landmark book *Slim Chance in a Fat World: Behavioral Control of Obesity*,[26] suggest that today's Americans in general are actually consuming slightly fewer calories than their predecessors. However, increased mechanization has meant decreased energy expenditure, and hence bulging waistlines as activity levels fail to compensate for calorie intake.

Researchers at New Mexico State University[27] have found that a weight-control program that emphasizes both changes in eating habits and exercise is more successful than a program that focuses on eating habits alone. Thus a strong recommendation in our BT program is that calorie reduction be coupled with planned daily exercise. But ask your doctor to determine what type of activity is right for you, considering your age and your general health.

How much difference can exercise make in your weight-reduction program? Stuart and Davis estimate that if an individual simply climbed the stairs to his/her fourth-floor office four times daily, this alone would result in a yearly weight loss of approximately nine pounds. Couple such exercise with daily walks, tennis, jogging, swimming, and planned calorie reductions, and weight loss would be considerably greater. Of course, depending on how heavy you are at the outset, it might still take weeks or even months until you begin to look the way you want. So don't expect the "overnight miracle"—unless you run the Boston Marathon daily for several weeks.

*Lard-producing machines.* When one considers all the mechanical conveniences that are used today, it is clear how overmechanization is translated into excess personal tonnage. These "energy saving" (read "lard producing") conveniences include: escalators, elevators, golf carts, riding mowers, snow removers, electric garage-door openers, electric can openers, ice crushers, electric fireplaces, store-bought fire logs, and worst of all, the underground parking lot. Increase your activity level by:

1. parking at the far end of the lot or several blocks from work
2. using the stairs rather than the elevator or escalator

3. walking to get the daily paper
4. exercising while watching TV (This also precludes eating during this time; running in place is an excellent choice, unless you have a neighbor beneath you.)
5. walking rather than taking a bus or cab
6. getting a dog (The walks will do you both good.)
7. joining exercise or reducing programs at the "Y" or other religious or community centers
8. taking hikes or riding a bicycle
9. developing an interest in cross-country skiing
10. becoming active in sports like tennis, swimming, skiing, and baseball

## DEVELOP AN EXERCISE PLAN

After discussing your exercise plan with your doctor to determine the parameters of healthful exercising, plan your weekly exercise schedule. One ambitious psychiatric resident used this plan:

Monday: 1. Walk up stairs to office three times.
2. Park two blocks away from hospital.
3. One hour of tennis after work.
4. Nightly exercise for fifteen minutes during TV time.

Tuesday: 1. Walk up stairs to office three times.
2. Park two blocks away from hospital.
3. One hour bicycle ride after work.
4. Nightly exercise for fifteen minutes while watching TV.

Plans for Wednesday, Thursday, and Friday were similar. The weekend afforded yet more opportunity.

## THE EXERCISE B→C CONNECTION

Like other learned habits, routine exercise requires contingent reinforcers or payoffs. To reinforce yourself while exercising, tell yourself (1) how much more youthful and vibrant you feel, (2) how good it feels to be active and alive. (3) how close to nature you are, and (4) how each day you're becoming trimmer and feeling more youthful. Picture yourself thinner in your mind's eye, and hold that image. Congratulate yourself for taking steps to shed those pounds and tone those sagging muscles. Need further payoffs? Construct a point system whereby each activity earns a certain number of points, which are later exchangeable for tangible rewards, such as favored activities or small gifts. Set a weekly goal for yourself in terms of points to be earned. Make your rewards contingent on reaching that goal, and use response cost, in graduated penalty levels, for failure to reach weekly goals. If two are exercising jointly, use the point system in tandem: Each manages the payoffs for the other. Of course, the delayed reward should be increasing fitness and weight loss.

## STRATEGY 3: The BT Way to Shop for Food

Caroline, a forty-three-year-old housewife and mother of five growing children, complained that no matter how hard she tried to avoid consuming cookies, potato chips, cakes, and ice cream, the mere sight of these snack foods in the refrigerator was too demanding to resist. Who, indeed, can resist a nibble at a half-finished carton of all-natural mocha mint chip ice cream? Since the sight of food is a most potent stimulus for eating, use response prevention: You can't eat what isn't there. *Proper weight control begins in the supermarket.*

Begin to recognize the pitfalls of supermarket shopping. Be on the lookout for the stimulus cues (food $A$'s) that are intentionally planned to pattern our shopping behavior. Remember that the fancy display cases, the elaborate and colorful packages, and the super-bright lighting are all intended for one thing: to induce you to buy and buy and buy. It is the consummate art of undersell. No salesman pestering you to buy his goods. Just foodstuffs in brightly colored packages that slyly attempt to seduce you. Never!! Fortified!! Richer!! appear in bold print on the package and attract our interest. The aware shopper comes prepared for the challenge and obeys the following rules of self-control:

- Don't shop when hungry. Dr. Stuart[28] found that overweight women who shopped after their dinner bought 20 per cent less than women who shopped before dinner.
- Bring a list with you and stick to it.
- Bring only enough money to purchase items on the list.
- Walk quickly through the market. A lingering mind is quick prey to the fancy displays.
- If you can avoid it, don't bring your children with you.

Children's attraction to sweets sets traps you might not be able to sidetrack.

- Don't make food shopping a high point in your day.
- Shop when you really don't have enough time to shop.
- Avoid aisles containing junk or snack foods. If it is not possible to avoid stimulus contact with these articles, walk quickly and keep your eyes focused straight ahead.

## ONE DOES NOT LIVE BY COOKIES ALONE

Do not buy foods that don't fit within your calorie-reduction plan. Having tempting or problem foods in the house sets up your reducing plan for hasty defeat. We often hear from dieters that having the cakes, cookies, and ice cream in the house is necessary for their kids, their spouse, their mother, their father, or even their cat! But do you really think you're doing these family members a favor? The child who is raised on seemingly unending supplies of snack foods will have a more difficult time unlearning these behaviors than children raised within caloric guidelines. The best way to stop smoking is never to have started; likewise childhood food overindulgence sets the stage for adult obesity.

## SEPARATE "ILLEGAL" FOODS

We are not, however, suggesting restriction of all snacking by other family members. It is *you*—not they—who are on the calorie-reduction plan. Still, there are things you can do to limit the presence and influence of these powerful *A*'s. Rather than having ice cream in half-gallon containers, the weight reducer might decide to give his or her children extra money to buy ice cream on their way home from school. Or a separate refrigerator in the basement might be used to separate "illegal" foods from other foods. *Refuse to serve as middleman in preparing food treats for your children at home.* Don't have them come to you to be served ice cream or cake, for as modern economics makes clear, the middleman usually reaps more than his share of profits. Many dieters buy snack foods desired by other family members but not desirable for them. You may also dissociate yourself from your family's snacking by being out of the house during preparation, consumption, and cleaning up. Use assertive behaviors to communicate the point that only foods that others like but you dislike can be kept in the house.

## DON'T BE A BASKET CASE

While food shopping, look at the baskets of other shoppers. For the most part, the people buying the large quantities of "junk food" are the very people who can afford it the least. The next time you see an obese shopper buying these foods, look down in your cart. Ask yourself: Am I going to control my behavior or not?

# STRATEGY 4: Redesigning the Stimulus Environment (Breaking the $A \rightarrow B$ Connection)

The work of Professor Schachter and his colleagues has shown how overweight people are oversensitive to environmental, food-related cues in regulating their eating behavior. To change your eating *B*ehavior, change the stimulus *A*ntecedents. Overweight people eat because of the sight, the smell, or the mere propinquity of food. Seeing others eating, passing by a restaurant or fast-food place, watching a TV food commercial, all cause overweight people in particular to begin thinking of eating. Thinking about something is an approximation to doing it and quite frequently leads to the behavior itself. Follow these methods for preventing inappropriate eating at its source—by manipulating the stimulus milieu through changing the eating *A*'s.

## STEP 1: RESTRICT THE STIMULUS FIELD

For the overeater, it often becomes second nature to eat while watching TV or studying. Since these food habits were learned, they can be unlearned. Begin to break these connections by restricting eating to one eating place. Don't engage in any other activity while eating. If you feel you must munch while watching TV, excuse yourself, go to your eating place—out of earshot from the TV—and eat. Never eat in the bedroom or living room. Don't eat while reading or talking on the telephone. Always eat while sitting down. In these ways you can begin to condition eating to a restricted area, thereby weakening the problem eating habit in other stimulus settings and breaking $A \rightarrow$ problem $B$ connections.

The beer drinker who wishes to cut down would also be well advised to break the $A \rightarrow B$eer connection. Drink only in one place, and never do anything else while drinking, such as

watching TV ball games or playing cards. Drink the beer out
of earshot, and eyeshot, of the TV. Keep the gusto in the
kitchen and not in the TV room!

## STEP 2: CONTROL THE GEOGRAPHY
## OF EATING

*Eliminate potent cues for snacking.* Consult your snacking
diary. Identify situations in which you eat excessively. Plan
your activities to avoid these danger areas as much as possible. If, for example, you eat routinely while studying, study
in the school library and in your kitchen. If TV viewing is
implicated, watch less TV; move the TV away from the
kitchen; or watch TV principally after meals, when you are
least hungry.

Locate situations in which you usually don't eat. Increase
your time spent in these eating-free activities. Many people
find that they avoid eating or thinking of food while attending class. If so, investigate the schools in your area for continuing education courses, particularly in the evening, to plan
your time more constructively.

*Avoid food cues.* The sights and smells of food are most
potent stimuli for overeating. Don't ever leave small "treats"
around. Keep food hidden behind cabinets. If possible, live
outside of olfactory and visual proximity to restaurants. Certainly do not watch TV with open cartons of cookies or
crackers.

*Embellish all acceptable foods.* Since the sight of food is a
potent *A* for eating, be creative with your salad dishes and
your cottage cheese specialties. Garnish them and make them
visually entertaining.

*Use smaller plates.* Overeating is often controlled by the
amount of available food, rather than the internal cues of
satiety. In particular, Americans often feel obliged to fill the
plate when serving. If you must, fill the plate, but a smaller
plate, and eat the whole portion. But why not simply break
the childish notion that you *must* finish your plate?

*Don't leave seconds on the table.* The physical proximity of
available food seconds is a strong enticement to overeat, particularly with pots and dishes that contain an apparently
unending amount of food. If you feel you must have seconds,

force yourself away from the table or the house first. These extra valuable seconds or minutes might give you time to reflect on whether you really want and need that extra food. Remind yourself of how you want to look and feel. You may also insist on making smaller dishes so that seconds are not available. The simple maxim that what isn't there can't be eaten should be applied wherever possible. As one of our wives suggested, "If you don't *make* cheesecake, you don't *eat* cheesecake." Unless, of course, you err by *buying* cheesecake.

*Avoid the kitchen area as much as possible.* The person who works about the kitchen is usually a confirmed nibbler. Enlist your family's help in your cause. Explain how important your weight control is, for appearance and health reasons. Enlist their help in cooking and washing dishes. Exchange these for other duties about the house, in territory less dangerous for you. Avoid walking through the kitchen, and always eat from a plate—not from a food container.

### STEP 3: USE *B*'s THAT COMPETE WITH EATING
### (BUILD *A*→NEW *B* CONNECTIONS)

Habits can be weakened by pairing a new *B* with the habit-related *A*'s. Use your snacking diary to determine the potent *A*'s for problem eating, such as TV watching or feeling angry or depressed. If these *A*'s can't be avoided or removed, then consider possible competing *B*'s that are incompatible with eating to take the place of eating. The following are examples:

| STIMULUS CONDITION (*A*) | COMPETING RESPONSE (new *B*) |
|---|---|
| TV viewing | Use exercise, gum chewing, loving a loved one, or progressive self-relaxation to interrupt the otherwise automatic eating chain. |
| Feeling angry | Avoid the kitchen, take a walk, think things out, or write down your feelings instead of eating. |
| Feeling depressed | Don't use food as a way of soothing your depression—it only winds up compounding it in the end. When feeling depressed, call |

up a friend, write down your feelings, go see a movie, or do something enjoyable. Attempt to find reinforcers elsewhere than in the kitchen. If the problem persists, contact a mental health professional and do something about your depression.

Routine use of these competing responses in such situations should reduce the likelihood of automatic food eating.

## STRATEGY 5: Avoid Deprivation

Stuart and Davis suggest that there are three types of deprivation conditions that are linked to problem eating. The first is food deprivation, the frequent use of meal skipping by the dieter. This tactic often backfires by inducing overindulgence at the next meal. *Rule 1:* Plan meals for particular times and eat every planned meal.

Second is energy deprivation. Overeating is often related to sleep deprivation and fatigue. *Rule 2:* Avoid fatigue-related overeating; maintain a regular sleeping pattern.

Third, overeating often results from boredom. *Rule 3:* Structure your time to engage in novel activities to reduce eating brought about by boredom. Don't use food to structure periods of boredom. Buy yourself a datebook and begin to fill it in with planned, nonfood-related activities. Become "involved." Do things. Avoid afternoon TV snacking. Join a midday or weekend exercise club. Play tennis. Become involved in volunteer or civic activities. Find a weight-reducing partner and do things together. Keep each other from temptation. Plan to be out of the house before meals, when you're usually most hungry. Leave housework, especially kitchenwork, for after meals.

## STRATEGY 6: Break Down Automatic Eating Habits

With the American emphasis on speed, fast eating has become an American ritual. Break down the habit of food shoveling. Attend to the acts involved in eating itself. Many overweight people eat more rapidly than normal-weight people, and it may take fifteen minutes or longer after the start of a meal before the filling effects of the food begin to be felt.[29]

In a novel experiment, Pennsylvania State University researchers[30] investigated the eating behavior of obese and nonobese people in a fast-food restaurant. Results showed that obese eaters took more bites, but chewed their food *less thoroughly* and *more quickly* than nonobese eaters. Follow these strategies to slow down the pace of eating and avoid gorging[31]:

1. Take smaller bites. Chew more thoroughly and slowly.
2. Chew and swallow all food before taking more.
3. Put down your utensils after every bite. This will help you to chew at a leisurely pace.
4. Slow down your eating pace through social conversation. And don't talk with food in your mouth. Take a while between bites.
5. Pay attention to the taste and texture of each bite. Each bite should be enjoyed, not simply passed on to make room for the next.
6. Take a short break from eating during the meal. Allow your body to begin to recognize the presence of food already consumed. When you return to eating, ask yourself if you *really* need to finish everything on your plate. Leave a portion to be enjoyed as a snack later on.

## ADDITIONAL EATING STRATEGIES

- Do not loosen your belt during or following a meal. If you've eaten too much, allow yourself to feel the consequences.
- Program your snacks. Haphazard snacking must be avoided. Don't become a nibbler who eats like a mindless robot. Schedule your snacks as well as your meals, and stick to your schedule. At first you might schedule snacks at one-hour intervals. Set yourself a goal of increasing this interval week by week, and reward yourself for progress toward your goal.

# STRATEGY 7: Program a Positive Weight-control Attitude

Use the Premack principle, explained in Chapter 7, to increase your motivation to maintain proper eating habits. Psychologist Lloyd Homme[32] has suggested writing motivating statements on index cards, one per card, which can become required reading *before* you engage in a high-frequency activity. Make these harsh statements. *The harder they hit, the more calories will fall.* Examples:

1. I feel sick when I see myself without clothes.
2. This extra weight means I'll never have any dates.
3. I can see that look in John's face when he looks at me.
4. A minute on the lips, a lifetime on the hips.

In addition to these anti-eating statements, construct producing statements, such as:

1. Each day I'm good I grow thinner and more attractive.
2. Look out, world! I'm no longer going to be an ugly duckling!
3. Everyone will be so proud of me when I shed those pounds.

High-frequency activities can range from brushing your teeth to TV watching, from going out of the house to reading. Select one. Then *each time* you are about to engage in this activity, first read to yourself one anti-eating and then one producing statement. These motivating statements will thus become part of your daily routine. As they begin to "sink in," your attitude toward permanent weight control should improve. Alternate the various statements and try to picture vividly the content of each statement. Continue to invent new statements to suit your own needs.

# STRATEGY 8: Imagine Successful Confrontations with the Devil

This technique prepares you to resist temptation by having you imagine successful confrontations with problem foods.

The method is based on the covert reinforcement technique originated by Professor Joseph Cautela of Boston College and adapted By Drs. Beatrice Manno and Albert Marston of the University of Southern California.[33]

Close your eyes. Imagine a highly desirable food. You're drawn to it. Before you know it, you're reaching for it. Just as you bring it to your mouth, you put it down. You imagine yourself saying, "I don't want it, I don't need it." You imagine yourself filled with pride, beaming at your accomplishment at resisting temptation. You're feeling wonderful inside. Imagine friends and family around you, patting you on the back. That special someone says, "I knew you could do it."

Use this imagination technique several times daily, changing the scene elements to include various problem foods. Also, vary the content to include each of the behavioral steps in the eating chain:

1. thinking of eating that problem food
2. seeing the food and feeling tempted
3. reaching for the food
4. putting the food in your mouth
5. beginning to eat the food

As you imagine each of the above behaviors, stop yourself in imagination. Imagine yourself rejecting the food, breaking the chain right there. Imagine feeling proud and wonderful. Imagine getting on that scale and hitting that ideal weight. Pour the imagined good $C$'s on! You may find it helpful to work backward in the eating chain over several weeks, starting with throwing the partially eaten food away (No. 5) and continuing backward until you vividly imagine rejecting the very thought of eating the problem food (No. 1). Repeat each scene as many times as you find helpful to reinforce the imagined good $B \rightarrow$ imagined good $C$ connection.

We have said that thinking about something is next door to doing it. Likewise, imagination is your private screening room for future public roles. Rehearsing rejection of inappropriate eating in imaginaton will help you to prepare for resisting problem foods in daily life. Tie these imaginings to daily life situations. Imagine that problem food facing you in the cafeteria food line, or when you visit your in-laws.

Use the following techniques to help you break the eating chain in daily life whenever you face the devil disguised as banana cake, pizza, and so on.

## STRATEGY 9: Resist Inappropriate Foods by Unhooking the Eating Chain

### LENGTHENING THE EATING CHAIN

The invention of the refrigerator-freezer made food gathering and preparing an almost effortless enterprise. No longer must you trudge down to the local store for a treat of ice cream or baked goods. Food processors delight in making convenience foods, such as packaged meat patties, TV dinners, or instant anythings. Our instant-oriented culture has created a monster: the consumer who can reach into his refrigerator and in a flash produce all kinds of tempting and calorie-laden treats.

To breakdown overeating habits, begin to prolong the problem-eating chain. Stretch out your food preparation. Before you make yourself an unplanned snack, set the kitchen timer for ten minutes—and wait it out. During this time, ask yourself if you really need that extra something. Give yourself time to engage in a response that is incompatible with eating, like taking a walk, showering, or making love. Even as you approach the refrigerator, you can stop yourself. Pause. Reflect on what you're doing. Is it really necessary? If you continue and begin to prepare the "illegal" snack, stop! Pause. Reflect. If you can prolong or interrupt the chain of behaviors that make up problem eating, you will be succeeding in breaking down automatic overeating habits. Even if you begin to eat, throw most of the portion out. *Better out than in.* And suffer the self-indignation of wasting food and money. By making the preparing of problem foods more effortful, they will begin to lose some of their compelling positive value. *Problem eating becomes work.*

If you do wind up eating, eat slowly, take breaks, chew thoroughly, and put down your utensils after each bite. And ask yourself: Is this really necessary?

### THE MAGIC OF PHOTOGRAPHY

Dr. Mary Harris[34] of Stanford University suggests that you look at an unattractive picture of your "fat self" in a bathing suit, the *you* you hate people to see, whenever you are tempted by inappropriate foods. Ask yourself: Does this *have* to be me?

## MOTIVATING STATEMENTS TO THE RESCUE!

Use your anti-eating and proreducing statements whenever tempted by "cookie fever" or "pasta panic." Remember that if you can interrupt or prolong the usual eating chain, you should be able to weaken improper eating habits.

You're walking through the cafeteria lunch line and suddenly spot that piece of chocolate cake seemingly waiting just for you. Merely looking at it seems to add calories. You're about to reach for it. But wait! You reach for your index cards instead. You read several of the motivating statements, first the anti-eating and then the proreducing statements. You've interrupted the eating chain, even temporarily, and brought the delayed consequences of overindulgence and self-discipline to the foreground. You're able to walk right by. As you do, reward yourself. Make a note that you'll buy a small gift for yourself or go to the movies tonight. You deserve it!

## THE BUG-IN-THE-EAR TECHNIQUE

A motivating statement may have greater impact if it is played back on a tape recorder rather than simply read. Have a tape machine readily available at home and/or at the office to play back during those ever-occurring problem-eating situations. Record direct instructions to resist, with further elaboration on the miseries of excess fat and the future joys of thinning down. Use an earphone if privacy is desired. The following instructions are illustrative:

*Stop!* Hands off! You eat that and you'll never be thin, never be popular. Others will continue to ignore you. You'll despise yourself and make yourself sick when looking in the mirror. *Resist!* You can do it! In no time, you'll be thinning down, becoming more attractive. You'll feel more youthful, with-it. Others will take notice of you. You'll look great in new clothes. Come on now, do something else rather than eat, and let the temptation pass. Take a deep breath and tell yourself to relax as you let the breath out. Now go do something incompatible with eating, like going for a walk or a drive, or exercising. Good going!

You may find it helpful to have that special someone you wish to please record the instructions.

We recognize the initial difficulties you'll have in learning to resist temptation. From the sight of the forbidden food, to reaching for it, picking it up, and bringing it to your mouth, this chain of behaviors has usually occurred so fluidly that you're seldom conscious of every step. These chain-breaking techniques will help you to unhook the problem-eating chain by making you more conscious of far-off goals and problems *now*. Each time you resist a forbidden food, pat yourself on the back, or reward yourself with a small gift or favored activity. By rewarding yourself contingently upon resisting temptation, the habits of resistance should strengthen. You may never pass by a piece of cake without a hint of desire, but you *can* learn to look and not touch—and to feel great about yourself as you do.

## Strategy 10: Oh, Boy, Am I Hungry! (Changing the Meaning of an $A$ in the $A \rightarrow B$ Connection)

The BT way to weight control is intended to produce gradual weight loss through the unlearning of self-defeating eating habits. Since the weekly weight goals are modest, feelings of hunger should be minimized. Yet, what can you do when hunger does strike? Dr. David Doty suggests that feeling hungry can be thought of as a signal that you are winning! Feeling hungry does not have to lead to panicky eating.

When you feel hungry internally, it means generally that you are in the process of losing weight, of using excess stored calories. Your hunger feelings are signaling that you can resist temptation with each passing minute. When you begin to feel hungry, say to yourself, "I'll take care of that in a few minutes, not just yet." Then divert your attention and continue with your previous activity. Over time, you will lose that sense of urgency when hunger strikes and be better able to exercise self-control.

## Strategy 11: Keeping It Off!

Proper weight maintenance is a lifelong occupation. Give away or alter all "fat" clothing so that there is no clothing available if you should begin to get heavy again. Or leave only the most unattractive fat outfits. When altering clothing, have excess material cut off rather than kept at the inside of the seam so that the alteration process is irreversible. Refuse to buy any larger-sized clothing if you begin to gain weight. Wear the tight clothing, feel the discomfort, look at yourself in the mirror, focus on those bulges, and go back to the BT program.

Don't be afraid to reinstate any or all parts of the BT program periodically to maintain your desired weight. Periodic booster sessions are most useful in regulating lasting weight control.

## WEIGHT CONTROL:
## A CONCLUDING NOTE

The BT approach to weight control is not a quicky device for shedding a few pounds. We have advocated no special diets or reducing devices. The worst mistake would be to use these *behavior-change* strategies for a few weeks, lose some weight, and then go back to the "real you." Soon enough, your weight would return to its original level and you would feel more disgusted as you conclude that this *new* approach failed like all the others. Adopt parts of the program permanently, particularly the BT strategies for marketing, exercise, slowing the eating pace, redesigning the stimulus environment, and chain-breaking to unhook problem eating chains, within your usual day-to-day eating habits to maintain lasting weight loss. Long-term success requires a commitment to practicing these new behaviors long enough and convincingly enough so that they become part of a different, more desirable, *real* you.

# 9

# BT STRATEGIES FOR KICKING THE CIGARETTE HABIT

"Doc, I want to quit, but I don't know how." Regardless of how long or how much you've smoked, or how often you've tried to quit, you can *learn* to become a nonsmoker. Numerous BT strategies have proven valuable to smokers in their attempts to stop smoking.

## A Deeply Ingrained Habit

Most confirmed smokers would testify that cigarette smoking is a most intransigent habit. It becomes more ingrained every day we smoke and becomes associated with thousands of activities. Some even smoke in their bathtub. If the puff is taken to be the crucial unit for reinforcement of the habit, a two-pack-a-day habit would result in approximately 146,000 opportunities for reinforcement or puffs per year![1]

The BT treatment of smoking, like other self-control programs, focuses on the *A*ntecedents and reinforcement *C*onsequences of the smoking act. In this chapter, you will learn to help yourself beat the habit by arranging your environment to weaken traditional smoking patterns and build habits of abstinence.

# Smoking and Cognitive Dissonance Theory

Though it has been estimated that two hundred thousand to three hundred thousand deaths per year occur prematurely because of cigarette smoking,[2] approximately one third of all adult Americans continue to smoke. Why, then, do so many people continue such self-destructive behavior?

Although most smokers would verbally admit that smoking is physically harmful, their continued smoking often reflects the implicit belief that *they* will not be one of the unfortunate. The attitude that "It's the other guy" who will be harmed by smoking is a popular protective delusion.

Cognitive dissonance theory, formulated by psychologist Leon Festinger of Harvard University,[3] suggests that people experience mental discomfort or dissonance when they hold two conflicting beliefs, or when their actions don't agree with their beliefs. The smoker is a case in point. Many smokers would agree that smoking is linked to lung cancer. Yet they continue to smoke. Certainly, the smoker doesn't wish to develop cancer, but his actions belie his beliefs. Cognitive dissonance theory suggests that when beliefs and actions are incompatible, the person will attempt to reduce the resultant dissonance or discomfort by changing either the actions or the beliefs to restore compatibility. Thus the smoker may decide to become an ex-smoker, or he may deny that smoking will harm *him*. How often have you heard the smoker say, "Look, I could stop smoking today and be run over by a truck tomorrow." Should he continue smoking, he may use the uncanny human capacity for self-distortion to reduce dissonance by changing beliefs to speculation, facts to fiction.

## AN EXAMPLE OF SELF-DELUSION

Drs. Lawrence Pervin and Raymond Yatko of Princeton University[4] found that while smokers and nonsmokers had similar knowledge about the relationship between smoking and lung cancer, the smokers tended to believe in their personal invulnerability. These smokers reduced dissonance by believing that their own smoking was at a "safe level" or that a cure for cancer would likely be found before they would be affected. The behavior of smoking remained the same, but personal beliefs were changed or distorted.

*What about you?* If you are a confirmed smoker, think of your own attempts to reduce cognitive dissonance. Some of the more common examples we have heard include, "I want to live fully while I'm young," "Cancer doesn't run in my family," or "The odds are on my side." An even more common rationalization is, "I can't help it, I just can't quit." Since this person believes in his own helplessness, dissonance is reduced. He deludes himself into thinking he has done all he can.

## ASSORTED ANGELS OF MERCY

Children are often taught that there are protective benevolent figures watching over them, like the good fairy, Santa Claus, or protective angels. As adults, we often incorporate these myths and believe implicitly, though we'd never admit it, that terrible and horrible things, such as cancer, can't happen to people like us who lead righteous lives. Ah, wouldn't that be nice?

This chapter is intended for the smoker who is no longer deluding himself or herself about the need to quit smoking: the smoker who would like to reduce dissonance by "extinguishing" his smoking and not his life or his rationality.

# Expectations: The Hidden Factor

People who expect to fail often wind up failing. This phenomenon is referred to as a self-fulfilling prophecy, which you read about with respect to sleep and sex problems earlier. One of the most significant factors in the success of antismoking programs is the presence or absence of a positive attitude. You must be able to say strongly, out loud, *and with others present:* "I will quit smoking, I *must* quit smoking." If not, it is unlikely you can make the commitment to breaking the habit. We congratulate you if you are ready to make this public commitment, and we invite you to proceed.

# Consult Your Physician

To increase your present level of commitment to quitting, consult your family physician to determine the effects of continued smoking on your health. Have your doctor discuss the effects on *your* health, not merely anonymous statistics. Discuss the connection between your smoking and your frequent respiratory symptoms: cough, sinus problems, phlegm, and shortness of breath. Many smokers avoid physical examinations to tune out knowledge of the harmful effects of their smoking. Don't fall victim to this self-defeating ploy.

## Should You Quit Cold Turkey or Gradually?

Opinion is generally mixed on whether it is more effective to quit all at once or to taper off. The BT strategies described in this chapter were, for the most part, designed for gradual reduction of the cigarette habit.

We find that a gradual method has advantages for many people. The cold-turkey or "sink or swim" method required such a dramatic change in behavior that a high failure rate is not unlikely. Frequent failure may compound a sense of weakness and futility. A gradual method allows for a series of small successes along the way. Each successive step is a small increase from the last, so that the probability of succeeding at each step is maximized. By using a gradual BT technique, bodily withdrawal effects are also minimized as you gradually adjust to lowered nicotine levels. Also, as with crash dieting, going cold turkey does not give you the opportunity to change the habit-maintaining Antecedents and Consequences of smoking. Gradual reduction allows you to reprogram the environmental context of the Behavior to strengthen long-term abstinence—that is, to change the ABC's of smoking in a systematic way.

Yet many people have found the cold-turkey method to suit them best. The challenge of man or woman against cigarette, winner take all, one final contest, appeals to our competitiveness. At present there are no precise methods for determining what types of smokers are best suited for quiting all at once or gradually. We suggest that you decide which method makes the most sense for you. If you do go cold turkey, and it doesn't work out, try the gradual-reduction method. You have nothing to gain but your health!

## Going Cold Turkey

If you decide to quit cold turkey, consider the following suggestions:

- Pick a time when your motivation is ripe for quitting, such as during an illness, or before or after a physical exam. Also, start in the morning, when you have already gone eight hours without a cigarette.
- Change your stimulus environment (*A*) during withdrawal, if possible. Take a vacation. Take a cabin in the woods. Get away from it all. And don't bring cigarettes with you.
- Moving time is also a good time to try for total abstinence, since the stimuli (*A*'s) in your new home have not been previously associated with your habit smoking. Do not permit ashtrays and other smoking paraphernalia in your new home. Make your new home an *A* for nonsmoking by not allowing the habit to develop there.
- Since all home furnishings act as subtle *A*'s for past smoking habits, change the furnishings or rearrange them if possible.
- Get rid of all stimulus trappings of cigarettes: cigarette packs, matches, ashtrays. Ask your guests not to smoke, or to bring their own paraphernalia. Never buy cigarettes, not even to test your willpower. Never carry matches or a lighter.
- Several weeks before withdrawal, begin to change your attitudes about smoking by using the directed-imagining techniques described later in the chapter.
- Structure your time to engage in activities that have been associated with nonsmoking, such as going to the movies, concerts, shows, evening courses, reading in the library, or visiting nonsmoking friends.
- Avoid people who smoke like the plague—a rather apt analogy. If your spouse smokes, try quitting together, or take separate vacations.
- Keep substitutes such as gum and mints easily available.
- Try to avoid shopping in stores where you previously purchased cigarettes.
- Tell friends and family members that you've quit smoking. The anticipation of loss of face if you resume smoking may be a strong incentive not to smoke.
- Use competing *B*'s to smoking, like progressive self-relaxation (PSR), exercise, gum chewing, or drinking glasses of water, whenever you feel the urge to smoke.
- Remind yourself repeatedly that the first few days of withdrawal are the hardest—your task will become progressively easier.

- Learn to use assertive statements to ask others who are smoking to excuse themselves from the room, or excuse yourself. Learn to refuse offers of cigarettes graciously.
- Read the rest of the chapter. You may find additional strategies that apply to your situation.

# GRADUAL SMOKING REDUCTION: PINPOINTING THE MOTIVE

## What Makes You Smoke?

The first step in unlearning the smoking habit is to investigate the *A*ntecedents that pattern your smoking behavior. The pioneering work of Dr. Daniel Horn of the National Clearinghouse of Smoking and Health[5] and social psychologists Bernard Mausner and Ellen Platt,[6] and our own work in the clinic, have helped us to identify several of the most common patterns.

### THE RITES OF PASSAGE

Cigarette smoking has long held the value of a puberty rite in our culture, an act that marks the transition, at least symbolically, from childhood to adulthood. Drs. Mausner and Platt have noted that smoking is associated by many people with freedom, daring, assertiveness, and attractiveness. Young smokers claim to want to be "with it," and smoking is believed to legitimize their claim to maturity.

We all know about the "virility" of the "Marlboro Man." In one research study, Dr. J. M. Weir[7] showed a group of students photographs of people with and without cigarettes. Compared to the male nonsmoker in the photographs, the smoker was seen as more adventurous, rugged, daring, and individualistic. He was also seen as less awkward, timid, and shy. Thus the social connotations of inhaling these burning plants may determine the decision to smoke or not.

### SELF-IDENTITY

It is often remarked that a poor man is really a rich man temporarily inconvenienced. The way in which we define ourselves is a determining factor in how we behave and the roles we enact. In your mind's eye, do you envision yourself with a cigarette in hand? Is it difficult to see yourself as a non-smoker?

Dr. Mausner[8] of Beaver College invited a group of college women who were interested in stopping smoking to attend an antismoking clinic. Much of the talk during clinic sessions was about the use of cigarette smoking as a device by which the students could develop and refine an image of themselves as bright, sophisticated, career-oriented young women. The clinic's almost total failure in inducing these young women to quit was reportedly due, in part, to the women's inability to redefine themselves as nonsmokers, since being a smoker was associated with all these desirable personal qualities.

## SMOKING FOR THE SAKE OF SMOKING

Functional autonomy is a term invented by Harvard psychologist Gordon Allport[9] to describe behavior that continues despite the fact that the original *A*ntecedents and *C*onsequences that initially shaped the behavior are no longer present. Functional autonomy is the psychological equivalent to the princilpe of inertia. The rich man who no longer needs to work continues to get to the office by eight. The retired policeman repetitively walks his old beat. This is functionally autonomous behavior. This principle is equally applicable to cigarette smoking. Although the "desirable" social factors such as "being with it" or being mature that are often involved in initiating our smoking may be long gone, our continued smoking may represent a functionally autonomous habit—a *B* now independent of the *A*'s and *C*'s.

For many people, the original social conditions that initiated their smoking are lost or forgotten. All that remains is the habit. There may be, in fact, little or no pleasure in smoking.

The habitual smoker may smoke almost without realizing it. We shall see that the first step in eliminating habit smoking is to increase the habit smoker's awareness of his smoking behavior.

## THE SOCIAL EMBRACE

Traditionally, cigarette smoking has been a means for creating a social atmosphere of warmth and sharing. From Gary Cooper offering cigarettes to men in the trenches, to Cary Grant lighting Joan Fontaine's cigarette, smoking sets the stage for social relations. Smoking thus becomes an *A*ntecedent for increased social *B*ehaviors. The antismoking advertising campaign ("Do you mind if I smoke?" "Yes, I do.") attempts to counter the belief that smoking should be a social pastime.

## SOCIAL PRESSURE

In a survey conducted by Lieberman Research, Inc.[10] for the American Cancer Society in 1969, it was found that 56 per cent of smokers but only 19 per cent of nonsmokers reported that most of their friends were smokers. Drs. Jerome Schwartz and Mildred Dubitsky[11] found that male smokers who successfully stopped smoking in a smoking cessation program were less likely to have wives who smoked and less likely to "smoke with a loved one" than males who continued smoking. It stands to reason that an antismoking program will be more successful if social pressure can be mobilized to reduce rather than to encourage smoking.

## PLEASURE AND CRAVING

Smoking pleasure is usually identified by smokers with taste, aroma, feelings of fullness in the mouth, sensations of smoke drawn through their respiratory system, and the tactile sensations of holding and manipulating a cigarette. Smoking has also been described as a source of stimulation, reportedly used by many people to provide a "quick lift." It is clear that the smoking habit may be maintained by an imbalance between the *immediate* pleasurable *C*'s of smoking and the *delayed* adverse-health *C*'s. Our BT strategy will involve redressing this imbalance.

It is often difficult to determine whether smokers light up to obtain pleasure directly or to avoid the displeasure of not smoking. Psychologists Theodore Sarbin and Larry Nucci[12] of the University of California at Santa Cruz noted that breaking the habit might be facilitated if the smoker could look upon displeasurable withdrawal effects as symptoms of a temporary and voluntary sickness—rather than as stimuli for renewed smoking. We shall consider this point further.

## STIMULUS CONTROL: THE
## $A \rightarrow B$ CONNECTION

Behavior (*B*) can be conditioned to certain environmental stimuli (*A*'s) if the behavior occurs routinely in the presence of such antecedents. This repetitive pairing of *A*'s and *B*'s allows us to exercise quick decision-making in certain situations, like stopping for a red light. However, undesirable behavior can be conditioned as well. Do you smoke (B) routinely while watching TV (A)? Does seeing others smoking (A) generate thoughts of smoking yourself (B)? Many stimuli in our environment have become A's for smoking, so that we almost reflexively begin to think of smoking (B) or reach for a cigarette when faced with these situations. Breaking the A→B connection will be discussed later.

## ANXIETY RELIEF

A college student may recognize a group of students awaiting an exam by the number of cigarettes present. Many smokers routinely attempt to allay feelings of anxiety through smoking. We've even heard, perhaps tongue-in-cheek, of a fellow who lit up to reduce his anxiety after he was told by his doctor that he had lung cancer. There exist many more constructive methods for reducing anxiety. Note the chapter on how to relax without tranquilizers.

# Self-recording to Discover the Cues for Smoking

This list of antecedent factors involved in smoking, though certainly not exhaustive, does suggest that smoking represents a combination of physiological, social, and psychological events. Your first task in the antismoking program is to attempt to identify the antecedent conditions (A's) that pattern your smoking habit (B's).

*Use a diary to record each and every cigarette smoked during a two-week baseline period.* Discover which smoking pattern best describes your habit. Are you a pleasure smoker? An anxiety-relief smoker? Your smoking record will give you clues to discover your pattern.

Have patience and record the following information for each cigarette smoked: *where you were, the time of day, whom you were with, what you were doing, and your mood.* In addition, code each cigarette in terms of the antecedent reasons or conditions for smoking described above. The following guide, based on prior research[13] and our clinical experience, summarizes these A's for smoking.

| Smoking Type | Examples |
| --- | --- |
| Habit (H) | "I just found myself doing it." <br> "The first thing I knew the cigarette was in my mouth." |
| Others doing it (ODI) | "Everyone in class was smoking." <br> "Everyone had a drink in one hand and a cigarette in the other." <br> "It was the social thing to do." |
| Pleasure (P) | "I looked forward to that after-dinner cigarette." <br> "I really like lighting up on a nice spring day." <br> "I liked holding the cigarette and having the smoke in my mouth." |
| Craving (C) | "I began to feel itchy for a cigarette." <br> "I just couldn't wait to get a cigarette." |
| Anxiety relief (AR) | "I got uptight, and the cigarette helped me relax." <br> "When I get upset, I reach for a cigarette." |
| Self-definition (SD) | "I wanted them to think I was grown up." <br> "Smoking makes me feel sophisticated." <br> "Everyone expects me to have a cigarette in my mouth." <br> "Cigarettes are part of me; I wouldn't go anywhere without them." |
| Stimulation (S) | "I needed a quick lift." |
| Stimulus control (SC) | "I always smoke when studying." <br> "Smoking and drinking just go together." <br> "At these business meetings I always wind up smoking." |

## GATHERING BASELINE DATA

Keep a smoking diary for two weeks. Record the what, when, where, and so on of each cigarette smoked. Also, code each cigarette in terms of the above categories, using the category initials. Since these categories are not exhaustive, you may wish to invent additional categories. If several categories apply to a particular cigarette, list them all. Discover the patterns that typify your smoking behavior. After several weeks you will be able to answer these questions: Are you generally an AR smoker? An ODI smoker? Or a P smoker? Do you generally smoke alone? Do you usually smoke during times when others are smoking? Do you smoke more during certain activities? Do you smoke more in the morning, afternoon, or evening?

Do not try to change your usual behavior in any way during the baseline recording—except for keeping records. Use the diary to record your smoking patterns during the baseline period only, but continue to record daily smoking frequency throughout the duration of the program. To record smoking frequency conveniently after the baseline period, many people note the number of cigarettes in the pack or packs at the start of the day and then at day's end. Each night chart the number of cigarettes smoked during the day on a frequency chart such as this:

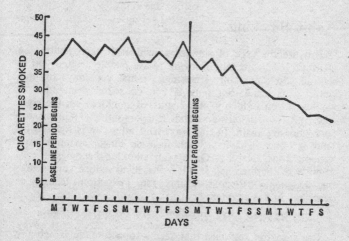

Continuous recording of smoking frequency is a critical element in the BT program, and provides its own reinforcement as you watch your daily rate descend. In fact, in one study at Wichita State University,[14] researchers found that one group of students who merely kept records of their smoking wound up decreasing their smoking rate!

# GRADUAL SMOKING REDUCTION: PROBLEMS AND SOLUTIONS

The following suggestions for changing the *ABC*'s of smoking are organized according to the particular types of smokers described above. Look at your baseline record. Which pattern or patterns best describe your habit? No one pattern fits each smoker exclusively. Therefore, all of the following suggestions should be helpful to you in designing your BT antismoking program.

To start breaking the cigarette habit, read through the chapter and design a program that you feel fits your particular situation. Don't be afraid to revise the program if the need arises. Incorporate the antismoking program in your daily routine. Structure a program that works for you!

## Habit Smoking

If you are the type of smoker who doesn't even realize the cigarette is in your mouth, begin to ask people around you to remind you that you're smoking. At first you may continue smoking as usual, but only if you consciously intended to smoke. If you suddenly "find" yourself smoking, put the cigarette out immediately and wait fifteen to thirty minutes before smoking again. In this way, your attention is focused on your smoking behavior. Smoking is no longer an automatic, "unconscious" activity. Once your smoking becomes a consciously deliberated act, it will be easier to reduce your smoking frequency through using the reduction techniques described in this chapter.

### TO BREAK THE HABIT, BREAK THE CHAIN

The smoking response that seems so automatic is actually composed of a series or chain of behaviors. If this chain can be prolonged or interrupted, the quantity of smoking may be reduced. Since smoking will become more effortful, it will lose some of its attractive value. *Each time* you find yourself reaching for a cigarette, ask yourself, "Is this one really necessary?" Remember, it's never too late to break the smoking chain until the cigarette is completely smoked. Even if you've started smoking, you can remove the cigarette and put it out!

The act of smoking a cigarette can be broken down into a chain of preliminary behaviors: (1) thinking of smoking; (2) reaching for the cigarette; (3) putting the cigarette in your mouth; (4) lighting the cigarette; and (5) inhaling the cigarette. Your antismoking BT strategy might be to interrupt the chain at each step. When you feel the "urge" to smoke, set the kitchen timer or a stopwatch for ten minutes. Don't reach for a cigarette until the time has expired. Use this time to reflect on whether you really need that cigarette. Give yourself time to engage in some competing response to smoking, like going for a walk or a drive without cigarettes, having something to eat, exercising, or doing progressive self-relaxation (PSR). Imagination at such times is a most useful distraction. For example, fantasize a romantic involvement with an attractive person who is nearby. If your attention can be diverted from your smoking "urge" by using a competing response, the temptation may pass more easily. Reward yourself if at the end of the ten-minute period you decide *not* to have that cigarette.

If you do reach for the cigarette, interrupt and prolong the chain further. Rather than having cigarettes and matches handy, put them in a remote place. Get one cigarette at a time only. Return to your original place. Hold the cigarette in your hand for several minutes before putting it in your mouth. Reflect. Is this cigarette really necessary? Then get up and get the match and return. Light the match, wait for it to burn down, and then light the cigarette. Wait several moments before inhaling. Put the cigarette in the ashtray between puffs. Even as you're smoking, ask yourself if it is really necessary and see if you can put it out, right then and there.

This chain-breaking technique illustrates how elongating a behavior chain can change an automatic series of effortless responses like smoking into a laborious, even frustrating task. Repetitive, habitual smoking becomes work and loses some of its attractiveness. "But I wouldn't enjoy smoking like that." We agree. We rest our case.

Begin to leave your cigarettes home for increasing amounts of time. Go shopping for one hour without cigarettes, then two hours, and so on. Don't carry change with you; this will deprive you of ammunition for vending machines. Leave your matches at home so that you will have to bother others for a light and earn an occasional frown or grunt (an ugly *C* for an unwanted *B*).

*The bug-in-the-ear technique.* To help you break the smoking chain in midstream, tape-record self-instructions to *Stop!* coupled with antismoking and proquitting statements. This brief tape would be played back, through an earphone if privacy is desired, whenever you feel tempted to smoke. The following instructions are suggestive:

*Stop that right there!* Catch yourself before it's too late! If you have that cigarette you'll be disgusted with yourself, you'll be letting yourself and your family down. You'll be drawing poisons into your lungs and making yourself emotionally and physically sick. Pause one moment and think. Think how proud you'll be to kick the habit. Remember that friend, you know, the one with the emphysema (or bronchitis). The one who smokes as much as you do. Do you want to turn out like that? How can you teach your children not to smoke when you do yourself? Shake off the temptation *now!* Go for a walk, take a drive, or reach for a fruit or glass of water instead. Do something else and let the temptation pass. Take a deep breath and tell yourself to relax on the outbreath. Now go do something else incompatible with smoking. Good going!

In summary, break down automatic smoking habits by:

1. attending to every cigarette smoked, so that smoking becomes a consciously deliberated act
2. attempting to elongate or interrupt the smoking chain
3. using competing responses to break the chain wherever possible

## Pleasure Smoking

Pleasure smokers must be sure that the immediate penalties (ugly *C*'s) for smoking outweigh the immediate benefits (unfortunate good *C*'s). Consider what would happen if you smoked in violation of the *No Smoking* sign on an airplane. Your steward or stewardess would yell at you and other passengers would frown and grunt disapproval (all ugly *C*'s). This would be especially ugly if you had wanted to ask the steward or stewardess for a drink during the flight. The pleasure of smoking would be reduced. One sanction, albeit extreme, against smoking was imposed in Turkey during the seventeenth century. The Turkish authorities prohibited the use of tobacco since it violated the laws of the Koran. A violator was subject to having his nose pierced, and the stem of his pipe passed through his nose. Then the violator was driven through town on a donkey.

How can you, a soon-to-be ex-smoker, arrange your environment to make the act of smoking socially as well as physically unhealthy? How can you provide ugly *C*'s? Consider the following ways to make smoking less pleasurable:

1. Adopt a low-tar, low-nicotine cigarette, particularly one with a difficult draw.
2. If part of your enjoyment comes from the physical sensation of fondling a cigarette, substitute worry beads or key chains. Many ex-smokers become pen chewers, which although socially distasteful, has not as yet been identified as carcinogenic.
3. Say to yourself each time you smoke, "I'm that much closer to lung cancer." Imagine the agonies of dying from cancer and undergoing fruitless operations.
4. Read the health message on the cigarette pack each time you smoke.

## DIRECTED IMAGERY

Imagine yourself smoking a "vomit cigarette."[15] Imagine growing progressively more nauseated. Elaborate the image. Visualize your lungs becoming blackened, filling with tar, your vessels clogged and heavy. Concentrate on the image not as a hypothetical event but as something actually happening to you *now*. Not to someone else, to *you!* Imagine becoming more disgusted with yourself for smoking again. The people around you, your family and friends, are disgusted with you. You see your young child playing with your cigarettes. Your child is going to take after you! You feel like filth. You feel you're going to throw up. Just then, imagine yourself throwing the cigarette down and breathing fresh air as if for the first time. You feel proud. Others congratulate you. You've kicked the habit! You're no longer a smoker, you're one of the lucky nonsmokers. You feel wonderful and proud. Everyone is so proud of you. Imagine your lungs getting clearer, your stamina returning, your doctor giving you a clean bill of health. Visualize walking through a pristine forest, being reborn.

Practice these directed imaginings, with your eyes closed, several times daily. Vary the content to include each of the behavioral steps in the smoking chain:

1. thinking of smoking
2. seeing a cigarette and feeling tempted to smoke
3. reaching for a cigarette
4. putting a cigarette in your mouth
5. lighting a cigarette
6. beginning to smoke a cigarette

As you imagine each of the above behaviors, switch quickly to imagining yourself becoming progressively more nauseous and feeling more disgusted with yourself. Then imagine rejecting the cigarette—breaking the chain right there, and feeling prouder, healthier, more self-satisfied. You may find it helpful to work backward in the smoking chain, in your imagination, over several weeks. Start with imagining yourself rejecting the cigarette after one or two puffs (No. 6) and continue backward in the chain until you vividly imagine rejecting even the thought of smoking (No. 1). Repeat each scene as many times as you find helpful to reinforce the imagined good *B*→imagined good *C* connection. And make sure to use the chain-breaking strategies described earlier to unhook the smoking chain in everyday situations.

Kicking the habit requires that you begin to view smoking in a new light: not as a harmless vice, but as a disgusting and corrupting habit that you reject as part of your personal identity. Although these imaginal exercises should be used several times daily to reorient your thinking about smoking, they are particularly useful as an additional chain-breaking technique to be used directly when you begin to feel the temptation to smoke.

Drs. Sarbin and Nucci suggest that your identity as a smoker must symbolically perish so that you can be reborn a nonsmoker. Your personal involvement in these directed imaginings should help prepare you for this conversion in real life.

## SELF-REWARD: A GOOD *B* DESERVES A GOOD *C*

The other side of the coin to making smoking less pleasurable is to increase the immediate benefits of cutting down by using a self-reward system.

*An open-ended self-reward system.* First, check your smoking-frequency chart to determine your average daily intake during the baseline period. During the first week of the active BT program, award yourself one point for each day you smoked one less cigarette than your average baseline rate, two points for two less, and so on. Make the earned points IOU's for tangible rewards or favored activities later on. Post daily records of points earned on the home refrigerator for other members of the family to see. Your stop-smoking task will be much easier if family members socially reinforce you for good performance via praise, approval, encouragement, and attention. They should also note poor performance in disapproving terms, though with implied encouragement, perhaps by saying, "Mary, yesterday was a terrible day, but we know you can do better today."

Establish a meaningful system for cashing in your earned points. You might decide that ten points earned during the week is worth a movie or a dinner out. Twenty points earned would be worth a more considerable prize. Remember that a self-reward system will only be effective if the rewards are contingent on the performance of the desired behavior. If these rewards occur naturally, and without regard to your smoking behavior, the system would be worthless for changing this behavior.

Make it progressively more demanding to earn rewards. The second week of the program, make each point earned equal a reduction of two cigarettes per day, the third week three, and so on. This way your reduction plan will not stagnate but will increasingly cut into your daily intake.

Consider giving money to charity as a self(less)-reward. Make out a check proportionate to the number of cigarettes reduced from your baseline rate during the preceding week. Make sure you reinforce your desired behavior with rewards (good *C*'s) that have meaning for *you*.

*A timetable self-reward system.* Rather than using an open-ended reward system, you might decide on a specific timetable for reducing your smoking rate. Self-rewards would then be contingent on meeting daily and/or weekly goals. The following system is illustrative:

GOAL: Reduce to five cigarettes daily
AVERAGE DAILY RATE DURING BASELINE: Fifteen cigarettes

| WEEK | WEEKLY GOAL |
|------|-------------|
| 1 | An average daily rate of fourteen or fewer cigarettes earns a five-dollar personal gift. |
| 2 | An average daily rate of thirteen or fewer cigarettes earns a ten-dollar personal gift, movie, or dinner out. |
| 3 | An average daily rate of ten or fewer cigarettes earns a twenty-dollar personal gift. |
| 4 | An average daily rate of five or fewer cigarettes earns a thirty-dollar personal gift. |

Use these four basic rules for shaping behavior toward your goal:

1. The first week's goal may be quite close to your baseline rate and the week-to-week steps small.
2. The initial weekly steps can be smaller than the latter steps.
3. As you approach your final goal, make your rewards larger and more compelling.
4. Progress each week toward your final goal. Don't get "stuck" on any one step, even if this means making steps quite small.

The weekly rewards must be contingent on meeting your cigarette quotas. If you routinely buy yourself gifts or treat yourself to favored activities, begin to tie your pleasures to your accomplishments. Withhold good $C$'s until you perform good $B$'s. If you didn't earn the weekly movie or dinner out, sit home on Saturday night and appreciate the unfortunate $C$'s of excess smoking.

To limit yourself to your daily cigarette quota, plan your next day's smoking schedule the night before. If your daily total calls for twenty cigarettes, you might decide to smoke one cigarette each hour between 9 A.M. and 5 P.M., and two each hour following until 11 P.M. To cut down further, begin to skip those hours during which you're usually least tempted to smoke. Structure those particularly dangerous hours, such as after work or after dinner, with smoking-competing activities: swimming, tennis, evening courses. To meet each week's goal, extend your smoking intervals accordingly—say, one cigarette every hour, then one every two hours, and so on.

When you reach your final goal, make the reinforcers harder to earn. Award yourself money or favored activities for *maintaining* that target level for two weeks straight, then three weeks, etc. Note that many people use a reward system like the timetable system to reduce smoking to a relatively low frequency rather than to attain complete abstinence. But there is no reason why you cannot contract with yourself to make the final week's reward contingent on complete abstinence. Read on to learn how to bridge the transition from low-frequency smoking to complete abstinence.

## ARE SELF-REWARDS CHILD'S PLAY?

Use your ingenuity to design a self-reward system that will effectively motivate you. Don't fall victim to the belief that these kinds of strategies are childish or just somehow beneath you. Self-reward systems merely concretize the most enviable practice of tying our pleasures to our accomplishments. Whenever you buy yourself a little something or treat yourself to dinner out for getting that report in on time or fixing the car, you're making use of self-reward strategies. In every sense, a self-reward strategy is a method for building effective self-discipline.

## RESPONSE COST: THE UNWANTED B→COSTLY C CONNECTION

Cancer, the potential ultimate response cost, is often too distant a possibility to be an effective smoking deterrent. A response-cost strategy, as explained in Chapter 7, can be an effective tool for reducing undesirable behaviors. *To create greater incentives for kicking the cigarette habit, use a response-cost strategy in tandem with a self-reward system.*

Begin by assessing yourself a fixed small amount, such as five cents, for each cigarette smoked. Don't just keep track of your assessments on paper. Have available a ready supply of change and assess yourself (an ugly *C* for an unwanted *B*) right on the spot, whenever you light a cigarette. At day's end, put the assessed money aside. Don't use it for any other purpose. Each week increase the assessment per cigarette. Every month, or perhaps every two weeks, make out a check for the total amount to one of your most hated organizations or political figures, or to your brother-in-law, or as a special tip to the newspaper boy or girl who never gets the paper there on time. Should you not trust yourself, allow a loved one to assess you each time he or she witnesses you lighting up. It's one way to help insure that your love will be lasting.

## The Premack Principle: Using Activities as *C*'s

The Premack principle has been used to help the smoker strengthen antismoking and proquitting attitudes.[16] To use the technique, first choose a high-frequency activity, such as using the bathroom, reading, or watching TV, as explained in Chapter 7. Then construct a list of five or ten antismoking statements, such as:

1. Smoking is a disgusting habit.
2. My smoking makes me feel sick about myself.
3. I'm that much closer to cancer by smoking each day.
4. I'm so ashamed that I can't or won't stop.
5. I feel terrible that the kids might pick up my habit.

Next, construct a list of five or ten proquitting statements, such as:

1. Each minute I don't smoke, my lungs grow clearer.
2. Food will taste so much better by not smoking.
3. Won't everyone be proud of me when I quit.
4. Quitting will put years on my life.
5. Good-bye cigarettes, good-bye cough, good-bye sore throat. . . .

Write each statement on an index card. Your task then is to use the high-frequency *B* that you select as a *C* for reading these antismoking and proquitting statements. The rule is to engage in the high-frequency *B* only *after* reading an antismoking and then a proquitting statement to yourself. These motivating statements will thus become part of your daily routine, each day strengthening your commitment to your stop-smoking program. Alternate the various statements, and invent new statements to avoid excessive repetition.

Avoid reading the statements in an automatic perfunctory

manner. Picture the content of the statement in your mind's eye, and elaborate the image. You might also find it useful to read several of these motivating statements when you feel the smoking "urge," to help you break the smoking chain right there.

The Premack principle can also be used in other ways. Select several high-frequency $B$'s, such as bathing, watching TV, or making yourself a snack. Then, before you engage in any of these activities, set a kitchen timer or a stopwatch for ten minutes. If you stop yourself from smoking during this ten-minute period, allow yourself to engage in the intended activity. If not, reset the timer and try again. Over time, increase the time interval to prolong periods of smoking abstinence. Set a schedule for increasing these time intervals. Progressively increase the time spent not smoking until it becomes more habitual not to smoke than to smoke.

## Anxiety Reduction

Does your smoking diary indicate that you use cigarettes to reduce anxiety, to take the edge off stress and tension? If so, study Chapters 2 and 3 to learn techniques for mastering anxiety and fears. Explore Chapter 5 to learn to relate more effectively with other people through assertiveness training, and without needing to build your self-confidence by smoking.

If today you have a test, a job interview, a new date, or any anxiety-arousing situation, exercise response prevention: Don't bring cigarettes with you. Use systematic self-desensitization at home beforehand, as explained in Chapter 3, to prepare for these fear-producing events. Use competing responses to smoking when faced with anxiety: PSR, taking a walk, breathing fresh air. Remember that the first few times you feel anxious or fearful and do not smoke are the most difficult, but that continued interruption should progressively weaken the anxiety $(A) \rightarrow$ smoking $(B)$ habit.

## Stimulus Control: Breaking the $A \rightarrow B$ Connection

The smoking habit often becomes conditioned to specific stimulus cues ($A$'s). By changing these cues, the habit can be weakened. Consult your smoking diary. Investigate when, where, with whom, while doing what, and in what mood you tend to smoke. For example, you may find that your smoking is concentrated during periods of study or reading. You may have convinced yourself that you can't possibly pick up a book without a cigarette in your other hand. It's time to uncouple these smoking connections.

## BUILD ADAPTIVE $A \to B$ CONNECTIONS

Begin to study for increasing amounts of time in a smoking-restricted area of the library. Reward yourself contingently for reading or studying in this smoke-free environment. At first, take smoking breaks in a lounge area some distance from your studying area. Then gradually extend the intervals between smoking breaks and use response cost and self-reward to motivate you to increase these nonsmoking intervals. As the nonsmoking intervals are extended, begin to use response prevention: Don't bring cigarettes with you every third day, then every other day, then every day. Remember to remove all stimulus cues ($A$'s) for smoking while studying. Remove from sight all matches, ashtrays, and cigarette packs. Study where others do not smoke.

## REMOVE POTENT SMOKING $A$'s AND DEVELOP COMPETING $B$'s

If your smoking is often associated with studying, begin your smoking-reduction program during a respite from study, such as a vacation (remove the $A$). When you return from vacation, interrupt the smoking habit through using $B$'s incompatible with smoking if you feel the smoking urge. Chew gum, drink glasses of water, suck candy or mints, take exercise or relaxation breaks. In addition, the American Cancer Society suggests that vigorous exercise is very helpful in relieving the immediate feelings of irritation many smokers feel when they miss a cigarette.[17] Or use progressive self-relaxation (PSR) as a competing, alternative $B$ in situations usually associated with smoking, or whenever smoking temptation begins to build.

To use PSR effectively, first develop relaxation skills as explained in Chapter 2. You should eventually be able to feel more relaxed by taking several deep breaths and saying "relax" softly on each outbreath. When you feel the smoking urge, use PSR to relax, then do something else—and leave your cigarettes behind.

A most effective competing response to cigarette smoking is pipe or cigar smoking. Though pipe and cigar smokers who don't inhale avoid contaminating their lungs with tars and nicotine, they do risk a higher incidence of mouth and lip cancers. Still, many smokers find that pipe or cigar smoking is an effective *halfway* stop between cigarette smoking and nonsmoking. Within several weeks or months, they find they are less "attached" to their pipes or cigars than they were to their cigarettes and are more easily able to give up smoking altogether. Others continue with the apparently less harmful habit.

Use your smoking diary to pinpoint particular trouble spots. Many smokers feel the urge to smoke most strongly following a meal. If so, use such competing *B*'s as taking in some fresh air or walking the dog following each meal to break this $A \rightarrow B$ connection.

Do you smoke when feeling angry or depressed? Learn to break these connections by writing down your thoughts or feelings, talking it out with someone, or going to a movie instead of smoking. If your smoking is associated with seeing others smoke, avoid the company of smokers during your withdrawal program. Don't allow others to smoke in your home. Remember that the sights and smells of smoking are powerful *A*'s to induce you to smoke. If your diary suggests that you usually smoke when alone, plan to spend more time with others. In the beginning stages of the program, spend more time in places where you usually don't smoke, such as movie theaters, museums, libraries, or even department stores. *Make your stimulus environment work for you in helping you to kick the habit.*

## RESTRICTING THE STIMULUS FIELD: USE OF THE "SMOKING CHAIR"

How does a behavioral psychologist help his wife stop smoking? One psychologist, J. Dennis Nolar,[18] used the principle of restricting the stimulus field (*A*'s) for smoking to best advantage. The treatment plan allowed Mrs. Nolan to smoke freely, but *only* if she smoked while sitting in one particular chair, a designated "smoking chair." The chair was placed so that watching TV or conversing with others was difficult. While smoking, Mrs. Nolan was not allowed to read, and no one was allowed to approach or speak to her. Thus smoking became a "pure" experience, unattached to other reinforcing events. This treatment plan, faithfully executed, resulted in a daily cigarette intake of twelve, or less than half her original intake. When the "smoking chair" was moved to an unused part of the cellar, her smoking rate dropped at first to five cigarettes daily, and then leveled off at approximately seven daily. Within several weeks, Mrs. Nolan became disgusted with her inability to stop smoking completely, whereupon she promptly quit altogether.

At the time of Dr. Nolan's writing, his wife had been free of cigarettes for six months. Since, prior to the behavioral program, Mrs. Nolan had tried unsuccessfully many times to quit voluntarily, we may presume that the program acted as a catalyst to weaken the habit sufficiently to make voluntary quitting less difficult. Dr. Nolan's treatment approach underscores the flexibility of behavioral strategies. Once you've learned the *ABC*'s of behavior, you can use your ingenuity to tailor innovative programs to your own special needs.

Most behavioral treatments of smoking rely on the belief that smoking cessation will be facilitated if the smoking response can be made more aversive than not smoking. In Mrs. Nolan's case, the social isolation (ugly *C*) contingent upon her smoking apparently lessened the perceived value of each smoke.

Employ this procedure yourself in your smoking-reduction program. Confine yourself to a restricted area while smoking, have no one talk to you, and engage in no other activities. However, should you be tempted to smoke and resist, reward yourself! Buy yourself something right on the spot, or put away gift money. Learn to make *not smoking* more desirable than smoking. Tip the balance in favor of nonsmoking!

University of Minnesota psychologist Alan Roberts[19] used an adaptation of the Nolan procedure on his own twenty-three-year-long, pack-a day habit. Previous attempts to quit had been notably unsuccessful. Dr. Roberts had noted that he rarely smoked in the bathroom, and hence this site was selected as the only allowable smoking place. One week later, Dr. Roberts restricted himself from reading or talking while smoking in the bathroom. Hence, the smoking act was removed from its usual association with reward consequences such as social interaction, TV viewing, and reading. Dr. Roberts notes that while he did not consciously attempt to reduce his smoking, his smoking rate was cut by 7 per cent within several weeks. Soon thereafter, he developed a cold, quit smoking entirely, and remained abstinent. His efforts were reported in a scientific journal seven months later.

## Others Doing It

Many of us feel compelled to smoke when we see others smoking around us. If you sense this stimulus control, remember to look carefully around you. Attend closely to the people who aren't smoking. The nonsmokers are usually in the majority! Support restrictive smoking actions in classes or other groups. Avoid socializing with smokers, particularly in the beginning of the BT withdrawal program. Begin to eat lunch with groups of nonsmokers. Arrange to do something else during your coffee break if your coffee break is really a cigarette break with coworkers. Don't sit in the smoking sections of theaters or airplanes.

## Stimulation

If you rely on cigarettes for that "extra lift," or to perk you up when you're feeling down, consider other ways of gaining this desired stimulation. The age-old remedy of a breath of cool air should help, as would a cup of coffee or caffeinated soft drink. Exercise should also help "get the blood flowing." Use self-reward (a good $C$ for a good $B$) to reward yourself for using one of these alternative $B$'s to smoking.

## Craving

Suppose someone were to invent a vaccine that would reduce the likelihood of heart disease or cancer among smokers. The vaccine would be freely available, though there would be one catch: It might cause discomfort, anxiety, or nausea for a brief period of time after its administration. Would *you* be interested in this potentially life-saving vaccine? In fact, this vaccine is readily available today! What is this miracle? Simply to stop smoking.

Though withdrawal effects may be unpleasant, they can be construed as constructive signs that your body is beginning to cleanse itself. You wouldn't avoid a potential life saver because of temporary side effects. Yet you continue to smoke out of fear of withdrawal. Maybe you've convinced yourself that withdrawal from cigarettes is so painful and unbearable that it's personally healthier to continue smoking. *Bunk!* Would you consider banging your head against the wall because it feels so good to stop? We think not. Yet the same kind of convoluted logic is used to rationalize continued smoking.

## WITHDRAWAL EFFECTS ARE TEMPORARY

Dr. Donald Frederickson[20] of the New York City Health Department Smoking Control Program suggests that the physical symptoms of withdrawal shouldn't cause alarm. They will likely subside in a matter of days or weeks. Some long-term smokers experience no withdrawal effects at all. However, you may wish to ask your physician to monitor your progress through the smoking-withdrawal program. Begin to conceptualize withdrawal—either tapering off or going cold turkey—as a temporary, voluntary sickness that should leave you feeling healthier and more alive.

## FEAR OF WITHDRAWAL

Researchers have found that what often best distinguishes smokers who manage to quit in antismoking programs from those who fail is that not smoking continues to be seen by the failures as more aversive than continued smoking.[21] *The fear of being without cigarettes outweighs the fear of potential cancer.* This fear of withdrawal is the overwhelming fear that often motivates continued smoking.

Almost everyone attempting to stop smoking believes that smoking is a bad thing. But as the junkie who uses heroin to ward off withdrawal effects, the habitual smoker smokes to avoid feeling the displeasurable effects of not smoking. "Thou shalt not feel uncomfortable at any time" becomes the habitual smokers' implicit commandment. Whenever queasy or nervous feelings compound their abstinence from cigarettes, they seek remedy through "just one more" smoke.

The next time you feel that craving urge to smoke, engage in a competing response: Reach for this book! In addition, use PSR, exercise, take a walk, have something to eat, make love, or engage in some other activity that is incompatible with smoking.

## THE USE OF DRUGS TO REDUCE CRAVING

There are a number of nicotine substitutes, several available over the counter. If you decide to use such drugs, do so in combination with the procedures outlined here, not as replacements for your active efforts. Be advised, however, that the majority of research studies testing various antismoking drugs (lobeline, hydroxyine, diazepam) have supported the conclusion that these drugs are no more effective than "sugar pill" placebos in helping smokers to stop smoking.[22]

## Self-identity

Do you feel that smoking makes you beautiful, sophisticated, "with it," or mature? Has smoking become part of your self-image? If your answer is "Yes" to these questions, Drs. Mausner and Platt[23] suggest you find people after whom you would like to model yourself who are either nonsmokers or ex-smokers. In fact, the evidence shows that the higher you go on the income and educational scales, the fewer smokers there are.

Begin to associate with people who similarly devalue smoking. Look closely at the smokers with the choking coughs, the tar-stained teeth and fingers. Ask yourself if these are the people after whom you wish to model your life.

Can you see yourself as a nonsmoker? Would it *really* be you? When a confirmed smoker gives up smoking, he sacrifices more than just a bad habit—he changes part of himself, part of his identity.

### THE ROLE OF HUMILIATION

Drs. Sarbin and Nucci[24] suggest that feelings of humiliation are prime catalysts for the conversion of personal identity from smoker to nonsmoker. Dr. David Premack[25] views humiliation as a key concept in accounting for the estimated twenty-nine million cigarette smokers who have spontaneously become nonsmokers. As Drs. Sarbin and Nucci suggest, at some point the soon-to-be ex-smoker becomes humiliated with his inability to quit, with his need to continue this "disgusting" habit. Perhaps the smoker sees his child following in his smoking footsteps, or he burns a hole in a favorite shirt or piece of furniture, or his doctor tells him of an ominous finding on his X ray.

Like the drinker who loses his job because of failure to limit alcohol intake, the humiliated smoker comes to see himself as immoral, wicked, and undeserving. He is defiling his own body. His personal concept of his own goodness is called into question. His belief that he can master his life and his habits becomes tenuous. This "humiliation shock," as Premack puts it, serves to mobilize him to action to restore his moral identity through renouncing the smoking habit.

As you recall, Mrs. Nolan used the smoking-chair method to help her reduce her cigarette intake significantly. Yet she was able to quit only when she became thoroughly disgusted with herself for continuing to smoke. She experienced a sense of personal humiliation, and decided to reconstitute herself anew as a reformed ex-smoker. This process of conversion from smoker to nonsmoker may be likened metaphorically to a process of death and rebirth.[26] In fact, many smokers succeed in quitting cold turkey by going on a "retreat" and reportedly returning a "new" person. At some point in their withdrawal program, soon-to-be ex-smokers must encounter this personal transition, denoted by feelings of humiliation, in which they succeed in saying, "I don't need them anymore. I don't want them anymore."

# TYING THINGS TOGETHER

The BT antismoking program guides the smoker to change the *ABC*'s of the smoking habit. The smoker reprograms his environment to weaken the *A*ntecedent and *C*onsequence connections that had been supporting his habit. The smoker engages in directed imaginings and silently reads antismoking and proquitting statements to change the perceived values of smoking and not smoking. He learns to interrupt or prolong the smoking chain, and further disrupts the habit. As the habit progressively weakens and intake declines, the smoker approaches a point at which he is psychologically better able to make the complete transition from smoker to nonsmoker. At this decision point, the smoker's personal sense of humiliation and outrage at his continued smoking form the basis for a final renunciation: "I'm no longer to be counted among the smokers." The techniques of directed imagery, self-reward, response cost, the smoking chair, social reinforcement, and so on, serve to heighten the smoker's feelings of humiliation for continued smoking—and feelings of pride and accomplishment for not smoking. These techniques set the stage and prepare the smoker for what in the end must be a personal commitment to change.

To foster this change, this identity conversion, use these techniques with a sense of commitment and involvement, and not with a "try it for a few days" attitude.

At present, there is no method for determining the best time for breaking completely with the habit. Certain persons might reduce their intake significantly and maintain themselves at this low level, never making the transition to total abstinence. Such smokers may continue to use the principles of stimulus control, such as never smoking during class, TV watching, reading, or only after predetermined intervals to maintain limits on the habit.

You may, like many others, try quitting several times before succeeding. In helping you adjust to abstinence, use the suggestions discussed earlier for quitting cold turkey. Also, continue to use the BT self-reward, response-cost program for several phase-out weeks following the attainment of complete abstinence—just to make sure.

One last note: Some smokers who quit report a modest, but often temporary, weight gain. Many do not. If you experience a lingering weight gain while quitting smoking, refer to the weight-control strategies described in the preceding chapter to keep those extra pounds off.

## The Case of Peter

Peter, a twenty-six-year-old high school English teacher, provided us with a striking example of the grief and the glory of the cold-turkey method for quitting smoking. *Peter's experience shows that regardless of whether you quit all at once or gradually, the ABC's of smoking can help you to quit permanently.*

Peter had quit smoking twice before, but had returned to the habit the first time after a two-month period, and the second time after a one-week layoff. His first return involved taking one cigarette when offered at a social get-together— "for the hell of it." He knew that smoking the one cigarette did not lead to the physical need to smoke more. So he began to smoke a few a day. Within two weeks, he was back at his prequitting level of two packs a day. He quit smoking the second time one week before final examinations in college. As the stresses of the examination period increased (potent smoking *A*'s), he found himself more strongly drawn to smoking, especially as he watched other students lighting up "to relax" (more $A$'s).

The third attempt to quit smoking arrived unexpectedly. He awoke one morning hacking. He reported that "two hours must have passed before I could catch my breath right." Once he caught his breath, he resolved "with every fiber of my being that I was never going to touch another damned cigarette again!" (humiliation shock).

He found many antismoking, proquitting self-statements to be of use during the first few days, when the physiological signs of withdrawal were at their worst. To counter these withdrawal effects, which he described as feeling "fingernails crawling inside my lungs . . . that could be quelled by one drag," Peter repeatedly used the following motivating assertive statements: "If I can get through the next three days, I won't be feeling the urge this strongly," "I am not, simply *not*, going to let some temporary discomfort in my throat and chest give me lung cancer or emphysema," "I am a human being and have the capacity to make decisions and stick to them!" "I am not a slave to my body! I can go without smoking if I choose to!" When the "pangs" of withdrawal were at their worst, he specifically focused on his fears of cancer (imagined ugly $C$'s), on his recollections of the morning he awoke "hacking my guts out" (remembered ugly $C$'s), and on the pride he could take in himself that despite withdrawal signs he was continuing his abstinence ("pat on the back" $C$'s).

Within three days the severest physiological withdrawal signs had passed, but the urge to inhale smoke, to be doing something with his hands, especially at habitual smoking periods (potent $A$'s), such as breaks between classes and following meals, remained strong. For the next couple of weeks he purposefully avoided the lounges in school where he and his colleagues had habitually smoked (removed potent $A$'s). Following meals he would again remind himself of all his reasons (good $C$'s) for quitting smoking and go for a walk rather than have a cigarette ($A\rightarrow$competing $B$). He rewarded himself for his abstinence by telling himself how "superior" he was to all the people he knew who wanted to quit but could not break the habit ("pat on the back" $C$'s). He allowed himself to bask in the warmth of his self-congratulations. He put aside the money he had used to spend on cigarettes, doubled it, and purchased luxuries that he normally would have avoided (self-reward $C$'s). He did mental calculations to determine the amount of money his nonsmoking would save in two years, in a decade, in forty years (long-term good C's).

He resolved never again to touch one cigarette. He has now discontinued smoking for three years. He admits that he still feels, though rarely, an urge to smoke, but that cigarettes actually appear to emit a foul odor at this point and that he adamantly conceptualizes himself as a nonsmoker (conversion in personal identity). He still occasionally focuses on other people who smoke despite their better judgment, and says to himself, "*I* was able to quit" ("pat on the back" C's). He has experienced no respiratory ailments since quitting cigarettes and feels that he has added years to his life. He remains very proud of himself (long-term good C's).

False modesty would be tragic—when you have made a great achievement, allow yourself to experience appropriate pride.

## If at First You Don't Succeed ...

Trouble-shoot the cause of the program's failure. Ask yourself: Were the self-rewards and response costs routinely applied and highly motivating? Did I follow the program regularly and with personal involvement? Were there parts of the program such as directed imagery I had trouble understanding or adapting? Did family and friends help by socially reinforcing me for abstaining? Did I really want to quit in the first place? Apply what you learn from your troubleshooting to redesign your antismoking program. Find the strategy that works best for you.

### THE CLINIC

You may decide that the peer pressure and mutual support of a group smoking clinic may be additionally helpful. Find an organized antismoking program in your community. The efforts of a group smoking clinic could certainly be used in tandem with the strategies described here. Or you may wish to form a group with your friends and/or family, using group pressure and mutual support to help each member design and carry through his or her BT plan.

### CONSULTING THE BEHAVIOR THERAPIST

You may decide to consult with a behavior therapist to enlist his or her help in designing your behavioral program and to teach you BT skills such as directed imagery, systematic desensitization, self-reward, self-punishment, stimulus-control techniques, and self-relaxation firsthand. In addition, behavior therapists are active in developing and refining additional techniques that require direct personal contact.

## If You Succeed . . .

Be forewarned: The recidivism rate in all types of antismoking programs is approximately 80 per cent within one year of treatment termination.[27] Generally, reaction to stress and social pressure are cited as the two key factors that lead to renewed smoking.[28] Should you fall back into old smoking habits, reinstate the BT program promptly and trouble-shoot problem areas. Doing without cigarettes is a lifelong effort and may require these periodic "booster sessions." Remember: Each day you delay, the habit becomes stronger.

Learn to deal with anxiety and stress through positive efforts, including assertiveness training and progressive self-relaxation. Reverse the tables with social pressure: Induce others in your social network to become quitters too. As two ex-cigarette smokers, we recognize personally the difficulties you face in kicking the habit, and warmly invite you to join the "IQ" club. Good luck.

# 10

# CONCLUDING NOTES

There is increasing recognition among mental health professionals of the efficacy of the direct approach to treating problem behaviors through BT. Literally thousands of research studies, ranging from case studies to sophisticated controlled experiments, have shown BT techniques to be successful in helping clients resolve problem behaviors.

## Results of BT

Several clinical studies of systematic desensitization for treatment of phobias have shown improvement rates of 92 per cent,[1] 85 per cent,[2] and 78 per cent.[3] In their study of sexual dysfunction, Masters and Johnson[4] have reported a 98 per cent success rate in treating premature ejaculation, 83 per cent in treating primary orgasmic dysfunction, and 77 per cent in treating situational orgasmic dysfunction. Dr. C. Chlouverakis of the State University of New York at Buffalo[5] has found that BT is more effective in controlling obesity than fad diets and also permits the client to avoid the hazards of medicinal, hormonal, and surgical methods for weight control. Dr. Albert Stunkard of the Department of Psychiatry of the University of Pennsylvania,[6] following review of the research evidence, agrees that BT is the most effective treatment of obesity available.

Throughout this book we have referred to many other studies that form the experimental foundation of the BT revolution. Yet research continues in virtually every major university to refine current methods and develop new techniques.

## Does BT Replace Other Forms of Therapy?

It has been our experience that many clients and many therapists presume that the practitioner of BT believes that his is the one legitimate therapeutic approach, just as practitioners of other therapies are dedicated to their approaches. This is not a view that we share. BT does not replace other therapies for people who seek to explore their feelings or their consciousness, to learn about their personal identity or their existential meaning, or to encounter their feelings toward themselves and others. *BT is an effective, problem-oriented technology of behavior change, a method of treatment that complements but does not replace other forms of therapy.* BT is a collection of therapeutic tools and not a new religion or philosophy of life. People undergoing long-term insight-oriented therapy may also wish to use reliable, scientifically validated BT programs to solve problems such as anxiety, fears, insomnia, nonassertiveness, sexual dysfunction, unwanted smoking, and overeating. We see no reason why a BT program to control such problem behaviors cannot be undertaken in conjunction with psychoanalysis or other therapies.

## The Movement Toward Cognitive Behavior Therapy

Behavior therapists are presently moving in the direction of synthesizing the study of man's inner and outer processes, his thoughts or "cognitions," and his observable behavior. The traditional focus in BT on the what, when, and wherefore of overt behavior is being expanded to examine the influences on behavior of man's inner creations—his thoughts, attitudes, beliefs, and fantasies. Throughout this book we have attempted to integrate these trends. We have described how reorientation of attitudes and the use of fantasy or imagination can lead to constructive behavioral changes. We have been aware that what a person says to himself about his behavior can be as significant to him as the behavior itself. This blending of the overt and the covert continues in our clinical work, which is perhaps best described by the more comprehensive term, *cognitive behavior therapy*.

# Behavior Therapy and Behavior Modification: The Client and the Contract

BT is often equated with behavior modification—"Behavior Mod"—and criticized as a tool for behavior control. BT, as this book makes clear, involves the application of the principles of learning to help clients unlearn their own problem behaviors. The relationship between behavior therapist and client is contractual and clear: The client draws on his therapist's expertise to help him master nagging problems in living. "Behavior Mod," as we see it, is a more general term than BT. Behavior modification includes BT, but may also include situations in schools, prisons, or mental hospitals in which the "client" may not have contracted for the services of the behavior modifier with informed and full consent. The teacher who uses gold stars or small gifts to selectively reinforce her students' "good" behaviors is employing behavioral principles in a systematic way, though student consent and comprehension of the system may be lacking. In other settings, selective reinforcement of behaviors that approximate normal speech has helped speech-impaired children to communicate more effectively. Few would assert that these noncontractual uses of learning principles are harmful, and many applaud their effectiveness. Yet when behavioral strategies are applied with unwilling or resistive participants, such as with prisoners or mental patients, or when such participants are coerced into "treatment," the ethical issues loom large indeed. When ethical concerns arise in such situations, we suggest that the behavioral programs in question be carefully screened by responsible members of the community, or in the courts to test their legality. Mental patients in many states now have the right to contest in court the use of unwanted psychotropic medications, and we feel that this libertarian movement should extend to all forms of treatment, including behavior modification, chemotherapy, work therapy, group therapy, and any other method that is unwanted by the recipient.

In this book such ethical concerns do not arise, since the reader contracts with himself to begin behavioral programs to solve problems in living.

## Behave Yourself

This book is an open invitation to you to become involved in solving your own problems by using the techniques of modern behavioral science. No longer must you sit back passively, waiting for anxieties and fears to go away, or trying to ignore them. No longer must you look upon undesired habits, such as overeating and smoking, as problems you are doomed to go on living with. By directly changing your behavior, you can remove obstacles to your own self-realization and enhance your self-respect.

# Notes

## 1

1. M. C. Jones, "Elimination of Children's Fears," *Journal of Experimental Psychology* (1924), Vol. 7, pp. 381-90; H. E. Jones and M. C. Jones, "Fear," *Childhood Education* (1928), Vol. 5, pp. 136-43.

## 2

1. W. B. Cannon, *Bodily Changes in Pain, Hunger, Fear, and Rage* (New York: Appleton, 1929).
2. A. M. Freedman, H. I. Kaplan, and B. J. Sadock (eds.), *Comprehensive Textbook of Psychiatry* (2nd ed.) (Baltimore: Williams & Wilkins, 1975); L. C. Kolb, *Modern Clinical Psychiatry* (8th ed.) (Philadelphia: W. B. Saunders, 1973); L. P. Ullmann and L. Krasner, *A Psychological Approach to Abnormal Behavior* (Englewood Cliffs, N.J.: Prentice-Hall, 1975).
3. Freedman, Kaplan, and Sadock (1975); Kolb (1973); Ullmann and Krasner (1975).
4. J. Dollard and N. E. Miller, *Personality and Psychotherapy* (New York: McGraw-Hill, 1950), pp. 355-63.
5. Dollard and Miller (1950), pp. 365-66.
6. B. B. Brown, *New Mind, New Body* (New York: Harper & Row, 1974).
7. E. Jacobson, *Progressive Relaxation* (Chicago: University of Chicago Press, 1938).
8. J. Wolpe, *Psychotherapy by Reciprocal Inhibition* (Stanford, Calif.: Stanford University Press, 1958) and *The Practice of Behavior Therapy* (New York: Pergamon Press, 1973).
9. D. Tasto and J. Hinkle, "Muscle Relaxation treatment for tension headaches," *Behaviour Research and Therapy* (1973), Vol 11, pp. 347-49.
10. C. B. Taylor, J. W. Farquhar, E. Nelson, and D. Agras, "Relaxation Therapy and high blood pressure," *Archives of General Psychiatry* (1977), Vol. 34, pp. 339-43.
11. G. L. Paul, "Physiological Effects of Relaxation Training and Hypnotic Suggestion," *Journal of Abnormal Psychology* (1969), Vol. 74, pp. 425-37.
12. Paul (1969); H. Benson, D. Shapiro, B. Tursky, and G. E.

Schwartz, "Decreased Systolic Blood Pressure Through Operant Conditioning Techniques in Patients with Essential Hypertension," *Science* (1971), Vol. 173, pp. 740-41.

13. D. Meichenbaum and D. Turk, "Cognitive-behavioral Management of Anxiety, Anger, and Pain," *The Behavioral Management of Anxiety, Depression, and Pain*, ed. P. O. Davidson (New York: Brunner/Mazel, 1976); D. Meichenbaum and R. Cameron, "The Clinical Potential of Modifying What Clients Say to Themselves," *Psychotherapy: Theory, Research, and Practice* (1974), Vol. 11, pp. 103-17.

14. D. C. Rimm, "Thought-stopping and Covert Assertion in the Treatment of Phobias," *Journal of Consulting and Clinical Psychology* (1973), Vol. 41, pp. 466-67.

3

1. Cannon (1929).
2. K. D. O'Leary and G. T. Wilson, *Behavior Therapy: Application and Outcome* (Englewood Cliffs, N.J.: Prentice-Hall, 1975), pp. 63-64.
3. O. Fenichel, *The Psychoanalytic Theory of Neurosis* (New York: Norton, 1945); A. H. Buss, *Psychopathology* (New York: Wiley, 1966).
4. H. J. Eysenck, "The Effects of Psychotherapy: An Evaluation," *Journal of Consulting Psychology* (1952), Vol. 16, pp. 319-24; S. Rachman, *The Effects of Psychotherapy* (New York: Pergamon Press, 1971).
5. J. B. Watson and R. Raynor, "Conditioned Emotional Reactions," *Journal of Experimental Psychology* (1920), No. 3, pp. 1-14.
6. A. Bandura and R. H. Walters, *Social Learning and Personality Development* (New York: Holt, Rinehart, & Winston, 1963).
7. D. E. Berlyne, *Conflict, Arousal, and Curiosity* (New York: McGraw-Hill, 1960).
8. S. R. Maddi, *Personality Theories: A Comparative Analysis* (Homewood, Ill.: Dorsey Press, 1972), p. 242.
9. T. G. Stampfl and D. J. Levis, "Essentials of Implosive Therapy; A Learning-theory-based Psychodynamic Behavioral Therapy," *Journal of Abnormal Psychology* (1967), Vol. 72, pp. 496-503; I. Marks, J. Boulougouris, and P. Marset, "Flooding versus Desensitization in the Treatment of Phobic Patients : A Crossover Study," *British Journal of Psychiatry* (1971), Vol. 119, pp. 353-75.
10. Wolpe (1958); Wolpe (1973).
11. Wolpe (1958); Wolpe (1973).
12. G. M. Rosen, R. E. Glasgow, and M. Barrera, "A Controlled Study to Assess the Clinical Efficacy of Totally Self-administered Systematic Desensitization," *Journal of Con-*

*sulting and Clinical Psychology* (1976), Vol. 44, pp. 208-17: H. H. Dawley. L. S. Guidry, and E. Curtis, "Self-administered Desensitization on a Psychiatric Ward," *Journal of Behavior Therapy and Experimental Psychiatry* (1973), Vol. 4, pp. 301-3; R. E. Phillips, G. D. Johnson, and A. Geyer, "Self-administered Systematic Desensitization," *Behaviour Research and Therapy* (1972), Vol. 10, pp. 93-96; N. D. Repucci and B. L. Baker, "Self-desensitization: Implications for Treatment and Teaching," eds. R. D. Rubin and C. M. Franks (New York: Academic Press, 1969).

13. D. C. Rimm and J. C. Masters, *Behavior Therapy: Techniques and Empirical Findings* (New York: Academic Press, 1974), p. 54.

14. Gradually prolonging exposure and the threshold method are both analogous to "progressive approach," as in A. J. Goldstein, "Separate Effects of Extinction, Counterconditioning, and Progressive Approach in Overcoming Fear," *Behaviour Research and Therapy* (1969), Vol. 7, pp. 47-56. In the threshold method, physical distance from the target stimulus or the target behavior is the dimension used in progressive approach, whereas in gradually prolonging exposure, the critical dimension is time. Progressive approach has also been shown to be effective in G. A. Kimble and J. W. Kendall, "A Comparison of Two Methods of Producing Experimental Extinction," *Journal of Experimental Psychology* (1953), Vol. 45, pp. 87-90. Both forms of progressive approach are preferable to the "sink or swim" method (labeled "stimulus flooding" or simply "flooding" in the technical literature) in that flooding is (a) painful and (b) probably ineffective as a method for reducing fear of unusually strong phobic proportions, as shown by M. Baum, "Extinction of an Avoidance Response Motivated by Intense Fear: Social Facilitation of the Action of Response Prevention (Flooding) in Rats," *Behaviour Research and Therapy* (1969), Vol. 7, pp. 57-62. The threshold method and gradually prolonging exposure may be conceptualized as *in vivo* forms of systematic desensitization, as discussed by Wolpe (1973); J. Wolpe and A. A. Lazarus, *Behavior Therapy Techniques* (New York: Pergamon Press, 1966).

15. A. Salter, *Conditioned Reflex Therapy* (New York: Creative Age Press, 1949).

16. Wolpe (1973); Wolpe and Lazarus (1966).

4

1. W. C. Dement, *Some Must Watch While Some Must Sleep* (San Francisco: Freeman and Company, 1972).

2. Dement (1972).

3. J. B. Raybin and T. P. Detre, "Sleep Disorders and Symptomatology Among Medical and Nursing Students," *Comprehensive Psychiatry* (1969), Vol. 10, pp. 452-62.

4. F. R. Freeman, *Sleep Research: A Critical Review* (Springfield, Ill.: Charles C. Thomas, 1972).

5. L. J. Monroe, "Psychological and Physiological Differences Between Good and Poor Sleepers," *Journal of Abnormal Psychology* (1967), Vol. 72, pp. 255-64; A. Kales and G. Cary, "Treating Insomnia," *Psychiatry*, Medical World News Supplement (Nov. 1971); P. A. Marks and L. J. Monroe, "Correlates of Adolescent Poor Sleepers," *Journal of Abnormal Psychology* (1976), Vol. 85, pp. 243-46.

6. M. Kahn, B. Baker, and J. M. Weiss, "Treatment of Insomnia by Relaxation Training," *Journal of Abnormal Psychology* (1968), Vol. 73, pp. 556-58; S. N. Haynes, S. Woodward, R. Moran, and D. Alexander, "Relaxation Treatment of Insomnia," *Behavior Therapy* (1974), Vol. 5, pp. 555-58; P. Nicassio and R. Bootzin, "A Comparison of Progressive Relaxation and Autogenic Training as Treatments for Insomnia," *Journal of Abnormal Psychology* (1974), Vol. 83, pp. 253-60. Note that our instructions for sleep induction include elements of progressive relaxation and autogenic training, both of which have been successfully used to induce sleep.

7. G. Weil and M. R. Goldfried, "Treatment of Insomnia in an Eleven-year-old Child Through Self-relaxation," *Behavior Therapy* (1973), Vol. 4, pp. 282-94.

8. J. L. Singer, *The Inner World of Daydreaming* (New York: Harper & Row, 1975).

9. Singer (1975), pp. 21-22.

10. In G. Gregg, "A Sketch of Albert Ellis," *Psychology Today* (1973), Vol. 7, p. 61.

## 5

1. Salter (1949).

2. *Human Behavior* (July 1973), p. 32.

3. H. Fensterheim and J. Baer, *Don't Say Yes When You Want to Say No* (New York: McKay, 1975).

4. S. A. Rathus, "Principles and Practices of Assertive Training: An Eclectic Overview," *The Counseling Psychologist* (1975), Vol. 5, No. 4, pp. 9-20; A. A. Lazarus, "On Assertive Behavior: A Brief Note," *Behavior Therapy* (1973), Vol. 4, pp. 697-99.

5. R. R. Sears, E. E. Maccoby, and H. Levin, *Patterns of Child Rearing* (New York: Harper & Row, 1957).

6. Watson and Raynor (1920).

7. A. Ellis, *Reason and Emotion in Psychotherapy* (New York: Lyle Stuart, 1962); A. Ellis and R. A. Harper, *A Guide to Rational Living* (No. Hollywood: Wilshire Book Com-

pany, 1973). Also see J. Wolfe and I. G. Fodor, "A Cognitive/Behavioral Approach to Modifying Assertive Behavior in Women," *The Counseling Psychologist* (1975), Vol. 5, No. 4, pp. 45-52.

8. Ellis and Harper (1973), p. 79.
9. Ellis and Harper (1973), p. 92.
10. Ellis and Harper (1973), p. 125.
11. Ellis and Harper (1973), p. 173.
12. Bandura and Walters (1963).
13. A. Bandura, D. Ross, and S. A. Ross, "Imitation of Film-mediated Aggressive Models," *Journal of Abnormal and Social Psychology* (1963), Vol. 66, pp. 3-11.
14. S. M. Johnson and G. D. White, "Self-observation as an Agent of Behavioral Change," *Behavior Therapy* (1971), Vol. 2, pp. 488-97.
15. S. A. Rathus, "An Experimental Investigation of Assertive Training in the Group Setting," *Journal of Behavior Therapy and Experimental Psychiatry* (1972), Vol. 3, pp. 81-86; S. A. Rathus, "Instigation of Assertive Behavior Through Videotape-mediated Assertive Models and Directed Practice," *Behaviour Research and Therapy* (1973a), Vol. 11, pp. 57-65.
16. R. D. Palmer, "Desensitization of the Fear of Expressing One's Own Inhibited Aggression: Bionenergetic Assertive Techniques for Behavior Therapists," *Advances in Behavior Therapy,* eds. R. D. Rubin, J. P. Brady, and J. D. Henderson (New York: Academic Press, 1973), pp. 241-53.
17. The "broken record" and "fogging" techniques have also been discussed in R. P. Liberman, L. W. King, W. J. DeRisi, and M. McCann, *Personal Effectiveness: Guiding People to Assert Themselves and Improve Their Social Skills* (Champaign, Ill.: Research Press, 1975); M. Smith, *When I Say No I Feel Guilty* (New York: Dial Press, 1975); J. V. Flowers and C. D. Booraem, "Assertion Training: The Training of Trainers," *The Counseling Psychologist* (1975), Vol. 5, No. 4, pp. 29-36.
18. Several studies have shown that subtle cues may increase and guide the content of people's remarks: J. Greenspoon, "The Reinforcing Effect of Two Spoken Sounds on the Frequency of Two Responses," *American Journal of Psychology* (1955), Vol. 58, pp. 409-16; W. S. Verplanck, "The Control of the Content of Conversation: Reinforcement of Statements of Opinion," *Journal of Abnormal and Social Psychology* (1955), Vol. 51, pp. 668-76; K. Salzinger and S. Pisoni, "Reinforcement of Verbal Affect Responses of Normal Subjects During the Interview," *Journal of Abnormal and Social Psychology* (1960), Vol. 60, pp. 127-30; J. D. Matarazzo, A. N. Wiens, G. Saslow,

B. V. Allen, and M. Weitman, "Interviewer mm-hmm and Interviewee Speech Durations," *Psychotherapy: Theory, Research, and Practice* (1964), Vol. 1, pp. 109-14.

19. Salter (1949).

20. Wolpe and Lazarus (1966).

21. See also Liberman et al. (1975); T. V. McGovern. J. Tinsby, N. Liss-Levinson, R. O. Laventure, and G. Britton, "Assertion Training for Job Interviews," *The Counseling Psychologist* (1975), Vol. 5, No. 4, pp. 65-68.

22. Analogous to "feeling talk" in Salter (1949) and "expression of feelings" in Rathus (1975).

23. Salter (1949).

24. D. Lack, *The Life of the Robin* (Harmondsworth, England: Pelican, 1953).

25. N. Tinbergen, *The Study of Instinct* (London: Oxford University Press, 1951).

26. J. Wolfe, "Short-term Effects of Modeling/behavior Rehearsal, Modeling/behavior Rehearsal-plus-rational Therapy, Placebo, and No Treatment on Assertive Behavior" (unpublished doctoral dissertation, New York University, 1975).

27. J. L. Wolfe and I. G. Fodor, "A Cognitive/behavioral Approach to Modifying Assertive Behavior in Women," *The Counseling Psychologist* (1975), Vol. 5, No. 4, pp. 45-52.

28. N. R. Carlson and D. A. Johnson, "Sexuality Assertiveness Training: A Workshop for Women," *The Counseling Psychologist* (1975), Vol. 5, No. 4, pp. 53-59.

29. Carlson and Johnson (1975), p. 53.

30. M. S. Horner, "Fail: Bright Women," *Psychology Today* (Nov. 1969), Vol. 3, pp. 36-38; M. S. Horner, "Toward an Understanding of Achievement-related Conflicts in Women," *Journal of Social Issues* (1972), Vol. 28, pp. 157-75.

31. S. A. Rathus, "A 30-item Schedule for Assessing Assertive Behavior," *Behavior Therapy* (1973b), Vol. 4, pp. 398-406.

32. S. A. Rathus and J. S. Nevid, "Concurrent Validity of the 30-item Assertiveness Schedule with a Psychiatric Population," *Behavior Therapy* (1977), in press.

33. Reprinted with permission from Rathus (1973b). Copyright © 1973 by Academic Press, Inc.

34. S. A. Rathus and J. S. Nevid, "Dimensions of Assertiveness," manuscript submitted for publications.

## 6

1. W. H. Masters and V. E. Johnson, *Human Sexual Response* (Boston: Little, Brown and Company, 1966), pp. 191-93.

2. W. H. Masters and V. E. Johnson, *Human Sexual Inadequacy* (Boston: Little, Brown and Company, 1970), p. 11.

3. Masters and Johnson (1970).

4. H. S. Kaplan, *The New Sex Therapy* (New York: Brunner/Mazel, 1974).

5. L. G. Barbach, *For Yourself: The Fulfillment of Female Sexuality* (Garden City, N.Y.: Doubleday & Company, 1975).

6. D. W. Briddell and G. T. Wilson, "Effects of Alcohol and Expectancy Set on Male Sexual Arousal," *Journal of Abnormal Psychology* (1976), Vol. 86, pp. 225-34.

7. Masters and Johnson (1970), pp. 93-94.

8. J. H. Geer and R. Fuhr, "Cognitive Factors in Sexual Arousal: The Role of Distraction," *Journal of Consulting and Clinical Psychology* (1976), Vol. 44, pp. 238-43.

9. Also see Kaplan (1974), pp. 305-6.

10. J. H. Semans, "Premature Ejaculation: A New Approach," *Southern Medical Journal* (1956), Vol. 49, pp. 353-57.

11. Masters and Johnson (1970).

12. Kaplan (1974), p. 210.

13. Kaplan (1974), p. 306.

14. Masters and Johnson (1970), pp. 102-6.

15. Kaplan (1974), p. 331.

16. Bandura, Ross, and Ross (1963); D. Grosser, N. Polansky, and R. A. Lippitt, "A Laboratory Study of Behavioral Contagion," *Human Relations* (1951), Vol. 4, pp. 115-42; Ross, "The Effects of Deviant and Nondeviant Models on the Behavior of Preschool Children in a Temptation Situation" (unpublished doctoral dissertation, Stanford University, 1962).

17. G. Kline-Graber and B. Graber, *Woman's Orgasm* (Indianapolis: Bobbs-Merrill, 1975), pp. 130-34.

18. Masters and Johnson (1970), p. 131.

19. Kaplan (1974), p. 324.

20. Kline-Graber and Graber (1975), pp. 38-39; A. C. Kinsey et al., *Sexual Behavior in the Human Female* (Philadelphia: W. B. Saunders, 1953), p. 373.

21. Masters and Johnson (1966); M. J. Sherfey, *The Nature and Evolution of Female Sexuality* (New York: Random House, 1972).

22. Masters and Johnson (1966), pp. 63-64.

23. Masters and Johnson (1966), pp. 118, 133, 134.

24. Masters and Johnson (1970), p. 227.

25. J. LoPiccolo, and M. A. Lobitz, "The Role of Masturbation in the Treatment of Orgasmic Dysfunction," *Archives of Sexual Behavior* (1972), Vol. 2, pp. 163-71.

26. Kaplan (1974).

27. Barbach (1975).

28. Kline-Graber and Graber (1975), pp. 37-39.

29. Kline-Graber and Graber (1975), pp. 92-94.

30. Barbach (1975).

31. Masters and Johnson (1966), pp. 66-67.
32. Masters and Johnson (1966), p. 63.
33. Kaplan (1974), p. 389.
34. Masters and Johnson (1966), pp. 66-67.
35. Masters and Johnson (1970), p. 240.
36. Masters and Johnson (1970), p. 300.
37. Masters and Johnson (1970), p. 307.
38. Kaplan (1974), p. 401.
39. Masters and Johnson (1970), p. 306.
40. Kaplan (1974), pp. 403-7.
41. Kaplan (1974), p. 405.
42. Kaplan (1974), pp. 412-28; G. T. Wilson, "Innovations in the Modification of Phobic Behaviors in Two Clinical Cases," *Behavior Therapy* (1973), Vol. 4, pp. 426-30.
43. A. Ellis, *Sex Without Guilt* (New York: Lyle Stuart, 1966).
44. Masters and Johnson (1966), pp. 118, 133, 134.
45. Kline-Graber and Graber (1975), pp. 37-38.
46. S. Freud, "Three Contributions to the Theory of Sex: The Transformation of Puberty," *The Basic Writings of Sigmund Freud,* ed. A. A. Brill (New York: Random House, 1938), Vol. 18, pp. 613-14.
47. Masters and Johnson (1966), pp. 118, 133, 134.
48. S. Fisher, *The Female Orgasm: Psychology, Physiology, Fantasy* (New York: Basic Books, 1973).
49. E. B. Hariton, "The Sexual Fantasies of Women," *Psychology Today* (1973), Vol. 6, pp. 39-44.
50. J. R. Heiman, "The Physiology of Erotica: Women's Sexual Arousal," *Psychology Today* (1975), Vol. 8, pp. 91-94.

## 7

1. Our *ABC*'s of behavior are analogous to the *ABC*'s used by E. B. Rettig and his colleague in E. B. Rettig, *ABC's for Parents* (Van Nuys, Calif.: Associates for Behavior Change, 1973); E. B. Rettig, and T. L. Paulson, *ABC's for Teachers* (Van Nuys, Calif.: Associates for Behavior Change, 1975). Albert Ellis also uses the acronym, in "The A-B-C's of Rational-emotive Therapy," *Humanistic Psychotherapy: The Rational-Emotive Approach,* ed. E. Sagarin (New York: The Julian Press, 1973).
2. Johnson and White (1971).
3. I. T. Rutner, "The Modification of Smoking Behavior Through Techniques of Self-Control" (unpublished master's thesis, Wichita State University, 1967).
4. D. Premack, "Reinforcement Theory," *Nebraska Symposium on Motivation,* ed. D. Levine (Lincoln: University of Nebraska Press, 1965).
5. J. R. Cautela, "Covert Sensitization," *Psychological Reports* (1967), Vol. 74, pp. 459-68; J. R. Cautela, "Covert reinforcement," *Behavior Therapy* (1970a), Vol. 1, pp. 33-50;

J. R. Cautela, "Covert Negative Reinforcement," *Journal of Behavior Therapy and Experimental Psychiatry* (1970b), Vol. 1, pp. 273-78.

6. Cautela (1970a).

7. L. H. Epstein and .G L. Peterson, "The Control of Undesired Behavior by Self-imposed Contingencies," *Behavior Therapy* (1973), Vol. 4, pp. 91-95.

8. J. I. Nurnberger and J. Zimmerman, "Applied Analysis of Human Behavior: An Alternative to Conventional Motivational Inferences and Unconscious Determination on Therapeutic Programming," *Behavior Therapy* (1970), Vol. 1, pp. 1-3.

9. D. L. Watson and R. G. Tharp, *Self-directed Behavior: Self-modification for Personal Adjustment* (Monterey, Calif.: Brooks/Cole, 1972).

## 8

1. U. S. Public Health Service, *Obesity and Health* (Washington, D.C.: U. S. Government Printing Office, n.d.).

2. J. Mayer, *Overweight: Causes, Cost, and Control* (Englewood Cliffs, N.J.: Prentice-Hall, 1968).

3. M. B. Harris, "A Self-directed Program for Weight Control: A Pilot Study," *Journal of Abnormal Psychology* (1969), Vol. 74, pp. 263-70; A. J. Stunkard, "The Management of Obesity," *New York State Journal of Medicine* (1958), Vol. 58, pp. 79-87.

4. D. Doty, "State University of New York at Albany Weight Reduction Program: Review Manual" (unpublished manual, State University of New York at Albany, 1974).

5. A. J. Stunkard, "Obesity and the Denial of Hunger," *Psychosomatic Medicine* (1959), Vol. 1, pp. 281-89.

6. A. Schachter and L. P. Gross, "Manipulated Time and Eating Behavior," *Journal of Personality and Social Psychology* (1968), Vol. 10, pp. 98-106; R. Goldman, M. Jaffa, and S. Schachter, "Yom Kippur, Air France, Dormitory Food, and the Eating Behavior of Obese and Normal Persons," *Journal of Personality and Social Psychology* (1968), Vol. 10, pp. 117-23; S. Schachter, "Some Extraordinary Facts About Obese Humans and Rats," *American Psychologist* (1971), Vol. 26, pp. 129-44.

7. Schachter and Gross (1968).

8. R. E. Nisbett, "Taste, Deprivation, and Weight Determinants of Eating Behavior," *Journal of Personality and Social Psychology* (1968), Vol. 10, pp. 107-16.

9. Goldman et al. (1968).

10. Harris (1969).

11. Stunkard (1958).

12. J. P. Wollersheim, "Effectiveness of Group Therapy Based upon Learning Principles in the Treatment of Overweight

Women," *Journal of Abnormal Psychology* (1970), Vol. 76, pp. 462-74.

13. D. B. Jeffrey, "A Comparison of the Effects of External Control and Self-control on the Modification and Maintenance of Weight," *Journal of Abnormal Psychology* (1974), Vol. 83, pp. 404-10.

14. B. Manno and A. R. Marston, "Weight Reduction as a Function of Negative Covert Reinforcement (Sensitization) Versus Positive Covert Reinforcement," *Behaviour Research and Therapy* (1972), Vol. 10, pp. 201-7.

15. Harris (1969).

16. Wollersheim (1970).

17. R. L. Hagen, "Group Therapy Versus Bibliotherapy in Weight Reduction," *Behavior Therapy* (1974), Vol. 5, pp. 222-34.

18. Wollersheim (1970).

19. Hagen (1974).

20. R. G. Romanczyk, P. A. Tracey, G. T. Wilson, and G. L. Thorpe, "Behavioral Techniques in the Treatment of Obesity: A Comparative Analysis," *Behaviour Research and Therapy* (1973), Vol. 11, pp. 629-40.

21. M. J. Mahoney, "Self-reward and Self-monitoring Techniques for Weight Control," *Behavior Therapy* (1974), Vol. 5, pp. 48-57.

22. Jeffrey (1974).

23. A. J. Stunkard, "New Therapies for the Eating Disorders: Behavior Modification of Obesity and Anorexia Nervosa," *Archives of General Psychiatry* (1972), Vol. 26, pp. 391-98.

24. Mayer (1968).

25. R. B. Stuart and B. Davis, *Slim Chance in a Fat World: Behavioral Control of Obesity* (Champaign, Ill.: Research Press, 1972).

26. Stuart and Davis (1972).

27. M. B. Harris and E. S. Hallbauer, "Self-directed Weight Control Through Eating and Exercise," *Behaviour Research and Therapy* (1973), Vol. 11, pp. 523-29.

28. Stuart and Davis (1972), pp. 79-80.

29. Harris (1969).

30. D. J. Gaul, W. E. Craighead, and M. J. Mahoney, "Relationship Between Eating Rates and Obesity," *Journal of Consulting and Clinical Psychology* (1975), Vol. 43, pp. 123-25.

31. Adapted from Stuart and Davis (1972); Harris (1969).

32. L. E. Homme, "Perspectives in Psychology: XXIV. Control of Coverants, the Operants of the Mind," *Psychological Record* (1965), Vol. 15, pp. 501-11.

33. Cautela (1970a); Manno and Marston (1972).

34. Harris, (1969).

## 9

1. W. A. Hunt and J. D. Matarazzo, "Three Years Later: Recent Developments in the Experimental Modification of Smoking Behavior," *Journal of Abnormal Psychology* (1973), Vol. 81, pp. 107-14.

2. B. Mausner and E. S. Platt, *Smoking: A Behavioral Analysis* (New York: Pergamon Press, 1971).

3. L. Festinger, *A Theory of Cognitive Dissonance* (Evanston, Ill.: Row, Peterson, 1947).

4. L. A. Pervin and R. J. Yatko, "Cigarette Smoking and Alternate Methods of Reducing Dissonance," *Journal of Personality and Social Psychology* (1965), Vol. 2, pp. 30-36.

5. D. Horn, *Smoker's Self-Testing Kit* (Washington, D.C.: Public Health Service Publication No. 1904, U. S. Department of Health, Education, and Welfare, 1969a); D. Horn, "Some Factors in Smoking and Its Cessation," *Smoking, Health, and Behavior,* eds. E. F. Borgatta and R. R. Evans (Chicago: Aldine, 1969b), pp. 12-21.

6. Mausner and Platt (1971).

7. J. M. Weir, "Male Student Perceptions of Smokers," *Studies and Issues in Smoking Behavior,* ed. S. V. Zagona (Tucson: University of Arizona Press, 1967), pp. 147-55.

8. B. Mausner, "Report on a Smoking Clinic," *American Psychologist* (1966), Vol. 121, pp. 251-55.

9. G. W. Allport, *Pattern and Growth in Personality* (New York: Holt, Rinehart, and Winston, 1961).

10. Lieberman Research, Inc., *The Teen-ager Looks at Cigarette Smoking* (unpublished report of a study conducted for the American Cancer Society, November 1967).

11. J. L. Schwartz and M. Dubitsky, "One-year Follow-up Results of a Smoking Cessation Program," *Canadian Journal of Mental Health* (1968), Vol. 59, pp. 161-65.

12. T. R. Sarbin and L. P. Nucci, "Self-reconstitution Processes: A Proposal for Reorganizing the Conduct of Confirmed Smokers," *Journal of Abnormal Psychology* (1973), Vol. 81, pp. 182-95.

13. Horn (1969a); Mausner and Platt (1971).

14. Rutner (1967).

15. M. K. Wagner and R. A. Bragg, "Comparing Behavior Modification Approaches to Habit Decrement Smoking," *Journal of Consulting and Clinical Psychology* (1970), Vol. 34, pp. 258-63.

16. Homme (1965); J. T. Tooley and S. Pratt, "An Experimental Procedure for the Extinction of Smoking Behavior," *Psychological Record* (1967), Vol. 17, pp. 209-18.

17. American Cancer Society, Inc., *If You Want to Give Up Cigarettes* (1970).

18. J. D. Nolan, "Self-control Procedures in the Modification of

Smoking Behavior," *Journal of Consulting and Clinical Psychology* (1968), Vol. 32, pp. 92-93.

19. A. H. Roberts, "Self-control Procedures in the Modification of Smoking Behavior: A Replication," *Psychological Reports* (1969), Vol. 24, pp. 675-76.

20. D. T. Frederickson, "How to Help Your Patient Stop Smoking," *National Tuberculosis and Respiratory Disease Association Bulletin* (1969), Vol. 55, pp. 6-11.

21. B. Mausner, "An Ecological View of Cigarette Smoking," *Journal of Abnormal Psychology* (1973), Vol. 81, pp. 115-26.

22. D. A. Bernstein, "The Modification of Smoking Behavior: An Evaluative Review," *Learning Mechanisms in Smoking*, ed. W. A. Hunt (Chicago: Aldine, 1970).

23. Mausner and Platt (1971).

24. Sarbin and Nucci (1973).

25. D. Premack, "Mechanisms of Self-control," *Learning Mechanisms in Smoking*, ed. W. A. Hunt (Chicago: Aldine, 1970).

26. Sarbin and Nucci (1973).

25. D. Premack, "Mechanisms of Self-control," *Learning Mechanisms in Smoking*, ed. W. A. Hunt (Chicago: Aldine, 1970).

26. Sarbin and Nucci (1973).

27. W. A. Hunt, L. W. Barnett, and L. G. Branch, "Relapse Rates in Addiction Programs," *Journal of Clinical Psychology* (1971), Vol. 27, pp. 455-56.

28. Mausner and Platt (1971).

## 10

1. This figure is based on an analysis of Joseph Wolpe's original clinical studies of systematic desensitization by G. L. Paul, "Outcome of Systematic Desensitization. I: Background and Procedures, and Uncontrolled Reports of Individual Treatments," *Behavior Therapy: Appraisal and Status*, ed. C. M. Franks (New York: McGraw-Hill, 1969).

2. This figure is based on an analysis of Arnold Lazarus' clinical studies with systematic desensitization by Paul (1969).

3. J. D. Hain, H. G. Butcher, and I. Stevenson, "Systematic Desensitization Therapy: An Analysis of Results in Twenty-seven Patients," *British Journal of Psychiatry* (1966), Vol. 112, pp. 295-307.

4. Masters and Johnson (1970).

5. C. Chlouverakis, "Dietary and Medical Treatments of Obesity: An Evaluative Review," *Addictive Behaviors* (1975), Vol. 1, pp. 3-21.

6. A. Stunkard, "New Therapies for the Eating Disorders: Behavior Modification of Obesity and Anorexia Nervosa," *Archives of General Psychiatry* (1972), Vol. 26, pp. 391-98.

Other SIGNET Books You'll Want to Read

☐ **BORN TO WIN: Transactional Analysis with Gestalt Experiments by Muriel James and Dorothy Jongeward.** This landmark bestseller has convinced millions of readers that they fere Born to Win! "Enriching, stimulating, rewarding . . . for anyone interested in understanding himself, his relationships with others and his goals."—*Kansas City Times*
(#E9590—$2.95)*

☐ **SUCCESS THROUGH TRANSACTIONAL ANALYSIS by Jut Meininger with a Foreword by Robert L. Goulding, M.D.** Here is the book that shows you exactly how you are interacting with others, what secret goals and desires are driving you, and how to understand the actions of those around you. This is the breakthrough book that makes I'M OK—YOU'RE OK work for you!
(#E7840—$1.75)

☐ **BIORHYTHMS: How to Live with Your Life Cycles by Barbara O'Neil and Richard Phillips.** Get in touch with your inner rhythms for maximum success and fulfillment in every area of life. This book shows you how to easily and exactly calculate your own personal biorhythm patterns and use them as invaluable allies rather than hidden enemies.
(#W7181—$1.50)

☐ **WOMEN IN SEXIST SOCIETY: Studies in Power and Powerlessness edited by Vivian Gornick and Barbara K. Moran.** "An important book because it is an intelligent attack on an antiquated, oppressive culture . . . a useful book for women's studies courses on women in literature, the socialization of women—in fact, for any course that teaches that the quest is not for the Holy Male, but for self-definition."
—Roberta Salper, *Ramparts* (#ME1351—$2.25)

☐ **FOR YOURSELF: The Fulfillment of Female Sexuality by Lonnie Garfield Barbach, Ph.D.** Here is a unique book that demonstrates in a step-by-step program how you can indeed take control of your life at its most intimate level—to achieve orgasm and a greater fulfillment of your sexual potential.
(#J8969—$1.95)

Buy them at your local
bookstore or use coupon
on next page for ordering.